Personal Property
of
Derek Basham

Advance Praise for *Critical SHIFT: The Future of Quality in Organizational Performance*

Lori and Annabeth have examined the past, present, and future of quality in a readable text. Quality professionals can learn how to become useful in helping their organizations become useful. I liked it.

Philip Crosby
Author of *Quality and Me: Lessons from an Evolving Life*

Critical SHIFT is a timely and insightful guide to where organizational performance is headed and provides the tools to succeed in the years to come. A must read for those who are determined to stay on top of where we are and where we are going in the evolution of quality.

Richard Y. Chang
President and Chief Executive Officer
Richard Chang Associates, Inc.
1999 Chairman of the Board: American Society for Training & Development

I found this book timely and helpful for me not only professionally, but personally, as I re-examine my career and broader life goals. The information and insights offered led me to a deeper level of self-examination and helped shed some light on important personal questions. *The Starburst Model*™ . . . helped me synthesize my thoughts into a coherent picture of how the various pieces of the quality integration puzzle fit.

Vern F. Campbell, P.Eng., MBA
Quality Coordinator
Manitoba Hydro

I have read the very impressive work of Lori Silverman and Annabeth Propst. It has given me renewed energy and a clarified sense of direction for our next efforts here at First Union.

Price Schwenck
North Florida Regional President
First Union National Bank

This book is a great blend of hard-nosed straight forward advice, mixed with a dash of theory and a tool kit for growth and transformation.

Marcy Fisher
Vice President, Organizational Development and Human Resources
Shell Technology Ventures, Inc.

With this book, the authors' have addressed a gap in the quality literature by exploring the future of the quality movement, its gyrations and transformations, and what's in store for quality professionals and practitioners. Picking up where the *ASQ Future Study* leaves off, *Critical SHIFT* parses the state of quality with the help of some of the leading management and quality thinkers, and pieces together clues of trends and forces which will shape organizational performance, work and work styles, and even job opportunities in the 21st century. This is a powerful guide for envisioning a contour on where we are and where we're headed.

Roberto M. Saco
Regional Quality Officer
American Express TRS Company

This book is a breakthrough in the understanding of what is needed to take companies to the next level of quality management. The authors have completed extensive research and have presented a logical and comprehensive roadmap for any sized company to implement a quality environment. They accomplish this with a masterful blend of insights, examples, and thought-provoking questions. Their *Starburst Model*™ encompasses all aspects of a company culture that is necessary to insure the successful integration of quality.

James L. Bossert
Vice President, Quality
Americas Region
Nokia Mobile Phones

We are tuned as consumers to expecting that new is best . . . the old is out, the new is in. And so it goes for management approaches. Is quality in or out? Is reengineering better than quality? *Critical SHIFT* presents us with a more useful view; one of transition and evolution. It guides in an evolutionary journey through past, present, and future management approaches, building as we go, toward even better methods.

Maury Cotter
Director, Office of Quality Improvement
University of Wisconsin–Madison

Critical SHIFT: The Future of Quality in Organizational Performance

Also available from ASQ Quality Press

Quality Problem Solving
Gerald F. Smith

Creativity, Innovation, and Quality
Paul E. Plsek

Root Cause Analysis: A Tool for Total Quality Management
Paul F. Wilson, Larry D. Dell, and Gaylord F. Anderson

Mapping Work Processes
Dianne Galloway

Quality Quotes
Hélio Gomes

Let's Work Smarter, Not Harder: How to Engage Your Entire Organization in the Execution of Change
Michael Caravatta

The Change Agents' Handbook: A Survival Guide for Quality Improvement Champions
David W. Hutton

Understanding and Applying Value-Added Assessment: Eliminating Business Process Waste
William E. Trischler

To request a complimentary catalog of ASQ Quality Press publications, call 800-248-1946.

Critical SHIFT: The Future of Quality in Organizational Performance

Lori L. Silverman

with Annabeth L. Propst

9/29/99

Derek,

Best wishes to you in your performance improvement initiatives!

Enjoy—

Lori Silverman

ASQ Quality Press

Milwaukee, Wisconsin

Critical SHIFT: The Future of Quality in Organizational Performance
Lori L. Silverman with Annabeth L. Propst

Library of Congress Cataloging-in-Publication Data

Silverman, Lori L., 1958-
Critical shift : the future of quality in organizational performance / Lori L. Silverman, Annabeth L. Propst.
p. cm.
Includes bibliographical references and index.
ISBN 0-87389-445-6
1. Quality of products—Management. 2. Quality assurance--Management. 3. Organizational effectiveness. I. Propst, Annabeth L., 1950- . II. Title.
HF5415.157.S62 1998 98-43101
658.5′62—dc21 CIP

The Starburst Model™ graphic designed by Juliana Morris, Pittsburgh, PA

10 9 8 7 6 5 4 3 2

ISBN 0–87389–445–6

Acquisitions Editor: Ken Zielske
Project Editor: Annemieke Koudstaal
Production Coordinator: Shawn Dohogne

ASQ Mission: The American Society for Quality advances individual and organizational performance excellence worldwide by providing opportunities for learning, quality improvement, and knowledge exchange.

Attention: Bookstores, Wholesalers, Schools and Corporations:
ASQ Quality Press books, videotapes, audiotapes, and software are available at quantity discounts with bulk purchases for business, educational, or instructional use. For information, please contact ASQ Quality Press at 800-248-1946, or write to ASQ Quality Press, P.O. Box 3005, Milwaukee, WI 53201-3005.

To place orders or to request a free copy of the ASQ Quality Press Publications Catalog, including ASQ membership information, call 800-248-1946. Visit our web site at http://www.asq.org.

Printed in the United States of America

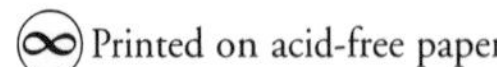
Printed on acid-free paper

American Society for Quality

Quality Press
611 East Wisconsin Avenue
Milwaukee, Wisconsin 53202
Call toll free 800-248-1946
http://www.asq.org
http://standardsgroup.asq.org

To performance improvement professionals who desire to make a profound difference in organizations and to my husband, Steven, who gives me unconditional support and love.
—Lori

To Tim for still being here.
—Beth

Contents

List of Tables and Figures

Preface

The book we intended to write and the one you have in front of you are quite different. We set out to write about the future of the quality professional. We began by interviewing people who we thought could give us interesting twists on the topic. Lo and behold, we realized that we were being challenged ourselves—challenged to explain how the historical development of the quality movement in the United States has influenced its current state and to discover the underlying issues behind the movement's most recent trends. We decided to embrace these challenges with great energy and proceeded to engage in numerous lengthy, animated conversations about them with our interviewees and between ourselves.

It wasn't until we compiled the data from these conversations that we realized a pattern was emerging. This pattern became even more evident after we decided to delve into literature on the workplace of the future. It eventually evolved into what we are calling the five fields of performance practice. We did not enter this endeavor to create a model that illustrates the role of quality practices in organizations or one that conjectures about the future of quality in performance improvement. Rather, our interviews and literature research surfaced information that led us to this outcome.

The Purpose of the Book

The purpose of this book is twofold. First, it will assist you and your enterprise in effectively preparing for and responding to the critical shift that is taking place in the practice of quality. As part of this purpose, it will also help you grasp the factors that are causing this shift to occur. Second, it will help you and your organization systematically integrate current and future operational and strategic initiatives into a cohesive framework that fosters quality and creates value. This unified framework will ultimately impact your organization's overall performance—by allowing it to more effectively use resources, accelerate the achievement of targeted results, and minimize conflicts between multiple initiatives.

Who This Book Is For

Critical SHIFT can be read from a variety of viewpoints. Individuals employed by organizations where quality and/or value creation are strategic objectives can use what they learn to coordinate and accelerate performance improvement efforts.

Those employed by organizations where quality is important in the performance of daily work (but has not been elevated to the strategic level) can introduce the strategic nature of quality and value creation to senior management. Individuals who belong to organizations that are not actively practicing quality approaches, or are entrenched in traditional inspection, will discover tools and methods that can make a difference in their workplace and personal lives.

Executives and leaders will find the framework presented in this book useful in communicating the synergistic purpose of multiple organizational initiatives. It will also help align these initiatives to achieve the results required by the organization's strategic plan. Individuals who work with enterprise leaders in the pursuit of performance improvement, including those employed in quality, organizational development, human resources, training, marketing, finance, engineering, and information systems, will be better equipped to help their organization

- realize the intended outcomes of individual initiatives,
- link together seemingly disconnected programs and efforts into a cohesive approach, and
- recommend future initiatives that strategically and operationally promote quality and value creation.

They will also be able to more effectively position themselves for future job opportunities. Employees responsible for the quality of products and services will become acquainted with a variety of tools and methods that they can employ in their daily work. Educators will find the information presented here helpful in designing organizational performance and quality management courses and degree programs.

Who We Are

What we bring to this book is a lifetime journey involving training, study, and experiences that have honed our abilities to collect and synthesize large amounts of seemingly disconnected information and data, to find patterns and possibilities within these, and to interpret them within the context of daily life. We each became familiar with the tools and methods of quality as employees over two decades ago. During this time, we experienced the internal challenges associated with improving performance and gaining commitment from senior management and entire organizations to pursue new initiatives. We also worked through how to link bottom-line performance to training and far-sweeping technology changes, and how to resolve complex business problems. Along the way we sought out formal educational opportunities that gave us insights into human behavior, business management, statistics, the hard sciences and mathematics, education and training, and the social sciences.

For the last decade we have worked as business owners and management consultants, helping organizations to achieve and maintain a competitive advantage in their marketplace by focusing on quality management, large-scale organizational change, and strategic management. Separately and together, our client experiences are in industries ranging from banking and financial services, to airlines, mining, continuous process, chemical transportation, trucking, fishing, steel, manufacturing, health care, bottling, medical equipment, engineering services, human resources consulting, higher education, retail sales, insurance, and the federal government, including the armed services. We, too, have grappled with issues facing quality management and performance improvement professionals including

- getting beyond the guru approach to management,
- achieving bottom-line results from quality initiatives,
- accelerating the pace of necessary business changes without losing people along the way,
- keeping alive critical initiatives with rotating senior management, and
- linking product and service quality to consumer value creation.

As we continue with this work, our vast network of colleagues keep us on our toes by continually introducing us to new perspectives and leading-edge thinking.

What we have acquired from the writing of this book is a different type of journey. It is a journey to the far reaches of our minds' universe that has prodded us to alter our most fundamental beliefs as they relate to our individual consulting work. It is a journey that will take us into our next lifetime. We invite you to open your hearts and your minds—and to join us as we explore the critical shift taking place in the practice of quality and its future in organizational performance.

Acknowledgments

Writing this book is the most challenging learning experience either of us has been involved with to date. Our learning was enhanced by the contributions of a multitude of individuals—those who graciously gave of their time and wisdom in response to our interview questions, and others who shared their unique expertise and insights on specific topics. These individuals are

Jill Adams-Rodeberg, Team Advisor, Midwest Express Airlines

Col. Liz Anderson, 302d Support Group Commander, 302d Airlift Wing, U.S. Air Force Reserve

Alan Backus, Quality Manager, Exide Electronics

Lon L. Barrett, Auditor, Boeing, and 1997–98 ASQ Spokane Section Chair

Paul B. Batalden, MD, Professor, Department of Pediatrics, Community, and Family Medicine, and Director, Health Care Improvement Leadership Development, Center for the Evaluative Clinical Sciences, Dartmouth Medical School; Director, Clinical Process Improvement and Leadership Development, Dartmouth–Hitchcock Medical Center; Vice President and Breech Chair, Department of Health Care Quality Improvement, Education and Research, Henry Ford Health System

Paul Borawski, Executive Director, American Society for Quality

Ellen Bovarnick, Senior Vice President, Quality, formerly of Florida Power & Light

William H. Braswell, Jr., Vice President, Quality Resources, Premera Blue Cross

Richard C. Buetow, Retired Senior Vice President, Motorola, Inc., and Motorola Director of Quality

Navin S. Dedhia, Chair, International Chapter, American Society for Quality

Linda Ernst, President, Training Resource

Lynda Finn, Senior Consultant, Oriel Incorporated

Tim Fuller, Partner, Fuller & Propst Associates

Dean A. Garner, Development Consultant, Wilson Sporting Goods

Cynthia Gentile, President, Applied Performance Strategies, Ltd.

Dana Ginn, Consultant, Cambridge Management Consulting

Howard Gitlow, Ph.D., Professor of Management Science, School of Business Administration, University of Miami

George J. Gliaudys, Jr., Colonel, Staff Judge Advocate, 63rd Regional Support Command, U.S. Army Reserve

Jack Gordon, Editor, *TRAINING* Magazine

Heero Hacquebord, President, Consulting in Continual Improvement

Lynne B. Hare, Director, Applied Statistics, Nabisco, Inc.

Lunell Haught, Ph.D., Owner, Haught Strategies
Carrie Hays, training and organizational development consultant, Yountville, CA
Harry Hertz, Director, National Quality Program, National Institute of Standards and Technology
Roger Holloway, Manager, ASQ Quality Press, American Society for Quality
Garry J. Huysse, Associate Director, Global Quality Improvement, Procter & Gamble
Jeff Israel, Principal, SatisFaction Strategies
Nancy M. Johnson, Ph.D., Vice President, Corporate Research and Development, American Family Insurance
Dr. George H. Labovitz, Chairman, Organizational Dynamics, Inc.
Barbara Lawton, Ph.D., Vice President, Business and Quality Processes, StorageTek
Thomas H. Lee, President Emeritus, Center for Quality of Management
Dr. Charles Liedtke, Owner, Strategic Improvement Systems
David Luther, Vice President of Finance and Administration, Green Mountain Energy Resources; Principal, Luther Quality Associates; Past President and Past Chairman, American Society for Quality
Sharon Lutz, Ph.D., Director, Integrated Analysis Team, Fairview Hospital and Healthcare Services
Tara Martin-Milius, CEO, Center for Corporate Learning
Nick Martino, Senior Consultant, Decision Strategies, formerly a quality engineer at a chemicals company
Thomas J. Murrin, Dean, A. J. Palumbo School of Business Administration, Duquesne University
Duke Okes, Management Consultant, APLOMET
Robert W. Peach, Principal, Robert Peach and Associates, Inc.
Dr. Curt W. Reimann, Senior Scientist Emeritus, National Institute of Standards and Technology
Randy Rossi, AVP, Business Banking Manager, Southwest National Bank
Lawrence Schein, Director, Total Quality Management Center, The Conference Board, Inc.
Louis E. Schultz, President, Process Management International
D. Scott Sink, Ph.D., P.E., Learning Leader, QPM, Inc., Past President of the World Confederation of Productivity Science and the Institute of Industrial Engineers
Lowell H. Tomlinson, 1996–98 Chair, Electronics Division, American Society for Quality
Marie Baucom Williams, President and CEO, Tennessee Quality
Fernando A. Yépez, Ph.D., Arthur Andersen LLP
A service quality consultant
A consultant in the field of statistics
Senior statistician
Vice President, Quality, Financial Services

The first pair of eyes that read through our initial manuscript were those of Steven Silverman. He coined the term "The Starburst Model™," for which we will forever be grateful. Juliana Morris, a gifted graphic artist, was able to turn our words (numerous times) into the starburst graphic.

Our first set of rewrites would not have been possible without the feedback we received from Nancy Johnson. Her strengths as a writer and public speaker helped us to arrive at the acronyms **SHIFT** and **CHAOS.** Many kudos to Sybil Sosin, who was the inspiration for the final organization of this book. She was also instrumental in how we elected to express the metaphor used to talk about The Starburst Model™ and the Inner Exploration questions scattered throughout the text. A special thank-you to Lisa Richardson, who provided insights on how to communicate some challenging topics, and to Mike Grennier, who, on a moment's notice, helped us to fully polish the final manuscript. Our appreciation to Maura May for her suggestion on the use of worksheets to make the book practical.

Bill Braswell, Lunell Haught, Mike Kenfield, Barbara Lawton, and Roberto Saco each provided us with insights on various parts of the manuscript we would not have had otherwise. Curt Reimann provided the impetus to cause us to ponder the reasons the quality movement has proceeded as it has and, without knowing it, he stimulated the conversations that led us to create the five fields of performance practice.

Roger Holloway, our knight in shining armor, rode into the picture just when we thought we might not be able to pull this book off. His never-ending enthusiasm for us and our work was the inspiration that kept us going. Those behind the scenes at Quality Press—Cathy Christine, Shawn Dohogne, Annemieke Koudstaal, Ken Zielske and others—as well as Lynn Steines and her colleagues at Shepherd, Inc. were also extremely resourceful and helpful, answering our numerous requests for information and assistance. Howard Gitlow, a prolific author, also shared with us his invaluable insights on the publishing process.

To Lou Schultz, Matt Nash, and Dr. Mohammed El-Sabbah our deep-felt gratitude for founding a firm that allowed us to meet each other and to develop the friendship and working relationship that would eventually lead to this book. And, finally, to Alan Backus who singularly was responsible for suggesting that we should write a book on the future of the quality profession. We did it!

Lori L. Silverman
Annabeth L. Propst
September 13, 1998

Introduction

During the last 20 years, we have watched as the practices surrounding the achievement of quality in products and services became one of the most rapidly and widely adopted business activities in organizations worldwide. Yet, in recent years, this once omnipresent business issue has all but vanished. This turn of events has already changed the lives of many professionals. In the future, it will alter the lives of many others, including you.

How This Book Was Developed

This book represents a compilation of data and information gleaned from a variety of sources. Over a period of several months in late 1997 and early 1998, we conducted depth interviews with 46 business leaders and experts in their respective fields to ascertain their views on trends in the quality movement, their organizations' quality initiatives and quality function, and the internal and external nature of the quality profession. Representative questions can be found in Appendix A. These individuals met at least one of the following five selection criteria:

1. They played a significant role in the advancement of quality in the United States and/or other countries.
2. They are known for their expertise in a specific aspect of quality or the quality movement.
3. They have written about or edited publications on the topics of quality, value creation, and/or organizational performance.
4. They assist and/or educate individuals and organizations on the planning, deployment, and implementation of quality and performance improvement.
5. They have actively participated in their organization's quality initiatives.

The information obtained in these interviews was grouped using the Affinity Diagram process—an approach that organizes and consolidates a large amount of verbal information into naturally forming clusters that bring to the surface the structure hidden behind the individual pieces of information.[1] The resulting clusters (i.e., themes) provided the conclusions presented later in this chapter, the trends expressed in chapter 2, and the chapter headings for Sections III, IV, and V. In addition, specific interview comments are woven throughout the text. These insights helped us to arrive at our conclusions about prior quality practices and our conjectures about the future of the quality movement and its role in organizational performance.

Other individual experts were contacted to provide their insights on a specific topic or issue. Their comments are interspersed throughout the manuscript.

In order to determine the forces impacting the workplace of the future (and consequently the practice of quality), we studied data on major trends—primarily in the United States—and reviewed the work of futurists and well-known management theorists. We synthesized this information into five forces using the Affinity Diagram process. These forces are presented in chapter 1 and provide the context within which we interpret the interview themes and provide recommendations in later chapters.

Section II describes five fields of performance practice. These fields resulted from the integration of the five forces impacting the workplace of the future and the interview themes. They are first introduced in chapter 2 and explained more fully in chapters 4 through 8.

During the writing of this manuscript, we conducted five conference presentations on the topics presented in this book to a variety of industries and professions. We also tested the five fields of performance practice with the leadership teams of several organizations. The feedback obtained from these interactions confirmed our findings and conclusions, and helped us to flesh out some of the details that support them.

Overall Conclusions

We have arrived at three overall conclusions about the future practice of quality in organizations. These conclusions are based on the collective results of the research and interviews (summarized in Section I, chapters 1 and 2) that we have conducted to date. They are supported by our personal experiences as management consultants working with over 60 organizations on their transformation efforts. Together, these conclusions serve as the backdrop for the content explored in Sections II through V.

According to Juran's classic, *A History of Managing for Quality,* quality, as a concept and in practice, has been around in some form since the beginning of recorded history.[2] It was apparent in China over 5000 years ago with the development of standard units and measurement calibration. The Chinese eventually developed a special department in the state administrative organization to control the production of handicrafts. Quality was evident in Egypt as portrayed in the pyramids, the Sphinx, and the Temple at Karnak. The Romans practiced quality in road building, and the ancient Greeks practiced quality in architecture and art. In the Middle Ages, quality was the province of the Guilds (perhaps the precursors of our modern-day professional societies). Since quality has been around for thousands of years in some way, shape, or form, it's safe to assume it will continue to survive for years to come.

Our first conclusion, therefore, is that the concept and practice of quality are timeless. From the information we have gathered it appears that "quality," as used within the context of "total quality management," has fallen out of favor. Some individuals would even go as far to say, "Quality is dead." What we have learned is that quality does not appear to be dead. It is going through a metamorphosis from the late 1970s when it came of age (more on this in chapter 2). Today it is already being called by other names, such as "performance management" and "operational excellence."

> "The future is performance management. The new vernacular separates out time, performance, delivery, organizational responsiveness/flexibility, and customer satisfaction. What is critically needed is a better integration of business disciplines with quality techniques, and the wisdom to know what expertise to call on at a particular point in time. By the way, do you still call it quality when it becomes everyone's job?"
>
> —Dr. Curt W. Reimann, Senior Scientist Emeritus, National Institute of Standards and Technology

Our second conclusion addresses what "the practice of quality" will look like when it has finished its metamorphosis. We agree with Dr. Howard Gitlow (as quoted in chapter 2) and others that the practice of quality will merge with the management field. As a result, the precepts of total quality management will completely transform the field of general management. No longer will management be merely the sum of its component disciplines—accounting, finance, marketing, human resources, operations, and so forth. The new management will synthesize into a total system focused on providing value to consumers, employees, and shareholders—as well as service to society.

> "I look for any opportunity to assure full ownership of quality for those who perform value-added work and even promote the *extinction of quality as a function* in those areas that are ready. In my career as a reengineering consultant I saw the potential for the field [of quality] to increase both in scope (business enterprise) and level of impact (whole organizational redesign). Today my role is one of facilitator of strategic change and convergence toward whole enterprise performance."
>
> —Alan Backus, Quality Manager, Exide Electronics

In the coming years, the inevitable result of this metamorphosis will be the reduction in the number of traditional quality professionals (i.e., those who work in quality departments or have the word "quality" in their job titles). This decrease in the number of traditional quality professionals and the concurrent increase in the number of quality practitioners is our third conclusion. We believe this outcome (supported by the American Society for Quality's futures study[3]) will occur for three reasons:

> "The quality professional could disappear or be modified (perhaps they will refer to themselves as change agents)."
>
> —Lawrence Schein, Director, Total Quality Management Center, The Conference Board, Inc.

1. Some of the functions currently assumed by quality professionals (e.g., quality training) will be absorbed into other parts of the organization.

2. Some of the functions will become part of everyone's daily work (e.g., data collection and interpretation).
3. The transformation of quality into performance management (or some other work) will restructure traditional quality roles.

The reduction in the number of traditional quality professionals does not mean that there will be a decrease in the number of people who are interested in quality. On the contrary, what we have discovered is that the number of *quality practitioners* (i.e., those who apply quality concepts, tools, and methods within their own work) is increasing.

> "I expect fewer traditional quality professionals, but those who exist should know what quality tools to use, how to use them, and how to interpret any findings."
>
> —Paul Borawski, Executive Director,
> American Society for Quality

In addition to these three conclusions, we believe that the world of work will be influenced by the environmental forces identified in chapter 1. Tomorrow's workplace will continue to become flatter, leaner, more flexible, more virtual, and more agile. Consequently, those who work in these environments will have to be more flexible, more knowledgeable, and engaged in continual learning. Undoubtedly these forces have significant implications for those who assist organizations in performance improvement.

How This Book Is Organized

There are five sections in this book. Section I—Trends and Forces Affecting Organizational Performance contains two chapters. The first chapter speaks to the five forces (summarized by the acronym **CHAOS**) that are impacting the workplace of the future. Chapter 2 explores five trends (summarized by the acronym **SHIFT**) resulting from the forces of **CHAOS** that are already under way in the practice of quality. One of these trends describes the five fields of performance practice that are the core of The Starburst Model™, the focus of Section II.

There are six chapters in Section II—Exploring The Starburst Model™. Chapter 3 provides an introduction to The Starburst Model™ and the use of the starburst metaphor. Chapters 4 through 8 are each devoted to one of the five fields of performance practice. These fields are Quality Assurance, Problem Resolution, Alignment and Integration, Consumer Obsession, and Spiritual Awakening.

Section III—Preparing to Use The Starburst Model™—covers three topics that enable individuals to apply the five fields of performance practice. Chapter 9 addresses the foundational skills and knowledge needed to work within all five of the fields. Chapter 10 outlines several ways to go about acquiring the skills and knowledge identified in chapter 9. Chapter 11 defines the leadership behaviors (summarized by the acronym **COMPASS**™) that need to be enacted by those with leadership responsibility for planning, implementing, and evaluating the five fields of performance practice or their individual components, which includes attention to the forces impacting the workplace of the future.

There are two chapters in Section IV—The Starburst Model™: Implications for Your Organization. They relate what organizations can do to realize the benefits of the five fields of performance practice. Chapter 12 discusses how to use The Starburst Model™ as a framework for promoting quality and creating value throughout the enterprise and ultimately achieving demonstratable performance improvement. Chapter 13 outlines a process for configuring a department or function to assist management in promoting quality and creating value as a means of improving organizational performance.

Section V—Your Career in Organizational Performance Improvement—presents actions that professionals who specialize in enhancing organizational performance can take to ensure their employability in the workplace of the future. Chapter 14 provides an approach for determining one's vocation, career, or job and the numerous steps involved in making a job and/or career change. Chapter 15 explores what it means to be an external consultant. It also examines whether to join an established firm, how to start a firm, and the daily challenges faced by those who are in this role today. Chapter 16 provides the steps for creating a personal action plan.

How To Read and Use This Book

It is important that you read all of Section I (chapters 1 and 2), and chapter 3 in Section II before launching into the rest of the book. These chapters, along with the three conclusions presented earlier, provide the foundation upon which the remaining chapters are written. With the exception of chapters 9 and 10, the rest of the chapters do not need to be read in order of presentation.

Throughout the book you will find questions labeled Inner Exploration and a series of worksheets. Working through these items will help you take the concepts, tools, methods, ideas, and recommendations and apply them to an organization and your specific employment situation. We urge you to spend time reflecting on these questions, completing the worksheets, and documenting actions for the future in order to obtain the benefits outlined in the Who This Book Is For section of the Preface.

> "Quality is dead, long live Quality! In my view, TQM has served its purpose. In my work with the University of CA Santa Cruz Extension, every five years we interview major customers in the Silicon Valley to integrate the Voice of the Customer into the support and education they need from the University. We recently found that organizations had internalized quality to fit their culture and had quality or quality-based goals in their business plans. They want people who are team

players, collaborative, and statistics savvy. Most businesses avoid the term quality—too much of a gag reflex. When quality was mentioned, they thought of measuring [and] of the traditional quality areas—reliability, design of experiments, etc. We learned that TQM is diffused, with no one focus, but that it is required in all functional areas. So in my view, if TQM is your game, change the name."

—Tara Martin-Milius, CEO, Center for Corporate Learning

Endnotes

1. Howard S. Gitlow and Process Management International, Inc., *Planning for Quality, Productivity, & Competitive Position* (Homewood, IL: Dow Jones-Irwin, 1990), 83.
2. Joseph M. Juran, *A History of Managing for Quality: The Evolution, Trends, and Future Directions of Managing for Quality* (Milwaukee: ASQ Quality Press, 1995).
3. ASQC Futures Team, *Quality, the Future, and You: An ASQC Consideration of the Year 2010* (Milwaukee: American Society for Quality Control, 1996), 14.

Section

I

Trends and Forces Affecting Organizational Performance

Section I introduces the trends and forces that are impacting the practice of quality and the success of organizational performance initiatives. Chapter 1 presents the five forces that are shaping the workplace of the future. These five forces—represented by the acronym **CHAOS**—describe the environment in which organizations will be operating over the next five to ten years. They are

- [C]hanging definition of work and the workplace,
- [H]eightened social responsibility,
- [A]ging baby boomers,
- [O]verarching demographic change, and
- [S]trategic growth through technology and innovation.

Chapter 2 introduces five overarching trends that have recently emerged in the practice of quality as a result of present environmental forces. These trends—represented by the acronym **SHIFT**—are influencing the manner in which organizations are approaching performance improvement. They are

- Quality goes [S]ofter,
- Quality goes into [H]iding,
- Quality goes [I]ntegrative,
- Quality goes [F]ar-flung, and
- Quality goes [T]echnical.

Together, these forces and trends are starting to mold the initiatives that organizations are embracing to achieve required business results.

CHAPTER 1

Living in the Workplace of the Future

> "You are already in the organization of the future. Today's stressful workplace is a symptom of something new being born within an older form. The task is not to predict the future and then work towards it. It is not even to run after an evolution that is already in motion. The real leadership challenge is to hasten that evolution by understanding its components and reinforcing its direction."[1]
>
> —Frederick G. Harmon, author of *Playing for Keeps: How the World's Most Aggressive and Admired Companies Use Core Values to Manage, Energize, and Organize Their People and Promote, Advance, and Achieve Their Corporate Missions;* formerly a senior executive with the American Management Association

Some of you may question whether it is possible to predict the future with any degree of accuracy. The data suggest it is. In the February 1997 issue of *THE FUTURIST,* Edward Cornish reviewed 34 forecasts made in the first issue (January–February 1967) and found that 68 percent of them reached fruition.[2] Inaccurate forecasts had failed to take into account shifts in the underlying factors that impacted the direction of future trends. Even though it may not be possible to predict the future with complete accuracy, these underlying factors need to be considered when preparing for future challenges.

Based on an extensive review of literature on the workplace of the future, this chapter highlights the five forces that will have an impact on it and the future practice of quality in the United States. It is likely that many of them will also play out in other developed nations such as Japan, as well as the nations of Europe and North America. The forces covered in this chapter (represented by the acronym **CHAOS**) include

Changing definition of work and the workplace,
Heightened social responsibility,
Aging baby boomers,
Overarching demographic change, and
Strategic growth through technology and innovation.

On the surface, it may appear as though we are living in a chaotic period in history. Change is occurring faster than ever before—around the world, financial markets are volatile, mergers are frequent, and technology development is rampant. The study of complex systems suggests that below the surface of these forces are hidden structures and patterns of interactions. Thus, chaos and order are part of the same system. We believe, as do Watts Wacker and Jim Taylor in their book *The 500-Year Delta,* that collectively these five forces—which are a part of the surface **CHAOS**—hint at the existence of some sort of convergence. We encourage you to think through the many possible scenarios that could result from this convergence and the potential impact these scenarios have on you and your organization.

CHANGING DEFINITION OF WORK AND THE WORKPLACE

Remember the days when you got a job in an organization by responding to a newspaper "help wanted" ad? You were likely interviewed by your potential boss and a representative from the personnel department. A job description detailed the roles and responsibilities you would be asked to perform. It also outlined where you were "positioned" within a specific department and the overall organization. Career paths and career ladders, especially for leadership roles and critical specialty areas, were spelled out. Human resource or career development specialists helped you determine the best way to progress up these defined rungs. Your gross pay and salary increases were defined by charts developed by an outside firm.

Today, changes in the nature of work and the workplace have altered the hiring process, as well as job responsibilities and the path toward career development. What are some of the reasons that account for these changes? For one, blue-collar and white-collar jobs are disappearing. Mergers, technology advancements, reengineering work, the desire to get goods and services more quickly to the marketplace, and the shrinking budget deficit (in terms of defense spending) have led to a permanent reduction of jobs in the United States.[3]

Secondly, multiple alternative work arrangements have been created by the transformation in organizational forms. Organizations are becoming smaller, globalized, virtual, and interdependent. More functions are being outsourced. They are shifting from tall (i.e., hierarchical) to flat (i.e., equal status), and vertical (i.e., functional) to horizontal (i.e., cross-functional). When entering a new job, it is not always clear what work a person has been hired to do. Individuals need to rely on their personal influence and expertise, relationship-building skills, and reputation to get work done since "reporting relationships" have become fuzzy or nonexistent.

Long gone is the reality of a singular job or company for life, as well as loyalty to a specific organization. Moreover, it is frequently difficult to identify who is an employee of the organization, since full-timers often work side-by-side with part-timers, contract employees, and temporary workers. The responsibility for defining one's career path resides with the individual, not the organization.

Definition of Work

> "An analysis of Census Bureau data . . . finds that nearly 30 percent of U.S. workers are now employed in 'nonstandard work arrangements' such as independent contracting, self-employment, part-time employment, or employment through temporary staffing firms. Fifty-eight percent of nonstandard workers are in jobs with substantial penalties and few benefits. . . . When asked, many nonstandard workers . . . say they'd prefer full-time work."[4]

A new definition of work is emerging. However, based on the above data, one wonders whether a majority of those in the workforce are willing to accept a new definition. How is the new definition of work altering the ways in which individuals approach their jobs and their careers? William Bridges, in his book, *JobShift: How to Prosper in a Workplace Without Jobs,* describes the new rules of employment, which include:

1. Employment is contingent on the achievement of organizational results. Therefore, everyone is a contingent worker, not just part-time and contract workers.
2. Because of ever-changing market demands, to stay employed workers must demonstrate their value to the organization in each successive situation they find themselves in.
3. Since employment is "contingent" on achieving organizational results, workers need to develop a mindset, an approach to their work, and a way of managing their own careers that closely mirrors that of people in business for themselves. They need to actively manage a life-long career and self-development plan, take primary responsibility for investing in needed insurance and retirement vehicles, and renegotiate compensation arrangements when organizational needs change.
4. Workers must be able to switch their focus rapidly from one task to another, work on several projects at once, work with people with very diverse backgrounds, work in situations where the group is the responsible party and the leader is only a coordinator, and work without clear position descriptions.
5. Workers need to be ready to move from organization to organization, and from project to project within the same organization. Organizations need to prepare themselves to handle the fallout of these moves.

6. To benefit itself, a wise organization will collaboratively work with contingent workers to make the work relationship beneficial to all involved parties. However, the "benefits" of this new work arrangement will probably be inherent in the nature of the work itself rather than add-on benefits, such as sick leave and health care subsidies. In addition, the organization must do its part to inform, train, and counsel people who are transitioning from the old to the new rules of employment. But, ultimately, it is the individual who must manage this transition.[5]

The new rules of employment encourage a focus on "You, Inc."[6] or "The Brand Called You™."[7] Loyalty to self carries with it three requirements: (1) adhering to personal values, (2) maintaining personal and professional integrity, and (3) striving for meaning and joy in work. Adhering to personal values is demonstrated when individuals do not engage in activities that they feel conflict with what is really "important in life." For example, one would not take a job that requires extensive travel if spending time with family is truly important. Maintaining personal integrity occurs when an individual's actions are consistent with what the person says to others. Maintaining professional integrity means that a person's actions and words are consistent with the codes of ethics prevalent within the individual's profession and industry affiliation. Underlying these two requirements is the need for work to be both meaningful and enjoyable. Individuals do not need to choose between loyalty to themselves and loyalty to their organization(s). They can be loyal to both. In fact, loyalty to an organization may very well increase with the strength of loyalty to self.

As was the norm prior to the Industrial Revolution, integrating life (personal development) and work (professional development) will again become customary. The skill sets that will help carry individuals forward in their career choices will be gained not only in traditional work settings, but in other venues in which they grow and learn. These venues include community service work, primary and secondary school-related activities, and involvement in professional/civic associations. Self-reflection and self-leadership are critical to making this integration work.

Organizational Structure

The changing definition of work, demographic trends (as described later in this chapter), and the application of new technologies will accelerate the need for new organizational designs. Three of these designs are: Organizations as chameleons, organizations as communities, and organizations as virtual entities. These organizational designs do not necessarily conflict with each other. In fact, there are many similarities among them.

Organizations as Chameleons[8]

Organizations need to continually reconfigure themselves to maintain a competitive advantage, much like children are able to quickly reconfigure transformer toys based on the moment (i.e., a warrior becomes a spaceship when it becomes time to flee the battle zone). The organization of the future will need to be as adaptable to its environment as chameleons are to theirs.[9] Organizational structure will follow the guidance of "both/and" versus "either/or" thinking. Enterprises will be "organized by function *and* product *and* [market] segment *and* distribution channel *and* customer to implement a series of constantly changing short-term advantages."[10] The challenges of a chameleon-like organizational structure are twofold. First, the structure must be created. Second, it must be implemented in such a way that all employees are comfortable with the high degree of ambiguity and flexibility that the structure brings forth. This type of structure does not ignore the importance of functional orientation. Functions are proposed as "the structure around which reconfiguration takes place . . . acting as 'homerooms' for those participating in projects and miniature business units [and] . . . as homes for experts and individual contributors."[11]

This type of chameleon, or fluidlike structure, necessitates the removal of boundaries and the introduction of policies to achieve the intended results. There are four types of boundaries that must be removed

1. vertical boundaries—those between levels and ranks of people;
2. horizontal boundaries—those between functions and disciplines;
3. external boundaries—those between the organization and its suppliers, customers, and regulators; and
4. geographic boundaries—those between locations, nations, cultures, and markets.[12]

Even though the concept of the "boundaryless organization" was first put forth by Chairman and CEO Jack Welch at General Electric in 1990, few organizations besides GE, Allied-Signal, Motorola, and others of a similar orientation have really put this sort of thinking into practice. In addition to boundary removal, aligned information, goal-setting, and human resource policies are needed for an organization to support the necessary mindset and the ability to continually reconfigure around internal and external capabilities.[13]

Organizations as Communities

> "The old language of property and ownership no longer serves us in modern society because it no longer describes what a company really is. [It] suggests the wrong priorities, leads to inappropriate policies, and screens out new possibilities. The idea of a corporation as the property of the current holders of its shares is confusing because it does not make clear where power lies. . . . Moreover, the language of property and ownership is an insult to democracy. . . . A public corporation should now be regarded . . . as a community created by common purpose rather than by common place. . . . The core members of communities are more properly regarded as citizens rather than employees or 'human resources'—citizens with responsibilities as well as rights."[14]
>
> —Charles Handy, author of *The Hungry Spirit, Beyond Certainty, The Age of Unreason,* and *The Age of Paradox;* formerly an oil executive, a business economist, and a professor at the London Business School

Organization as community is a second type of organizational structure that is beginning to emerge in business settings. What does it mean to develop corporations as communities? A community, in the broadest sense of the word, has a constitution that recognizes the rights and responsibilities of its different constituencies and puts forth a method of governance. It is something to which one belongs. However, in and of itself, a community truly belongs to no one. The organization as a community is not an instrument of its owners, nor are its people an instrument of the organization. Employees are referred to and treated as members who are selected by and freely choose to join the organization. Its suppliers, distributors, and customers are associates and treated as partners. Its owners are called and treated like investors. If an organization pursues becoming a learning organization, implied in this transformation is the concept of organization as community. However, this does not imply that a learning organization functions as a community, given the definition provided here.

There are some philosophical underpinnings for the creation of community. "Implicit within the process of community . . . are systems thinking and long-term thinking, equal responsibility for the development of community, flexibility and continuous learning, inclusively, encouragement for everyone to assert his or her leadership abilities, and commitment to authenticity and truth-telling."[15] These guiding principles direct the types of practices that need to be displayed within the organization.

There are also two major prerequisites for the creation of community. They are the development of a new social contract (based on the new rules of employment referenced earlier) and the use of self-managed teams.

First, what is needed is ". . . a new contract, a new way of spelling out the responsibilities of financiers, workers, and managers and of their relationship[s] to each other."[16] Charles Handy refers to this contract as a "citizen contract"[17] while Rosabeth Moss Kantor calls it a "new social contract."[18] This new contract, focused on the individual, would provide clear definitions of everyone's rights, responsibilities, and relationships to each other, including a redefinition of the role of management. In this contract, the organization "should show people what [it] is willing to do to help them build their own futures. It should be an explicit statement of how much people are valued. And it should be a commitment to specific actions and specific investments in people."[19] Each party commits to and accepts responsibility for making the agreement work (a measure of loyalty), and consents to the process for changing it as the organization evolves over time.

Once this new social contract has been put in place, it becomes imperative to develop groups of individuals who are able to carry out the work. "Workplace community is the culmination of highly evolved self-managed teams becoming a living organization. . . . Community is established when teams truly acquire the skills and are empowered to make all necessary decisions regarding their own work. And, through their representatives on a board of stakeholders, decisions are made regarding the future of the company and matters of governance."[20] A 1997 *IndustryWeek*

Census of Manufacturers survey (conducted in the United States) found that "despite the proven success of teaming employees . . . nearly one-fifth of all facilities across the country have none of their production employees participating in empowered or self-directed teams. Not quite 23 percent of the plants reported a majority of their workforce empowered and only 4.4 percent of plants (122 facilities) report a 100 percent-empowered workforce."[21] The challenges in this area are enormous. Even though we recognize the value of self-directed teams, there are still a number of obstacles to their implementation—workforce skill levels, time for formal training, turnover rates, and unionization—that need to be overcome for workplace community to take hold.

Why would organizations desire a sense of community in the workplace? Organizational actions such as downsizing and restructuring have shattered the rules of employment surrounding work as we knew it. With them went morale, loyalty, and productivity. By committing to the individual in the form of a new social contract, organizations are hoping to (a) realize the full potential of people who choose to work toward a common purpose; (b) create equitable, productive, participative, and satisfying workplaces; and (c) enrich the lives of people who work in them by creating meaningful work. Most people have experienced a feeling of community during times of organizational crisis. The challenge is to formalize what is meant by community so that it does not disappear as it usually does once the crisis passes. The challenge is also to recognize the value of a "self-organizing system of small, self-managed units, enjoying wide participation, with decisions originating from the bottom up."[22] Organization as community and a new social contract for employment are both explored further in chapter 8.

Organizations as Virtual Entities

What characterizes a virtual organization? What may come to mind is a small, hierarchically flat organization that owns the core business, and is linked to its employees and many independent suppliers by a common product(s)/service(s), business strategy, set of expectations and practices, and communications systems. These relationships can also include distributors, outsourcing partners, and customers. The linkages formed between these various enterprises are not meant to be permanent; they can be reformulated based on the needs of all involved parties. Alignment is a concept that is key to the success of this type of organization. Without a common frame of reference, breakdowns can and do occur.

The traditional "command and control" approach to business is "being replaced by, or intermixed with, all kinds of relationships—alliances, joint ventures, minority participations, partnerships, know-how and marketing agreements—all relationships where no one controls and no one commands."[23] Because of this shift in power, it is not always clear as to what is inside and what is outside of the main organization's boundaries.

"The growth of virtual organizations will be fueled by three factors: (1) the rapid evolution of electronic technologies, which are facilitating the digital, wireless

Derek Boshan

transfer of video, audio, and text information; (2) the rapid spread of computer networks; . . . and (3) the growth of telecommuting, which will enable companies to provide faster response to customers, reduce facility expenses, and help workers meet their child- and elder-care responsibilities."[24] There are several issues that arise with the growth of virtual organizations. They include how to recruit, orient, and train employees; how to communicate expectations; how to plan, organize, and delegate work; how to involve everyone in making decisions; and how to manage information and address information overload. Virtual organizations appear to be the hallmark of the Information Age, also known as the Knowledge Economy.

A New Era Is Under Way

Over 10,000 years ago, workers were hunters and gatherers. The Hunter-Gatherer Era has since given way to at least three different types of economies. The first, called the Agricultural Economy, lasted thousands of years.[25] The Industrial Economy, which began around 1750 when steam engines appeared in England, followed it and lasted only a couple of hundred years. Most of the tools and methods associated with traditional quality improvement emerged during this era. The third type of economy, often referred to as the Information Age, started somewhere around 1950. It is projected to last anywhere from 30 to 40 years (at its peak) to 100 years in length overall.[26,27] Some suggest that the percentage of the U.S. Labor force employed in Information Age-related work will grow to about 50 percent within the next 50 years (i.e., about the middle of the twenty-first century).[28]

In the Information Age, people are the source of power in organizations since the "product" of their work is knowledge and the application of it. This source of power has been called "intellectual capital." To be effective, knowledge workers need to be able to question fundamental assumptions, use critical thinking skills to assess what is in front of them, and manage hoards of information. Technical expertise in many fields has a half-life that is far shorter than it was ten years ago, and it is shrinking daily. Consequently, the recency of learnings and experience in technical areas carries more importance than work experience. Concepts surrounding "the new science"—chaos theory, complex systems, and interdependency—have also taken hold during this era. These concepts have had an impact on generating new organizational designs (as described earlier in this chapter). For example, telecommuting has become possible because people can connect to the workplace via electronic communications. Telecommuting allows individuals to once again integrate their personal and work lives.

One societal challenge of this economy revolves around the disparity between the "have's" and the "have-not's" relative to access to knowledge and information. A second challenge, for the workplace, is the need to rethink traditional approaches to coaching, mentoring, and motivating workers.

As we enter the new millennium, the roots of another economy appear to have already started to take hold in the world of business. This new economy has been referred to as the Existential Era[29] or Dream Society.[30] Its emergence as a percentage of the United States labor force has hovered around five to ten percent over the past 50 years, and, it is anticipated to peak at about 50 percent around the year 2150.[31] "One view . . . that seems to be emerging is that consciousness is causal, that the inner experiences of individuals, including intuitions, emotions, creativity, and spirit are vastly more important than the world of the senses alone. [S]cientific discoveries, coupled with the experience and yearnings of many of us, have moved us to a view of the world that is characterized by wholeness and connection and of the primacy of inner wisdom and inner authority."[32] Individuals will search for meaning in work, thus necessitating a new set of organizational values. As mentioned earlier, work (which will be viewed as play) and leisure will be intertwined. Material consumption and its overt display will give way to other types of status symbols. These will include what some consider to be scarce today—satisfaction, domestic contentment, and spiritual experiences.[33] The source of power will move from knowledge workers who provide intellectual capital to storytellers who provide stories that produce "dreams" for public consumption.[34] The Nike television ads featuring Michael Jordan, Tiger Woods, and Olympic gold medal recipients are recent examples of this shift in power.

Inner Exploration

1. How will the changing definition of work affect your organization's business performance?
2. Describe the type of organizational structure embraced by your organization today. What challenges exist because of this structure? What type of structure do you think would better support your organization's business?
3. What impact will the Information Age continue to have on your organization's business performance? What impact will the transition to the Dream Society have on its future business performance?
4. What steps has your organization taken (or does it plan to take) to put the new social contract for employment in place?

HEIGHTENED SOCIAL RESPONSIBILITY

> "The old paradigm has always measured wealth strictly as financial assets derived from productivity and profit. This kind of thinking has focused on short-term exploitation and competition, the traditional balance sheet and financial statement, and a quick return for stockholders. The new paradigm explores a different concept of wealth based on intellectual capital and social accounting. Proponents are also developing a sense of value based on a corporation's contribution to global responsibility, the health of the planet, and the personal fulfillment of its employees, in addition to the financial rewards of its stakeholders."[35]

What is causing the increased interest in corporate social responsibility and accountability? Perhaps it is customers who are becoming more demanding of the organizations whose products and services they purchase. Perhaps it is the community in which the organization is located that has become jaded due to downsizing and restructuring efforts, as well as environmental pollution. Perhaps the pressure being applied by external public constituents is becoming more overt. Or, perhaps it is the enlightened personal values and philosophy of the organization's owners. In any case, an organization's commitment, and that of its leaders, to social responsibility can only serve to make the world a better place.

To the Planet

As a result of the Industrial Revolution, with its apparent disregard for the environment, there has emerged an increased focus on the health of the planet. If we believe that the world needs to be managed as a living, breathing system composed of many interconnected parts, then it becomes imperative to develop a sustainable society. A sustainable society, according to Lester Brown of the Worldwatch Institute, "is one that satisfies its needs without diminishing the prospects of future generations."[36] This type of thinking implies a shift toward economic activity that increases human welfare and is based on ecologically focused corporate values.

From an environmental perspective, individuals and organizations will be concerned not only about the impact of waste and emissions; they will also be concerned about better utilization of raw materials. The world's supply of raw materials will no longer be viewed as infinite, and it will become essential, for personal and organizational financial health, to eliminate or minimize by-product waste. Environmental issues will be accorded strategic priority. Economic growth and environmental protection will be managed in concert.

One approach to integrating economic growth and environmental protection is zero-emissions manufacturing, or complete elimination of waste by reusing or recycling all the raw materials a factory takes in.[37] Gunter Pauli launched the Zero Emissions Research Initiative (ZERI) in April 1994 at the United Nations University Office in Tokyo to put together zero-emissions technology and document its performance benefits. While zero emissions may not be cheaper, its proponents claim it can help an organization to make more money. Namibia Brewers Ltd. in Tsumeb, Namibia, is the first company to commit to building a plant based on zero-emissions principles. As a "fully integrated biosystem . . . the complex will produce seven times more food, fuel, and fertilizer than a conventional operation, and create four times as many jobs."[38] Perhaps zero emissions is a way for organizations to strategically distinguish themselves from others in their industry. This approach is discussed further in chapter 8.

To Society

> "Overall, supply now outstrips demand. In the past, consumers had to make trade-offs among cost, quality, and convenience. No more. Since the late 1980s it is possible to have it all. When the consumer can conveniently get high quality at

low cost, then what is the next demand? I think it could be argued that it is social responsibility on the part of the company that produces goods and services. Consumers don't have to do business with a company that pollutes, or exploits workers, or is racist. We can know 'the bad guys' easily. The Internet has Web sites that allow unhappy customers to tell the world."

—Nancy M. Johnson, Ph.D., Vice President, Corporate Research and Development, American Family Insurance

The philosophy that guides socially responsible organizations is one in which the organization transforms itself into a community where work takes on deeper meaning and satisfaction. Inherent in this philosophy is the belief that organizations are defined by their roles in society, not just by their offerings or brand image.

Socially responsible organizations such as The Body Shop (natural cosmetics), Tom's of Maine (natural personal care products), and Ben & Jerry's (ice cream and yogurt) commit to a higher purpose. This higher purpose is grounded in their values and guiding principles, and goes far beyond their stated mission and vision statements.[39] Out of 100 international company reports evaluated by SustainAbility for the United Nations Environmental Programme, The Body Shop's Values Report 1997 scored the highest rating for the second year in a row by engaging in unusual efforts to integrate social and environmental reporting with significant stakeholder engagement.[40] In the case of Tom's of Maine, the company's products are all developed using nonanimal testing methods and made using natural ingredients.[41] Ben & Jerry's meanwhile, is dedicated to the creation and demonstration of a new corporate concept of linked prosperity. It gives away 7.5 percent of its pretax earnings to projects that are models for social change.[42] These organizations recognize that they exist to serve society. The values that are a part of this recognition are themselves different. They include beliefs such as "responsibility for the whole, importance of the common good, equality through freedom of expression and equal rights, respect for all life, and unconditional caring."[43]

Improving economic performance needs to be balanced with producing social benefits and results. Based on a series of case studies and interviews conducted in preparation for the 1995 U.N. World Social Summit in Copenhagen, Denmark, it appears that there is a positive correlation between corporate social responsibility (including environmental, ethical, and social impact) and corporate strategy for sustained and improved competitiveness.[44] Traditional financial measures of success and associated approaches to leadership and work need to be redefined to promote socially compelling agendas that may not be economically rational.

This sense of social responsibility does not develop overnight. In the coming years, corporations will experience increasing pressure to explore and redefine their ethics. The Ethical Accounting Statement is one tool that has been used since 1988 in about 50 Danish private and public organizations to introduce and maintain value-based management and organizational ethics.[45] Another tool is the Sunshine Standards for Corporate Reporting to Stakeholders. It is used by the Stakeholder

Inner Exploration

1. What does your organization need to do to comply with the social responsibility agenda?
2. What degree of alignment exists between the organization's business decisions and the social responsibility agenda? What systems need to be put in place to ensure alignment?
3. What types of leadership behaviors are required to promote social responsibility?
4. Does your organization have a statement of higher purpose? If not, what do you think the statement should say?

Alliance (representing more than 15 million individuals) and calls for detailed corporate disclosure of information on numerous items, such as

- "indictments and citations for regulatory violations during the previous five years
- "warnings regarding unusual contamination and adulteration exposure and risks during production, shipping, marketing, and storage of products
- "customer satisfaction measures appropriate to the organization's products and industry
- "layoff records for the previous five years
- "medical data on past accidents, injuries, illnesses and medical complaints.
- "hires, promotions, and average total compensation by gender and race, tabulated by job level/classification."[46]

Social Accountability 8000, the new international and inter-industry standard whose development has been driven since 1997 by The Council on Economic Priorities Accreditation Agency, also focuses on workplace conditions and is designed to promote fair and humane labor practices.[47] To achieve sustainability of the planet, doing what is in the long-term interest of the world will need to replace doing what is best for the organization or a small portion of society. Demands will be placed on boards of directors to align with new social accountabilities, new business relationships, and more diverse memberships. More importantly, individuals will want to see what value a potential employer adds to society before committing to work for it. The concept of social responsibility and accountability, and the use of social responsibility audits, are covered further in chapter 8.

AGING BABY BOOMERS

> "Just over the horizon looms a demographic time bomb for the nation's employers and no one has figured out yet how to defuse it."[48]

The U.S. population is aging. The baby boomers (those born between 1943 and 1960[49]) are getting older and having fewer children. The number of people aged 65 and older will double between 1990 and 2025, an increase from around 30 million to approximately 62 million people.[50] "If the current birthrates are kept constant, by the year 2035, nearly a quarter of the United States population will be elderly people."[51] This trend is occurring not only in the United States, but in most of the industrialized world.

If baby boomers retire at the traditional retirement age of 65 and follow the same age-related spending patterns that their parents did (with peak family spending occurring between the ages of 45 and 49[52]), their aging could have dramatic effects on the economy. It is predicted that the aging of the baby boomers in the United States, Germany, and Japan will trigger a global depression from late 2008 to 2023 due to a decrease in spending spurred by their desire to work less.[53] Even if the aging of the United States population does not contribute to the potential for a global depression, it will definitely impact the demand for various products and services, especially those in the healthcare industry. In addition, it is conceivable that these social forces will also cause elderly parents to move into the homes of their children or motivate them to form shared-living arrangements.

Will the assumption about baby boomers retiring at age 65 hold true? A number of social forces are now converging that could allow people to continue working past the traditional retirement age. These forces include

- more older people wanting to work and desiring to be useful
- healthier older people and less physically demanding work
- older people financially needing to work
- mid-life changes, as well as regular exits from and reentry to the workplace, becoming more common due to increased career education
- older workers becoming more desirable and necessary.[54]

As a result of these social forces, ". . . retirement as we now know it will soon disappear. The past tendency toward early retirement will slow and finally reverse itself, at first in a few industries, and eventually across the whole workforce."[55] Perhaps when people take advantage of early retirement, they will not retire for life, but begin second (or third) careers.

Aging of baby boomers, when combined with the new rules of employment, suggests "the cycle of work" mindset which is still pervasive in our society, will also need to be confronted. This cycle of work mindset states that, ideally, schooling (either completion of high school or college) is followed by a very lengthy period of active employment, which is followed by unemployment (i.e., retirement), and always by aging.[56] But, what if schooling (both training and education)

Inner Exploration

1. What impact will the aging of the baby boomers have on your organization's performance?
2. What changes will your organization need to make to address the changes in workforce composition with aging baby boomers?
3. How will your organization's recruitment and retention efforts, and its reward and recognition systems, need to be altered to handle the changing age composition of those available for hire?
4. How will your organization deal with the retirement shortfall—pension plans, social security, and Medicare/Medicaid?

happened continuously throughout one's adult life? What if unemployed workers of all ages were called "workers in reserve" rather than "unemployed"?[57] And, what if professional organizations to which they belonged, as funded by private organizations, helped these "workers in reserve" to assess their situation, provided them with retraining at adult educational institutions, and paid them a salary?[58] These retrained individuals could then either be rehired by their former organizations or by other firms that desired a specific set of skills, knowledge, and experiences. Not only would this approach start to address the labor shortages projected in the coming years, but it would also allow individuals the opportunity to more easily come and go from the workforce. This approach assumes, of course, that professional associations and adult educational institutions are at the leading edge of what is occurring in the specific industry(ies) they represent.

There is nothing that we can foresee in medical advancements or technology that has the ability to reverse or stop this aging trend in the next decade or two. As a result, there is no denying that we are running headlong into a labor shortage in nearly all sectors of our economy that most of us and our organizations have not even begun to prepare for.

OVERARCHING DEMOGRAPHIC CHANGE

The aging of the workforce is a problem in the United States and other developed countries, but it is not a world-wide issue. It is predicted that in the year 2000, the world population will be 6.1 billion; approximately 31 percent of the population will be under the age of 15, with a median age of 26.1 and an average life expectancy of 63.9.[59] By the end of the next century, it is anticipated that the world population will approach 11.5 billion.[60] "If we assume that a lowering of the death rate at each age continues at the same pace as it did in the 1980s, children born in 2015 [in developed countries] could expect [on average] to live into their 90s."[61] Since most of the world population will be in underdeveloped countries that are without the resources or technologies to feed and care for them, it is possible that, in 2000, a 20-year period of population megadisasters will be triggered due to famine, drought, crop failures, mismanagement, and warfare.[62]

While the entire world is moving toward overpopulation, the developed countries (Japan, and the nations of Europe and North America) are trending toward underpopulation.[63] This underpopulation of the developed countries poses some serious workplace issues, when combined with the aging of the baby boomers. For example, if the developed countries become underpopulated, they will most likely need to import workers from underdeveloped countries to handle their labor shortages. This phenomenon would accelerate the diversity trends of the past few decades. In the United States, these imported workers would be not only culturally different, but less likely to speak English. It is important to recognize that today "migration is at an all-time high around the world and is likely to increase in the future . . . about 125 million people now live outside their birth country—roughly equal to the entire population of Japan or 2 percent of the world population."[64]

There are factors other than the importing of workers from underdeveloped countries that are also sparking an increase in workplace diversity in the United States. By the year 2000, blacks, Asians, Hispanics, and other minorities are anticipated to account for 26 percent of the workforce.[65] Projections suggest that ethnic minorities may account for 30 percent of the total U.S. population by 2033, if low birth rates and illegal immigration continue at current rates.[66] Gender diversity is also on the rise. If current trends continue in the United States, non-Hispanic white males will represent less than 40 percent of the workforce by the year 2005, down from 60 percent in 1960.[67] By the year 2000, over 60 percent of adult women in the United States will be working, which equates to nearly one-half of the American workforce.[68] In 1990, approximately four out of ten working women had children.[69] There is no reason to believe these ratios will not continue. Thus, the boundaries between the workplace and the home will continue to blur, raising additional child care and insurance issues. In addition, the practice of leadership will also be influenced by increasing numbers of minorities and women in the workplace.

Inner Exploration

1. How will the increasing diversity of the workforce affect your organization?
2. What is your organization doing to ensure that pay, employee benefits, recognition, and rewards meet the needs of a diverse workforce?
3. What types of education and preparation will be required in your organization to maintain and enhance current levels of performance? What will be the best ways to deliver education and job training to a diverse workforce?

STRATEGIC GROWTH THROUGH TECHNOLOGY AND INNOVATION

> "Focusing on growth, rather than the game of strategy innovation, is likely to destroy wealth rather than create it. The reason is simple. There are as many stupid ways to grow as there are to cut: acquisitions that destroy value (Sony and Matsushita in Hollywood), market share battles that lower industry profitability (the airlines' perennial favorite), and megabucks blue-sky projects (think Apple and Newton) are just a few examples that should illustrate the danger of go-for-broke growth strategies."[70]
>
> —Gary Hamel, chairman of Strategos and visiting professor at the London School of Business, co-author of *Competing for the Future*

Creating and maintaining a sustainable competitive advantage in one's marketplace through cost management and the achievement of strategic imperatives is not enough. Many organizations also desire continued growth in revenue and market share. Going "global" has enabled these organizations to grow over the past decade. However, for some of them, increasing competition has slowed this growth. To achieve growth and continued differentiation, organizations are looking toward the heightened use of technology and strategy innovation.

Even though computer technology has strongly influenced people's lives, organizations have only begun to explore the myriad ways in which it can transform the workplace of the future. Further exploration needs to include using computer technology to (a) advance strategic issues, (b) enhance deliberations and communications at more advanced levels, (c) redefine organizational boundaries, (d) create communities of learning, and (e) enhance daily on-the-job training. Other technological implications at work include solving transportation gridlock, using artificial intelligence in practical applications, and applying expert systems in routine work.

It is possible that everything around us will become "smart"—that is, responsive to its external and internal environment via either sensors or materials that are sensitive to physical variables. Already we are seeing the use of "smart" cards in addition to debit and check cards, and "smart" fabrics that can keep us cool in hot weather and warm in cool weather.

Innovation has made an impact in many other areas as well. Breakthroughs in nanotechnology, genetic engineering, disease control, and fiber optics are currently being realized. Each of these applications opens up new streams of revenue growth for those organizations that are able to capitalize on them. However, just because something is technologically possible does not mean that it should proceed. The use of technology must occur in a socially responsible manner. For example, a majority of the people who responded to the September 1997 American Society for Quality/Gallup Survey do not necessarily see technological networking and communications capabilities as a prerequisite for leading a better life.[71] Future innovations and technological change should be, if not absolute prerequisites to a better life, at least contributors in some way.

> "The top 10 innovative products for 2006, as selected by Battelle researchers include: (1) genetaceuticals (the combination of genetic research and pharmaceutical responses), (2) personalized computers, (3) multifuel automobiles, (4) next-generation television (digital, high-definition, with clarity approaching that of a movie screen), (5) electronic cash, (6) home health monitors (for aging baby boomers), (7) smart maps and tracking devices, (8) smart materials, (9) weight-control and antiaging products, and (10) never-owned products (i.e., leasing of computers, major household appliances, etc.)."[72]

"The acceleration of technological progress has created an urgent need for a counterballast—for 'high touch' experiences. . . . High touch is about getting back to a human scale."[73] For example, the Internet allows individuals to converse in "chat rooms" and send greeting cards to others; the Concorde provides quickened transportation for those who have a short window of opportunity to meet face-to-face; and computer technology has allowed some car owners immediate access to trouble-shooting car problems and a "concierge" who can provide directions.

Technology is also responsible for "technoshrink"—the continuing shrinking of time and space.[74] This shrinkage has motivated the move to a global economy that has, in turn, influenced downsizing initiatives, marketing through facsimile, and the movement of some jobs overseas. Many businesses are now operating on a 24-hour-a-day basis. Some observers call this phenomenon "24-×-7"—referring to the fact that early mornings, evenings, and weekends are regarded as seamless phases of a new, never-ending business stretch. This change is spanning all facets of economic life worldwide.

Technology, in and of itself, is an enabler of change. It initiates change and allows us to respond to it. Technology has become an important part of our ability to be productive at work and achieve a higher quality of life outside of work. While technology may cause an innovation to be possible—such as the processing speed of supercomputers—at times it also becomes the solution to unanswered consumer wants and needs.

What prevents many organizations from pursuing innovation? Some reasons include deeply ingrained assumptions and beliefs, comfort levels in dealing with change, tunnel vision when looking at market and competitor information, and a culture not beholden to creativity. Now more than ever it is important for organizations to achieve innovation in product, process, and service as a means of value creation. This implies a move from innovation as a part of research and development to innovation as an integral part of everyone's daily work. Consequently, organizations will need to embrace a systematic approach to the generation and screening of innovative ideas that can be taught to all employees.

Inner Exploration

1. What does the phrase "strategic growth" mean in terms of your organization's ability to achieve and sustain a competitive advantage? What initiatives are currently under way in your organization that fall under this definition of "strategic growth"?
2. What impact are technology and innovation having on your organization today? How will your organization use technology and innovation in the future? What impact will this have on the organization's long-term performance?

Strategy innovation "is the capacity to reconceive the existing industry model in ways that create new value for customers, wrong-foot competitors, and produce new wealth for all stakeholders."[75] To ensure strategy innovation, breakthrough value-creating strategies need to be an outcome of the strategy creation process. This type of outcome suggests a radical, new look at the process of developing strategic plans.[76] Many of today's approaches to planning provide little more than "more of the same" packaged a little bit differently. To create strategic growth implies, at a minimum, an approach to planning that involves (a) large portions—if not all—of the organization and one's industry in thoughtful conversations, (b) a predisposition to experiment with new approaches, and (c) a belief system that values discovery learning.

FUTURES STUDIES IN QUALITY AND TRAINING

Two recent futures studies have been conducted that relate to the workplace of the future and the practice of quality. These studies were conducted by the American Society for Quality (ASQ) and the American Society for Training & Development (ASTD). ASQ's study took a look at year 2010 and answered the questions, "Where is Quality heading and how will the future impact ASQ, its members, and other users of Quality, both now and in the future?"[77] Nine key forces and four resulting scenarios are summarized in the booklet titled *Quality, The Future, and You.* ASTD's study put forth three scenarios that addressed how smart products, interconnected workers, and intellectual capital will influence each other in 2020. The organization also gleaned data about the top ten trends most likely to affect the future of training professionals.[78] To read more about these trends and the scenarios created by ASTD, we encourage you to obtain a copy of the November 1996 issue of *Training & Development.*

The ASQ study supports the three conclusions outlined in the Introduction and the five forces of **CHAOS** presented in this chapter. It also addresses globalization; the speed at which organizations adapt to change; the application of quality tools and techniques to education, health care, and the public sectors; and increased customer focus as demonstrated through mass customization and an intolerance for defects. The ASTD study also supports the five forces of **CHAOS.** It encourages training departments to focus on outputs (improved performance) rather than inputs (classes, number of people trained, etc.), and more on interventions in performance improvement and human performance management. In addition, it concludes that corporate training departments will change dramatically in size and composition, thus increasing the need for outsourcing and partnering arrangements; that the American workforce will be more educated; and that work systems will become integrated and high-performance.

CONCLUSION

As Frederick G. Harmon suggests in his comments on the first page of this chapter, each of us is already in the organization of the future. Each of us has a role in helping others to increase their understanding of the significance of the five forces of **CHAOS**

[C]hanging definition of work and the workplace,
[H]eightened social responsibility,
[A]ging baby boomers,
[O]verarching demographic change, and
[S]trategic growth through technology and innovation

so that they can make better-informed decisions relative to future actions. It is apparent that what many people and their organizations are doing today is not enough. This is the challenge that lies in front of us.

> "Today in the quality world there are a new set of rules that are grounded in three premises. (1) Many quality techniques have matured and are no longer sufficient to get attention. (2) Information technology is dramatically changing the way work gets done with implications for the quality professional. For example, every customer can be its own segment; supply chains are seamless. My impression is that quality has not kept up; it is not using state-of-the-art information technology strategies. (3) Globalization of markets, organizations, and supply chains. You can source and sell anywhere. For example, India has 100,000 programmers at work exporting programs to the world via the Internet. How do you manage a team via the Internet? How do you manage the supply chain when you have virtual suppliers linked by data but you rarely see them?"
>
> —David Luther, Vice President of Finance and Administration, Green Mountain Energy Resources; Principal, Luther Quality Associates; Past President and Past Chairman, American Society for Quality

Endnotes

1. Frederick G. Harmon, "Future Present," in *The Organization of the Future,* eds. Frances Hesselbein et al., (San Francisco: Jossey-Bass Inc., Publishers, 1997), 239.
2. Edward Cornish, "FUTURIST Forecasts 30 Years Later," *THE FUTURIST* (January–February 1997), 48.
3. William Bridges, *JobShift: How to Prosper in a Workplace Without Jobs* (Reading, MA: Addison Wesley Publishing Company, 1994), 5–6.
4. "The Price of Freedom," *TRAINING* (November 1997), 12.
5. Bridges, *JobShift: How to Prosper in a Workplace Without Jobs,* 50–52.
6. Richard J. Leider, "The Ultimate Leadership Task," in *The Leader of the Future,* eds. Frances Hesselbein et al., (San Francisco: Jossey-Bass Inc., Publishers, 1996), 189–198.
7. Tom Peters, "The Brand Called You™," *Fast Company* (August–September 1997), 83–94.
8. Doug Miller, "The Future Organization: A Chameleon in All Its Glory," in *The Organization of the Future,* eds. Frances Hesselbein et al., (San Francisco: Jossey-Bass Inc., Publishers, 1997), 119.
9. Miller, "The Future Organization: A Chameleon in All Its Glory," 119.
10. Jay Galbraith, "The Reconfigurable Organization," in *The Organization of the Future,* eds. Frances Hesselbein et al., (San Francisco: Jossey-Bass Inc., Publishers, 1997), 92.
11. Galbraith, "The Reconfigurable Organization," 96.

12. Ron Ashkenas et al., *The Boundaryless Organization: Breaking the Chains of Organizational Structure* (San Francisco: Jossey-Bass Inc., Publishers, 1995), 3.

13. Galbraith, "The Reconfigurable Organization," 92–93.

14. Charles Handy, "The Citizen Corporation," *Harvard Business Review* (September–October 1997), 26, 28.

15. Kazimierz Gozdz, "Building Community as a Leadership Discipline," in *The New Paradigm in Business: Emerging Strategies for Leadership and Organizational Change,* eds. Michael Ray and Alan Rinzler (New York: G. P. Putnam's Sons, 1993), 116.

16. Charles Handy, "Unimagined Futures," in *The Organization of the Future,* eds. Frances Hesselbein et al., (San Francisco: Jossey-Bass Inc., Publishers, 1997), 382.

17. Handy, "The Citizen Corporation," 28.

18. Rosabeth Moss Kantor, "Restoring People to the Heart of the Organization of the Future," in *The Organization of the Future,* eds. Frances Hesselbein et al., (San Francisco: Jossey-Bass Inc., Publishers, 1997), 148.

19. Kantor, "Restoring People to the Heart of the Organization of the Future," 148–149.

20. John Nirenberg, "From Team Building to Community Building," *National Productivity Review* (Winter 1994/95), 54.

21. George Taninecz, "Best Practices and Performances," *IndustryWeek* (December 1, 1997), 29.

22. William E. Halal, "Organizational Complexity," in *Encyclopedia of the Future, Vol. II,* eds. George Kurian and Graham Molitor, (New York: Simon & Schuster Macmillan, 1996), 683.

23. Peter F. Drucker, "Introduction: Toward the New Organization," in *The Organization of the Future,* eds. Frances Hesselbein et al., (San Francisco: Jossey-Bass Inc., Publishers, 1997), 2.

24. Robert Barner, "The New Millennium Workplace: Seven Changes That Will Challenge Management and Workers," *THE FUTURIST* (March–April 1996), 14.

25. Linda Groff, "Social and Political Evolution," in *Encyclopedia of the Future, Vol. II,* eds. George Kurian and Graham Molitor, (New York: Simon & Schuster Macmillan, 1996), 855.

26. Groff, "Social and Political Evolution," 855.

27. William Halal, "The Rise of the Knowledge Entrepreneur," *THE FUTURIST* (November–December 1996), 14.

28. Halal, "The Rise of the Knowledge Entrepreneur," 14.

29. Halal, "The Rise of the Knowledge Entrepreneur," 14.

30. Rolf Jensen, "The Dream Society," *THE FUTURIST* (May–June 1996), 9.

31. Halal, "The Rise of the Knowledge Entrepreneur," 14.

32. Michael Ray, "Introduction: What is the New Paradigm in Business?" in *The New Paradigm in Business: Emerging Strategies for Leadership and Organizational Change,* eds. Michael Ray and Alan Rinzler, (New York: G. P. Putnam's Sons, 1993), 3–4.

33. "Report from the Futurist: Watts Wacker," *Fast Company* (October–November 1997), 40.

34. Jensen, "The Dream Society," 9–10.

35. Herman Bryant Maynard, Jr. and Susan E. Mehrtens, "Redefinitions of Corporate Wealth," in *The New Paradigm in Business: Emerging Strategies for Leadership and Organizational Change,* eds. Michael Ray and Alan Rinzler, (New York: G. P. Putnam's Sons, 1993), 36.

36. Frijof Capra, "A Systems Approach to the Emerging Paradigm," in *The New Paradigm in Business: Emerging Strategies for Leadership and Organizational Change,* eds. Michael Ray and Alan Rinzler, (New York: G. P. Putnam's Sons, 1993), 234.
37. Steve Butler, "Green Machine," *Fast Company* (June–July 1997), 114.
38. Butler, "Green Machine," 115.
39. I. Somerville and John Edwin Mroz, "New Competencies for a New World," in *The Organization of the Future,* eds. Frances Hesselbein et al. (San Francisco: Jossey-Bass Inc., Publishers, 1997), 67.
40. "Company & Values: Welcome to the Body Shop Values Report," www.the-body-shop.com/values/valuesrep.html (1998).
41. "The Tom's of Maine Story," www.toms-of-maine.com/people/tkstory.html (1995–1996), 2.
42. "Everything You Ever Wanted to Know About Ben & Jerry's," www.benjerry.com/aboutbj.html (March 1998), 1.
43. Richard Barrett, "A Corporate Values Revolution," *Perspectives on Business and Global Change,* Vol. 10, No. 3 (1996), 53–55.
44. Kim Møller, "Social Responsibility as a Corporate Strategy," *Perspectives on Business and Global Change,* Vol. 11, No. 1 (March 1997), 49.
45. Pruzan Peter, "The Ethical Accounting Statement," *World Business Academy Perspectives,* Vol. 9, No. 2 (1995), 40, 44.
46. Ralph Estes and Subashini Ganesan, "The Stakeholder Alliance: A New Bottom Line," *Perspectives on Business and Global Change* (December 1997), 70.
47. Elizabeth R. Larson and Bonnie Cox, "Social Accountability 8000: Measuring Workplace Conditions Worldwide," *Quality Digest* (February 1998), 26.
48. Sue Shellenbarger, "Firms Try Harder, But Often Fail to Help Workers Cope With Elder-Care Problems," *Wall Street Journal* (June 23, 1993): B1, as referenced in S. Crampton, J. Hodge, and J. Mishra "Transition—Ready or Not: The Aging of America's Workforce," *Public Personal Management,* Vol. 25, No. 2 (Summer 1996), 243.
49. Jay A. Conger, "How Generational Shifts Will Transform Organizational Life," in *The Organization of the Future,* eds. Frances Hesselbein et al. (San Francisco: Jossey-Bass, Inc., Publishers, 1997), 19.
50. S. Crampton, J. Hodge, and J. Mishra, "Transition–Ready or Not: The Aging of America's Workforce," *Public Personal Management,* Vol. 25, No. 2 (1996), 244.
51. L. Bronte and A. Pifer, *Our Aging Society, Paradox and Promise* (New York: W. W. Norton & Company, 1986), 4.
52. Harry S. Dent, Jr., *The Great Boom Ahead* (New York: Hyperion, 1993), 26.
53. Dent, Jr., *The Great Boom Ahead,* 35.
54. Mercedes M. Fisher, "The Last of the Baby Boomers and Their Prospects for Climbing the Corporate Ladder of Success," in *FutureVision: Ideas, Insights, and Strategies,* ed. Howard F. Didsbury, Jr. (Bethesda, MD: World Future Society), 6–7.
55. R. Mowsesian, *Golden Goals, Rusted Realities* (Far Hills, NJ: New Horizon Press, 1986), 183.
56. Bertrand H. Chatel, "Unemployment and Underconsumption in the 21st Century," in *FutureVision: Ideas, Insights, and Strategies,* ed. Howard F. Didsbury, Jr. (Bethesda, MD: World Future Society, 1996), 44.
57. Chatel, "Unemployment and Underconsumption in the 21st Century," 43.

58. Chatel, "Unemployment and Underconsumption in the 21st Century," 45–46.
59. George Kurian and Graham Molitor, eds., *Encyclopedia of the Future, Vol. II,* (New York: Simon & Schuster Macmillan, 1996), 1052.
60. Carl Haub and Steven Gurley, "Population Growth: Worldwide," in *Encyclopedia of the Future, Vol. II,* eds. George Kurian and Graham Molitor (New York: Simon & Schuster Macmillan, 1996), 740.
61. Elizabeth W. Markson, "Longevity," in *Encyclopedia of the Future, Vol. II,* eds. George Kurian and Graham Molitor (New York: Simon & Schuster Macmillan, 1996), 575.
62. Kurian and Molitor, eds., *Encyclopedia of the Future, Vol. II,* 1052.
63. Peter F. Drucker, "The Future that Has Already Happened," *Harvard Business Review* (September–October 1997), 20.
64. "Surge in Global Migration," *THE FUTURIST* (January–February 1997), 40.
65. Joseph Coates, "Workforce Diversity," in *Encyclopedia of the Future, Vol. II,* eds. George Kurian and Graham Molitor (New York: Simon & Schuster Macmillan, 1996), 1006.
66. Coates, "Workforce Diversity," 1006.
67. Joseph H. Boyett and Jimmie T. Boyett, *Beyond Workplace 2000: Essential Strategies for the New Corporation* (New York: Dutton, 1995), 79.
68. Boyett and Boyett, *Beyond Workplace 2000: Essential Strategies for the New Corporation,* 80.
69. Boyett and Boyett, *Beyond Workplace 2000: Essential Strategies for the New Corporation,* 81.
70. Gary Hamel, "Strategy Innovation and the Quest for Value," *Sloan Management Review* (Winter 1998), 9.
71. *Promise vs. Payoff: Consumer Attitudes on Quality in the Age of the Networked Society* (Milwaukee: American Society for Quality, 1997), 1–2.
72. Stephen Millett and William Kopp, "The Top Ten Innovative Products for 2006: Technology with a Human Touch," *THE FUTURIST* (July–August 1996), 16–19.
73. "Report from the Futurist: John Naisbitt," *Fast Company* (December–January 1998), 44.
74. Harmon, "Future Present," 243–244.
75. Hamel, "Strategy Innovation and the Quest for Value," 8.
76. Hamel, "Strategy Innovation and the Quest for Value," 10.
77. ASQC Futures Team, *Quality, the Future, and You: An ASQC Consideration of the Year 2010* (Milwaukee: American Society for Quality Control, 1996).
78. Laurie J. Bass, George Benson, and Scott Cheney, "The Top Ten Trends," *Training & Development* (November 1996), 28–42.

CHAPTER 2

Quality Today: Recognizing the Critical **SHIFT**

"Quality got jump-started in the 1980s triggered by the Japanese threat. Our pride and our pocketbook were hurting. This set the stage for Dr. Deming and others. Quality appeared as the salvation of American industry, but hit a plateau in the mid-1990s. The people who were going to do it were doing it, not talking about it. It is still a driving force in business but people are not talking about it or treating it as something amazing."

—Jack Gordon, Editor, *TRAINING* Magazine

"During the late 1970s and 1980s it was the 'summer of quality.' Quality went into a very early autumn in the very early 1990s. From 1991 to 1994, it was the winter of quality. From late 1994 through 1995, it was the spring of quality. Today, we are in the late spring. Quality is on the rise, but it doesn't look the same. Today, quality must be very strategic and produce results. When summer comes again, quality might just be called 'management.' But, incredibly good times could postpone the summer."

—Howard Gitlow, Ph.D.,
Professor of Management Science,
School of Business Administration,
University of Miami

Just when you think you have the field of quality figured out, it changes. This is also true of the data that emerged on the performance of quality initiatives in the early to mid-1990s that caused people to say, "Quality is dead!" Were all quality initiatives and programs merely separate fads, as their detractors claim, or the natural progression and maturation of a single unified body of knowledge?

Based on a variety of perspectives about the past, the present, and the future of quality, this chapter discusses five overarching trends already underway in the field of quality. This **SHIFT** is represented by

Quality goes **S**ofter,
Quality goes into **H**iding,
Quality goes **I**ntegrative,
Quality goes **F**ar-flung, and
Quality goes **T**echnical.

It appears that these five trends are related to the five forces of **CHAOS** identified in chapter 1. For example, "quality goes softer" seems to be the result of the issues surrounding organizations as community (part of the changing definition of work and the workplace) and heightened social responsibility. "Quality goes integrative" appears to have its roots in the changing definitions of work and the workplace and heightened social responsibility (grounded in a systemic view of the world).

It is often easier to see trends in hindsight, rather than being able to predict them several years in advance. However, it is not unusual for the seeds of the next trend or advancement to be buried within existing practice. It is clear that there has been a natural progression within the quality field over the past twenty years.

QUALITY GOES **SOFTER**

The softer side of quality acknowledges that long-term sustained business results can no longer be achieved without attending to the social, psychological, and emotional needs of employees. What may be causing this? For several years, organizations have been asking employees to do more with less. They have been tapping into a smaller pool of qualified job applicants who are being heavily recruited by competitors. Jobs and pay have become commodities, with skilled people readily able to find employment wherever they choose. In addition, those born between 1961 and 1981 (i.e., Generation X) crave a sense of belonging that they did not receive because of splintered family structures.[1] Consequently, organizations must differentiate themselves on the basis of culture to retain employees or spend significant dollars ramping up new hires. To reduce costs and increase efficiencies, organizations must manage themselves as an interconnected system, which requires their employees to successfully work together in teams, communicate across functional and organizational boundaries, and maintain a win-win mentality.

> "In 1997, the Union of Japanese Scientists and Engineers (JUSE) changed its mission from 'increasing customer satisfaction' to 'increasing customer satisfaction and increasing employee satisfaction.' The implication of this change is that JUSE expanded its emphasis on the people side of quality beyond the wonderful concept of the quality control circle. In effect, the Japanese are incorporating Dr. Deming's theory of management into Japanese TQC."
>
> —Howard Gitlow, Ph.D., Professor of Management Science, School of Business Administration, University of Miami

Derek Bosham

It has taken organizations a long time to realize that the level of external customer satisfaction is related to the level of employee satisfaction. This is especially true in industries such as healthcare, air travel, hospitality, retail, and education—where the customer is an integral part of many work processes. The key question is "What are the components of employee satisfaction?" This issue is no different from determining the components of customer loyalty and initiating behaviors to create more loyal customers. The challenge is in measuring employee satisfaction and tying it directly to profitability, and in recognizing that it is not a one-dimensional subject (i.e., there are differences due to culture, lifestyle, and demographic factors). Take Sears, for instance. In late 1992, its worst year in history, Sears embarked on a massive turnaround plan. Part of this transformation included the development of an employee-customer-profit model (Sears Total Performance Indicators—a form of the balanced scorecard) based on its objectives in three categories: A compelling place to work, to shop, and to invest. This model demonstrates that a five-point increase in employee attitude (as measured through an employee survey) will drive a 1.3 point increase in customer satisfaction, which in turn drives a 0.5 percent improvement in revenue growth.[2] Sears also found that ten of the questions on its employee survey, specifically those on personal growth and development and empowered teams, have a higher impact on employee attitude, and ultimately customer satisfaction. It appears that the very tools and techniques that are used by quality and marketing professionals to identify customer requirements and monitor their satisfaction can be used to examine employee requirements and monitor their satisfaction. As always, to examine and monitor is not enough—it is also important to anticipate and act on the employees' *future* wants and needs.

If an organization says it believes that (a) employees come to work wanting to do their best (i.e., no one wants to fail), (b) they desire meaningful work, (c) they are inherently good people, (d) they can be trusted, and (e) the process/system is a key determinant of their performance, then its human resource policies and systems should be consistent with these beliefs. Yet, in many organizations, human resource policies are inconsistent with some, if not all, of these basic tenets. Until organizations align these policies and systems with the beliefs they espouse (often stated as values or guiding principles) as well as those beliefs held by a diverse work group, employees will continue to hear conflicting messages. These conflicting messages influence performance because employees are not always clear about how to act in a particular work situation. Until this alignment issue is corrected, training programs and improvement initiatives will not achieve their intended results.

> "Quality started in the late 1970s with a quality assurance type of system based on military specifications. This is the foundation of today's ISO 9000. Today, the trends are twofold. Total quality management (TQM) is a system that makes you competitive. Second, the people emphasis occupies a lot more space than in the 1980s. You have to understand how to mobilize people and align

> their purposes with the organization. You also have to manage the organization as a system composed of four parts—purpose, function, structure, and process. Future trends will move us to softer areas to address questions such as 'How do you manage people's interactions?' 'How do you understand what words mean to people?' and 'How do you coach people?'"
>
> —Thomas H. Lee, President Emeritus,
> Center for Quality of Management

The adage, "what gets measured gets done" also plays a significant role in employee performance. If one were to use an enterprise's operating assumptions to create an organization-wide measurement system, what would the measures suggest about how the enterprise views its employees? In addition, how would these assumptions match up against the values and guiding principles of the organization? According to a 1994 survey of 54 members of the Total Quality Management Center done by The Conference Board, the top four responses to the question "What Are Your Two Biggest Challenges in Supporting Teams vs. Individuals in the Next Three Years?" were: (1) placing accountability for results of team activities, (2) developing effective team leaders, (3) performance management, and (4) recognition programs (the last two items tied for third).[3] These data and the questions asked here suggest that the design of any system or work process needs to consider human behavior and motivation.

Inner Exploration

1. How does your organization monitor employee satisfaction? What improvements could be made to this system?
2. What efforts are under way to enhance employee growth, performance, and knowledge acquisition?
3. What is the organization doing to enrich employee interactions?

How can organizations ensure that when individuals with diverse backgrounds are brought together to work, either face-to-face or virtually, the resulting interactions are effective and constructive? Just as the basic tools of quality are necessary but not sufficient to achieve significant gains in process performance, so are the basic tools of communications necessary but not sufficient to achieve significant gains in learning and teamwork. Articulating and challenging assumptions, and understanding the symbolic meaning of language, are just a few of the areas that organizations need to explore in the future. In addition, mentoring and coaching systems that are based on looking forward rather than backward in time become imperative in helping individuals to realize their full potential.

Flatter, smaller, web-like, fluid, boundaryless, collaborative, and virtual are all terms used to describe the nature of the structure needed for organizations to respond quickly to external pressures and customer needs. The underlying implication is that any employee's job could change dramatically in a short period of time. This type of change necessitates continual learning on the part of every employee, and systems to support this level of learning. It also requires a willingness to let go of those things that are no longer relevant or useful (i.e., willful forgetting). The issues it raises are numerous. They include: how to facilitate improvements in virtual teams, managing a quality assurance system in a constantly changing environment, and interpreting time-ordered data when the underlying system continually fluctuates.

> "Organizations will be flatter and smaller, but less distinct. It will be harder to draw organizational boundaries."
> —Louis E. Schultz, President, Process Management International

QUALITY GOES INTO **HIDING**

The word *quality* began to fall into disfavor in the early 1990s. Quality efforts were discontinued, quality initiatives were renamed, and large quality departments were dismantled. The word *quality* is conspicuously absent in conversations, even in situations where the tools and methods of quality are used regularly. However, this absence does not mean that organizations have abandoned quality practices. In fact, many organizations continue to practice quality management. Thus, it looks as though quality has gone "into hiding."

There appear to be four reasons for this phenomenon. First, the word *quality* triggers bitter memories for many front-line employees. In the mid-1980s, when quality initiatives became popular, employees were led to believe that they would have control over making changes to their work, be able to work on problems of significance to the organization, and be heard and recognized for their contributions. While some enterprises may have engaged in actions that met these expectations, many did not. The leaders of these organizations did not fully understand what was required to support this level of participation from their employees. Therefore, the word *quality* reminds front-line employees of false expectations and failed efforts.

> "Today, I use the 'q' word less and less. The word 'quality' just has too much baggage now and creates more bias and surfaces old paradigms for many."
> —Alan Backus, Quality Manager, Exide Electronics

Second, leaders of major enterprises face several dilemmas with regard to quality initiatives. If an individual is newly appointed to a senior leadership position, that person is expected to do something different, even if current initiatives haven't yet paid out. This is especially true in organizations that are in the throes of financial, market share, or customer problems. Consequently, a newly appointed senior leader may be directed to introduce novel approaches. In many cases this means changing or eliminating "quality initiatives." Another dilemma is related to a common paradigm in business that implies senior leaders either do not require much training or do not have time for training. Thus, they receive little or no instruction in the new concepts, tools, and methods associated with the initiatives they themselves introduce. It is therefore not surprising that, under stress, they fall back into habits associated with old management approaches rather than using new concepts and practices. Finally, leaders are under pressure to achieve rapid results. If these results are not forthcoming immediately, they must appear to be doing something to rectify the situation. Thus, when quality initiatives did not achieve their intended results rapidly, these individuals abandoned them in search of the next "quick fix."

The third reason quality has gone into hiding is related to the quick fix mentality—a disposable attitude toward management practices. This is often referred to as the "program-of-the-month" syndrome. Even before a practice can take hold and provide results, it is abandoned in favor of the next fad. Thus, once quality had been discarded, it was not acceptable for an organization to reintroduce it under the same guise. As a result, management consultants who value quality practices were motivated to repackage them under new names in order to remain in business.

Inner Exploration

1. How do employees and organizational leaders refer to *quality* in their conversations?
2. What is written about the organization's quality practices in its publications (including electronic communications) and customer materials?

> "We have seen a period of 15 years in which QC [Quality Control] and SPC [Statistical Process Control] have moved to TQM. Now we are moving to integration with business strategy. We use all the tools but we don't call it quality anymore."
>
> —Lawrence Schein, Director, Total Quality Management Center, The Conference Board, Inc.

The final reason why quality has gone into hiding is found in those organizations where quality thinking has achieved a level of "unconscious competence."[4] For these organizations there is no longer a need for people to talk about "doing it." Quality concepts, tools, and methods are intertwined with the work of the organization. Using these tools and methods is part of the job, not separate from it. For example, data on key customer requirements are collected daily and fed back within 24 hours to those whom it impacts; financial data are displayed on control charts and not acted upon unless the data signal the need to take action; daily work procedures are documented, flowcharted and used to train new hires; and front-line work groups meet regularly to assess improvement opportunities and make necessary changes without approval from management. Unfortunately, many enterprises believe they are at the level of "unconscious competence" when they really are at the level of "unconscious incompetence."

QUALITY GOES **INTEGRATIVE**

Quality practices were introduced and applied in American firms in a piecemeal fashion. Instead of addressing the entire management system—as many Japanese organizations did through their use of daily management, cross-functional management, and policy management[5,6]—a number of organizations in the United

States implemented the tools and methods without an appreciation for the overall system. The need to view quality as integrative (i.e., addressing the entire management system) is best understood by examining its history in the United States.

The last 30 years have brought about a dramatic evolution in both the content of quality initiatives and the methods by which they are implemented in organizations. Prior to the late 1970s, quality meant quality control. It encompassed inspection, conformance, and sorting out defects. Very little emphasis was placed on monitoring work processes or preventing problems. Quality was delegated to lower-level staff functions consisting of inspectors and quality engineers. Inspection—both incoming and outgoing—and 100 percent testing were the predominant methods of controlling quality.

Several things happened in the late 1970s that catapulted the issue of quality into the public limelight. First, American industry began to feel the pressure of increased competition from the Japanese on the basis of initial product quality, price, and overall reliability. Second, in 1979, Philip Crosby wrote *Quality Is Free,* in which he categorized the costs of quality and showed that the cost of prevention could be significantly lower than (a) the cost of detection and (b) the cost of failure in the absence of prevention.[7] Finally, in 1980, NBC aired the white paper *If Japan Can, Why Can't We?* which introduced Japanese quality practices to the American public. These events firmly launched quality into its next era—defect prevention.

> "Quality was launched with the 1980 NBC White Paper *If Japan Can, Why Can't We?* Since then, there has been a technical shift from detection to prevention to value creation through learning, sharing, and applying knowledge."
>
> —Barbara Lawton, Ph.D., Vice President,
> Business and Quality Processes, StorageTek

Defect prevention, spearheaded by the American automotive industry and characterized by the use of basic quality tools (i.e., run charts, control charts, histograms, etc.) and SPC, rapidly evolved and expanded in the 1980s. Control charts—both correctly and incorrectly used—proliferated. Organizations initiated massive training programs for all production employees. Some early results accumulated, spurring additional expansion of the quality movement.

By the late 1980s, defect prevention was absorbed into TQM. At the time, TQM rapidly grew to encompass teamwork, empowerment, strategic planning, service quality, and quality of management. Two distinct organizational structures emerged in organizations practicing TQM—steering teams/quality councils and self-managed teams. Neither was universally effective. Steering teams and quality councils were, in effect, parallel structures that ensured a conflict between the practice of TQM and the day-to-day functioning of the business. Self-managed teams were organized around the work; however, in most cases the necessary support structures and systems were not in place for them to be fully successful. Massive training efforts continued, and were expanded to include a variety of TQM concepts and methods. This training was delivered to all parts of the organization, including top management.

> "In the 1970s the hot topic was productivity. In the 1980s it was TQM. In the early 1990s it was reengineering. In the future we will see emphasis on attractive quality creation."
>
> —Louis E. Schultz, President, Process Management International

During this same time frame, ISO 9000 appeared on the horizon, making TQM even broader in scope. As a result, many quality professionals started to gravitate to those specialties that were most comfortable to them, since it was not easy to be an expert in all areas. In general, one group opted for the quality systems route (which may or may not have included ISO 9000), and a second group gravitated toward more global business issues (which included strategic planning and change management). This appeared to a number of organizations as a splintering of the quality movement.

> "In the 1980s and 1990s the word quality was stretched so far it was hard for people to get their arms around it. Those who had mastery of all of its meanings . . . and the larger strategic and competitiveness context . . . got into the boardroom. When ISO hit, many quality professionals rallied around the associated conformity concepts because there was a marketplace need. The word quality shrunk to its earlier meaning. Professionals focusing on conformity issues, by and large, were not in the boardroom. Today, quality is seen as much narrower than it was about a decade ago."
>
> —Dr. Curt W. Reimann, Senior Scientist Emeritus,
> National Institute of Standards and Technology

Soon afterwards, organizations began to notice that TQM efforts that had been underway since the early to mid-1980s were not producing the expected bottom-line results. By the early 1990s, the need for results drove organizational leaders to search for other answers. These included reengineering, "the new science" (i.e., principles of chaos theory and self-organization), learning organizations, and personal principle-centered change (such as that promoted by Stephen Covey's materials). "Recent reports, supported with viewpoints expressed by the founders of the reengineering movement, claim that more than 70 percent of reengineering efforts have failed to achieve their purposes."[8] Who knows if any of these other approaches will be able to deliver better business results?

Perhaps there is another route to take—one that embraces "both/and" rather than "either/or" thinking. What if many, if not all, of the tools and methods that have been bantered about over the past 20 years are actually part of a single, coherent picture? What if there are significant synergies to be gained through using them in concert with each other? What if there exists a unified way to organize and apply these seemingly disconnected approaches in order to achieve the business results that organizations have not yet realized?

In this book, five fields of performance practice are identified as surfacing by the mid-1990s. Their collective purpose is to achieve and sustain market leadership and competitive advantage over extended periods of time. We have labeled these fields Quality Assurance, Problem Resolution, Alignment and Integration, Con-

itual Awakening (see Figure 2.1). It is important to note
ıutually exclusive or sufficient in and of themselves. In
that the specific practices within the fields—when they
r—can produce synergies, and ultimately accelerate busi-
scribe each of the fields of performance practice here; a
n can be found in chapters 4 through 8.

:ice, "Quality Assurance," emphasizes basic quality assur-
its aim product and service conformance to customer
ıge that organizations face in this field of practice is that
gained through ISO 9000) can often be achieved in envi-
:ct rates exist. All organizations need some form of a qual-
ıuse it operationally defines how the work is performed
: foundation for improving and maintaining gains in per-
is field are standardization, organization of the work area
ng management of a documented quality system.

ractice is "Problem Resolution." Efforts within this field are directed at solving today's problems quickly, without jeopardizing long-term business success. However, sometimes the need to achieve results within a given time frame sacrifices rigor. For example, processes may be reconfigured without actual customer input (because it takes too long to get the data). While some of the work in this arena

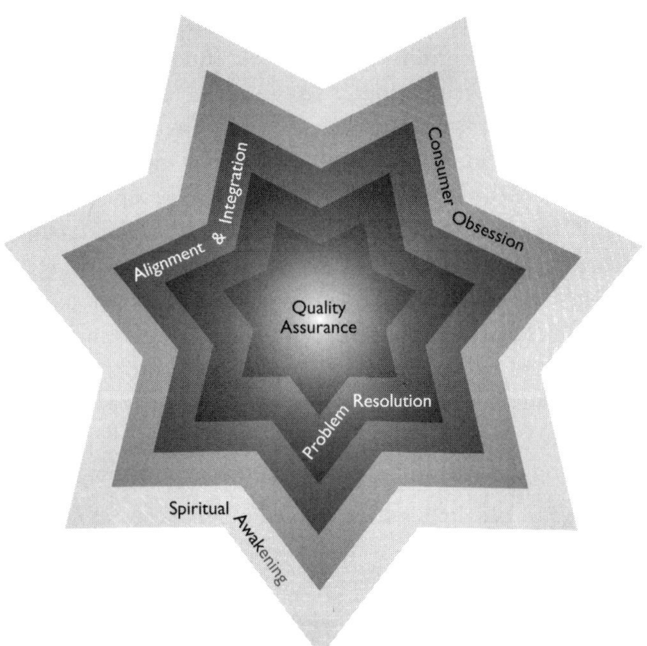

Figure 2.1
The Five Fields of Performance Practice

may be tied to the vision and strategic objectives of the organization, it is more often grounded in the organization's purpose or mission—what the organization currently is paid to provide to customers. Included in this field are process improvement practices, and constraint management and Six Sigma tools. In this field of practice, training of the workforce still appears to be the predominant means of implementation.

> "During the 1980s and into the early 90s, implementing total quality management was considered primarily a process of training. The implication was that if we could just train lots of folks and get them to understand the concepts of quality, as well as to use the tools of process improvement, all would be well. In many cases the training in quality concepts generated a lot of enthusiasm and excitement on the part of employees, and the establishment of small functional and cross-functional teams yielded some initial results.
>
> "But the critical success factor for the successful deployment of total quality is the ongoing commitment of senior management. If the quality process is not linked to strategic objectives, it will not capture the sustained attention of senior executives.
>
> "TQM becomes a way of life for an organization when it includes the alignment between the four elements of organizational performance—strategy, customers, people, *and* processes. It is the alignment between and within each of these elements that results in world-class performance."
>
> —Dr. George H. Labovitz, Chairman,
> Organizational Dynamics, Inc.

The third field of practice is "Alignment and Integration." This field focuses predominantly on the articulation, alignment *and* integration of all organizational elements. It links customer requirements to overall strategy and organization-wide measures, to key organizational systems, to daily work processes, to supplier requirements, to organizational structure and culture, and to employee well-being and satisfaction. This is the first field of performance practice that moves quality into the realm of "management." However, it contains more than the Japanese approach, which is composed of daily management, cross-functional management, and policy management. It includes managing the organization as a system and focusing on the organization's cultural elements—its assumptions, values, and guiding principles—and how they intertwine with the more strategic and operational aspects of the business. Critical to this field are the identification and modification (or removal) of policies and practices that prevent people from taking actions that are in concert with the organization's overall strategy.

The fourth field of practice, which we call "Consumer Obsession," addresses many of the strategic issues raised—but not resolved—by existing TQM practices and other disciplines such as marketing and organizational development (commonly referred to today as organizational effectiveness). These unresolved issues include what it truly means to create value for consumers, employees, and shareholders; methods and techniques for anticipating future consumer wants and needs; assessing brand meaning; the ongoing use of competitive intelligence information; employing a systematic approach for innovation; and continual organizational renewal. It is our belief that business leaders are indeed aware of the need to tackle these unresolved issues. However, they are hampered by the absence of clear operational definitions, and the methods and tools to address them. For example, there is no singularly agreed-upon definition of value creation in any discipline.[9] Upon close inspection of the tools and methods that are being marketed today to address these issues, it is not unusual to find traditional market research, process management, product development, and change management techniques and approaches once again being repackaged and relabeled.

> "Over the past 10 to 20 years, there has been a migration from the use of total quality tools by *individuals* in technical units (e.g., manufacturing and product development), to *organizational* use in technical areas, to *broad* use of quality principles and approaches in all areas of the corporation. During this period of transition, total quality has evolved from a rigid TQM prescription to a set of flexible approaches and principles that can help the organization achieve its business objectives and, in fact, survive. The current trend toward value will accelerate and the focus will be on value-added business results. Total quality, per se, will be transparent and the focus will be on applications for solving real business issues and problems."
>
> —Garry J. Huysse, Associate Director,
> Global Quality Improvement, Procter & Gamble

The fifth field of practice, "Spiritual Awakening," addresses the need to attend to individual and organizational spirit. Use of the word "spiritual" is not synonymous with "religion." Instead, its meaning is taken from American Indian literature. Spiritual is defined as "the greater self and all-that-is are blended into a balanced whole, and in this way the concept of being that is the fundamental and sacred spring of life is given voice and being for all."[10] However, religion must be recognized as a type of diversity that has impacted and will continue to impact our workplaces. The aim of this field of practice is to improve life for everyone on the planet and to manage the planet as a total system. Included here are organization as community, a new social contract for employment, and social responsibility and accountability. To deny this field of practice is to deny that basic human needs have a role in designing organizations (e.g., in determining the organization's values) and that organizations have an obligation to fulfill some of these needs (e.g., provide meaningful work).

Inner Exploration

1. What type of quality assurance system is in place in your organization?
2. How effective are the organization's improvement projects?
3. What level of alignment exists between the organization's mission, vision, values, guiding principles, market strategy, and long-term objectives?
4. What is your organization doing to learn more about topics such as value creation, brand meaning, assessing future consumer wants and needs, competitive intelligence, organizational renewal, and innovation?
5. What actions is your organization taking to learn about the impact of spirituality in the workplace?

QUALITY GOES FAR-FLUNG

"Overseas, the terminology of TQM seems to be more appropriate and 'in vogue.'"
—Lawrence Schein, Director, Total Quality Management Center, The Conference Board, Inc.

The practice of quality is reaching the far corners of the Earth—it has become far-flung. In 1980, individual membership in the American Society for Quality's (ASQ) International Chapter (outside North America) was about 1,100, with approximately 50 countries represented. In 1998, individual membership is more than 6,400 and the number of countries has grown to more than 80.[11]

There is increasing interest in quality throughout the rest of the world, especially in Europe, Asia and the Pacific Rim, and South America. This interest appears to be driven by several factors. The first factor is the global marketplace. When an organization can buy anything anywhere and can sell anything anywhere, it begins to realize the importance of basic quality practices. The second factor has to do with competition from both small domestic organizations (within national boundaries) and large multinational companies. Multinational companies are locating facilities in underdeveloped or less-developed countries because of reduced labor costs. These facilities are requiring their local suppliers to be ISO 9000 or QS 9000 certified. Because of these supplier requirements, ISO 9000, QS 9000 and the Malcolm Baldrige National Quality Award are getting a lot of attention outside of the United States. After Public Law 100-107 created the Malcolm Baldrige National Quality Award in 1987, 37 countries, Puerto Rico, and Western Europe developed their own national quality awards, some of which are modeled after the Baldrige.[12] Finally, many organizations and countries are realizing that their continued survival depends on providing high-quality products and services. This objective is problematic in many small and medium-sized companies because they do not always have the resources to implement required quality practices.

"Because of the global economy, we need to expand to a world-wide core of organizational performance standards that are universal. In Tennessee, we have developed an eighth category in our quality award that looks at global competitiveness. Global issues are relevant, even for small companies and schools. The question we're facing is, 'How do you bring organizations in Tennessee to a place where they can be competitive in the global arena?'"
—Marie Baucom Williams, President and CEO, Tennessee Quality

Many countries are mounting national efforts to increase quality awareness. These efforts include national quality conferences, seminars, radio shows, school essay contests, outdoor posters, and the distribution of pamphlets about quality in open-air markets. For example, Korea and India have begun to sponsor national quality efforts. The United Nations has declared the second Thursday in November as World Quality Day, but it has not received a lot of publicity. The European

Organization for Quality (EOQ) sponsors European Quality Week, which coincides with World Quality Day. More than 30 countries participate in this week-long event.

Inner Exploration

1. What strategies does your organization have to compete in the global marketplace? How effective are they?
2. How many languages are spoken by organizational leaders? Employees? How familiar are they with the customs of other cultures?

There are a number of different ways that countries use to educate citizens on various quality practices. For example, the University of New Zealand offers a degree in quality; some private organizations offer certificate programs. Organizations such as the Singapore Quality Institute provide quality correspondence or diploma courses. In India, a trust has been established to publish books on quality; they are distributed free of charge to any organization within the country. Spain and Brazil are starting to push the publication of quality books in their native languages to make them accessible to a greater number of people.

> "We have seen a dramatic increase in the need for us to supply information about quality on an international basis. Our international book sales, as well as our sale of translation rights, have increased significantly over the past three years. We see no reason for this increase to slow down."
>
> —Roger Holloway, Manager, ASQ Quality Press, American Society for Quality

Organizations in the United States need to incorporate an international perspective into strategic planning, marketing, product development and training activities. It has been noted that when Americans speak about market share, they typically speak in terms of the domestic market. However, in overseas firms, when employees speak about market share, they normally talk about worldwide market share. How can American firms effectively compete against those who have a broader perspective? And how can one be so sure that "best practices" are housed within the United States or U.S.-based companies?

> "By 2010, many of the underdeveloped countries (such as China and India) will have made dramatic strides in product quality. Their education and literacy levels are rapidly increasing and will continue to increase in the coming years. This will enable them to move forward rapidly on other fronts. They will have caught up with the U.S. in terms of product quality unless we do something dramatically different. And their rate of change will be much faster—they will be trying to do in 10–15 years what we did in 50. Their momentum could carry them ahead. Africa and the Middle East, with a few exceptions, are still lagging. I don't think that they will be able to do much because of their political and economic instability. Political stability is the key to being able to make rapid strides in quality."
>
> —Navin S. Dedhia, Chair, International Chapter, American Society for Quality

QUALITY GOES TECHNICAL

The basic tools of quality are no longer sufficient to achieve the levels of performance that today's organizations are seeking in order to maintain market leadership and competitive advantage. As a result, significant cost savings have been realized through the use of highly sophisticated, technical, statistically based tools. For example, in 1995 alone, $350 million in annualized cost savings and a 61 percent reduction in defects resulted from 2400 process improvements at AlliedSignal.[13] General Electric, under the leadership of Chairman and CEO Jack Welch, expects its Six Sigma effort to contribute an extra $10–$15 billion annually in revenue and cost savings from 1997 to the year 2000.[14] The underlying assumption in these two organizations is that the proper use of the Six Sigma approach, and its accompanying technical tools (e.g., contingency tables, t-tests, design of experiments, and regression analysis), will lead to defect rates of less than 3.4 defects per million, which will ultimately lead to increased profitability and market share.

> "Organizations will continue to mature in their understanding of what I call Grand Strategies; pushing for results on all fronts rather than just on single fronts. I suspect we will find organizations getting more sophisticated and disciplined in their approaches. Six Sigma, for example, will probably be the next big programmatic push."
>
> —D. Scott Sink, Ph.D., P. E., Learning Leader, QPM, Inc.,
> Past President of the World Confederation of Productivity Science
> and the Institute of Industrial Engineers

The technical tools listed above are often referred to as "black box tools" because people need only be grounded in the basics of statistical theory or the calculations underlying their usage in order to employ them in the workplace (assuming this information teaches them how to think critically about the meaning of the data input and the resulting output, and the consequences of tool misuse). The resurgence of sophisticated technical tools (popularized by Motorola in the late 1980s) has become possible because of the prevalence of sound, relatively foolproof, user-friendly statistical software. Thus, it is now feasible for large numbers of people throughout an organization to apply these tools in their daily work. Journals such as *Quality Progress* and *Quality Digest* periodically publish software directories that highlight the types of programs mentioned here.

> "In the past, quality was viewed in a functional way; we will now move more strongly into integrated systems. High quality will be the standard—an expected part of business. It will be required just to enter the competitive arena but will not be sufficient to survive. In the future, there will be more emphasis on technical tools such as design of experiments and other statistical methods because the easy stuff has been done. High-powered tools are necessary to go to the next levels of performance."
>
> —Tim Fuller, Partner, Fuller & Propst Associates

More frequently than not, the basic tools of quality (i.e., run charts, control charts, Pareto charts, etc.) alone cannot provide the level of sensitivity and analysis required to study complex systems and make improvements in areas where the magnitude of the effect is small (e.g., where defects are already being measured in parts per million). Since most, if not all, organizations are complex systems, the use of sophisticated technical tools will become more important in the achievement of business results. However, this does not mean that organizations should stop using the basic tools of quality. The "basics" are now "table stakes"—those organizations that do not use them must employ them as their fee for entrance in the competitive worldwide marketplace; those who have them can do more.

Inner Exploration

1. Where are Six Sigma approaches and black box tools used in your organization? How effective is their use?
2. Who has the expertise to use these tools and approaches?

OTHER THOUGHTS

This chapter has focused on five overarching trends that have emerged in the practice of quality, or what is coming to be known as the practice of management. Their impact will be felt in all management disciplines (e.g., accounting, finance, marketing, operations, human resources, etc.). These trends may appear paradoxical, and in fact they are. Going technical and going soft are happening at the same time. So are going hidden and going far-flung. These paradoxes, which are becoming more commonplace, require people to hold opposing viewpoints as valid. Imagine the implications this will have on organizational initiatives.

SHIFT

- Quality goes [S]ofter
- Quality goes into [H]iding
- Quality goes [I]ntegrative
- Quality goes [F]ar-flung
- Quality goes [T]echnical

The five trends discussed in this chapter are inevitable—they are already apparent today. In the future, these trends will continue to develop and new ones will emerge. They do not exclude other trends in the quality field that have been under way for some time. Some of these other trends, and their link to what we have discussed here, are best summarized by the following quote.

> "I have noticed three major trends in the quality field: definition, expansion, and integration. First, the definition of quality along with the substance it brings to organizations has evolved from a conformance and defect reduction scope to a more strategic and systemic definition to enable businesses to provide customer value and internal performance. Second, adoption of quality principles and tools has expanded in fields outside of manufacturing, notably health care, education, and government.

Small businesses have also picked up the use of quality improvement strategies, scaled to their situation. Third, to me, the most interesting and challenging trend in the quality field is this whole idea of integration, which is playing out in two ways—integration with other fields of study (business management and organizational development) and integration into the fabric of organizational practices."

—Alan Backus, Quality Manager, Exide Electronics

Endnotes

1. Watts Wacker and Jim Taylor, with Howard Means, *The 500-Year Delta: What Happens After What Comes Next* (New York: HarperCollins Publishers, Inc., 1997), 200.
2. Anthony J. Rucci, Steven P. Kirn, and Richard T. Quinn, "The Employee-Customer-Profit Chain at Sears," *Harvard Business Review* (January–February 1998), 82–97.
3. Anna S. Powell, *Quality Outlook* (New York: The Conference Board, Inc., Fall 1994), 15.
4. John W. Newstrom and Edward E. Scannell, *Games Trainers Play* (New York: McGraw Hill Book Company, 1980), 141, 143.
5. Howard S. Gitlow and Shelly J. Gitlow, *Total Quality Management in Action* (Englewood Cliffs, NJ: PTR Prentice Hall, 1994).
6. George Labovitz, Y. S. Chang, and Victor Rosansky, *Making Quality Work: A Leadership Guide for the Results-Driven Manager* (New York: HarperCollins Publishers, Inc., 1993).
7. Philip B. Crosby, *Quality Is Free* (New York: New American Library, 1979).
8. Susan Albers Mohrman et al., *Tomorrow's Organization: Crafting Winning Capabilities in a Dynamic World* (San Francisco: Jossey-Bass Inc., Publishers, 1998), 205.
9. C. Whan Park, Deborah MacInnis, Steven Silverman, and Bernard Jaworski, "A Value-Based Conceptual Framework Linking the Marketing Mix and Marketplace Exchange" (unpublished working paper, January 1998).
10. Paula Gunn Allen, *The Sacred Hoop* (Boston: Beacon Press, 1992), 55.
11. Conversation with Julie Gosselin, Membership Administrator, American Society for Quality (June 22, 1998).
12. National Institute of Standards and Technology, *Foreign/International Quality Award Descriptions* (June 22, 1998).
13. "Seeking Six-Sigma Status at AlliedSignal," *Leading Voices in Quality,* Report No. 1159–96-CH (New York: The Conference Board, Inc., 1996), 17.
14. Ann Walmsley, "Six Sigma Enigma," *Report on Business Magazine* (October 1997), 3.

Section

II

Exploring The Starburst Model™

Now that the **SHIFT** that is occurring in the practice of quality and its causal forces have been explained, the relationships between quality, value creation, and other performance improvement initiatives can be explored. Section II introduces and describes The Starburst Model™, a model that will help you and your organization systematically integrate current and future operational and strategic initiatives into a cohesive framework that promotes quality and creates value, and ultimately, improves business performance.

Chapter 3 explains the starburst metaphor, and illustrates how the five forces of **CHAOS** (presented in chapter 1) and the five fields of performance practice (presented in chapter 2) fit together in the model. In chapters 4 through 8 the five fields of performance practice are presented in detail—Quality Assurance (chapter 4), Problem Resolution (chapter 5), Alignment and Integration (chapter 6), Consumer Obsession (chapter 7), and Spiritual Awakening (chapter 8). Each of these chapters elaborates upon one field—its purpose, desired outcomes, significant underlying concepts, most commonly used tools and methods, and shortcomings as a field of performance practice. While the concepts, tools, and methods are overviewed in the field of performance practice where they are first used, it is important to realize that they may have application in other fields as well.

Finally, at the end of each of these chapters, there is the opportunity to evaluate your organization's level of deployment of field-specific concepts, tools, and methods, and to address the continuing impact of the forces of **CHAOS** on that field of performance practice. These assessments serve as the foundation for applying The Starburst Model™ to your organization in chapter 12.

CHAPTER 3

Introduction to The Starburst Model™

"Models, of course, are never true, but fortunately it is only necessary that they be useful. For this it is usually needful only that they not be grossly wrong. I think rather simple modifications of our present models will prove adequate to take account of most realities of the outside world."[1]

—George E. P. Box

CHAOS

- [C]hanging definition of work and the workplace
- [H]eightened social responsibility
- [A]ging baby boomers
- [O]verarching demographic change
- [S]trategic growth through technology and innovation

This chapter introduces The Starburst Model™ (Figure 3.1). It is a combination of the five forces of **CHAOS** (presented in chapter 1) and the five fields of performance practice—Quality Assurance, Problem Resolution, Alignment and Integration, Consumer Obsession, and Spiritual Awakening (presented in chapter 2 and more thoroughly explained in chapters 4 through 8).

The Starburst Model™ is based on the metaphor of the starburst galaxy. Metaphors, such as "the woman sailed into the room," "puppy dog eyes," or "the child bleated pitifully," provide a shorthand approach for understanding one portion of reality in terms of another, evoking powerful images while employing very few words. For example, the phrase "the woman sailed into the room" tells us about the way she moves, even though she does not have a sail and is not moving across the water. While metaphors can help individuals to understand a piece of reality by attaching to something familiar, metaphors can also be misleading because, by their very nature, they ignore certain aspects of reality (e.g., the color of the woman's hair) or impose distortions (the woman is not being propelled by the wind).

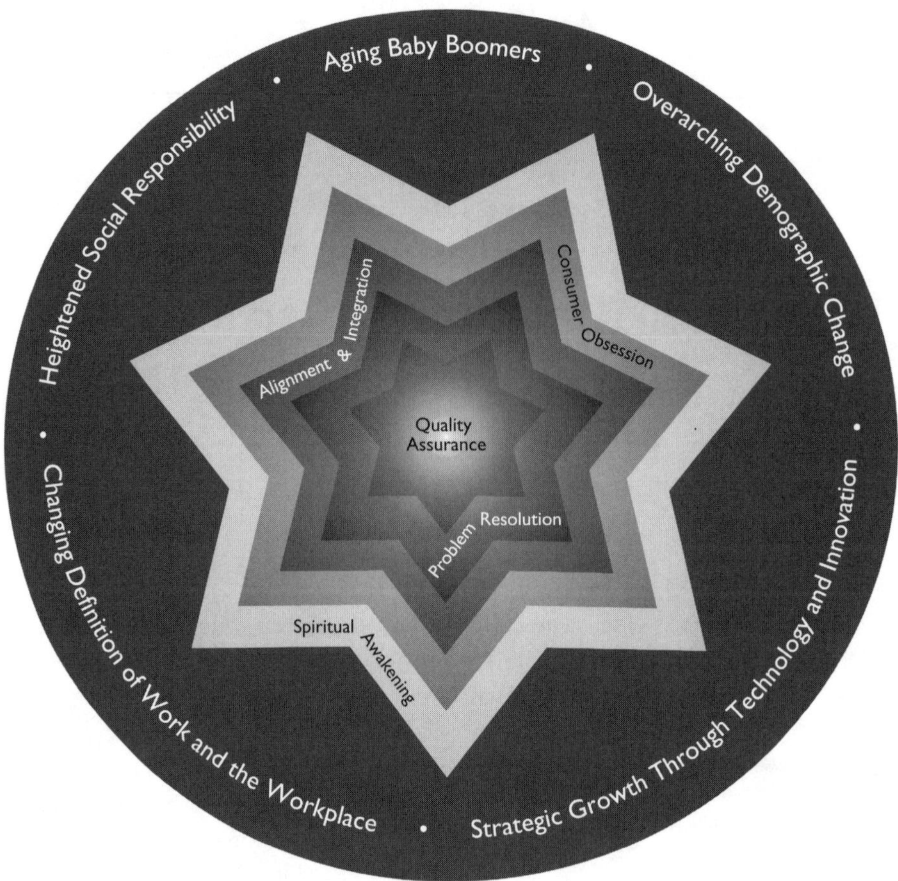

Figure 3.1
The Starburst Model™

WHY A STARBURST?

Starburst galaxies furiously convert solar masses of gas into stars—onwards of 20 times the rate of star formation in the Milky Way Galaxy.[2] Phases of violent star formation are known as starbursts.[3] They produce large numbers of massive stars and release enormous amounts of sustained energy over time as a result of disruptive forces in a galaxy. It is from this natural phenomenon that The Starburst Model™ was derived. In the process of visualizing the five fields of performance practice, they came to be seen as individual stars which (as explained later in this chapter) are intertwined.

Following this metaphor, it becomes clear that the five forces of **CHAOS** encircle these five stars as they continually influence the development and maturation of each field. In The Starburst Model™, the forces of **CHAOS**—**c**hanging definition of work and the workplace, **h**eightened social responsibility, **a**ging baby boomers, **o**verarching demographic change, and **s**trategic growth through technology and innovation—are the workplace forces that are disrupting organizations in the global business environment (i.e., the galaxy). Newborn stars (i.e., potential fields of performance practice) form quite regularly in starburst galaxies. Some of them die before they actually become stars (and are known as brown dwarfs).[4] Some are in the early stages of development. Others have already burned out.

The order of the stars, starting at the center and moving outward, mirrors the order of historical appearance of the five fields of performance practice. Over several decades, each field of performance practice emerged to serve a purpose—to meet the needs and challenges that existed in organizations at that particular point in time. As a specific field matured, and as past workplace forces continued to disrupt organizations, needs and challenges developed that could not be addressed by the existing field(s). This spurred the development of new concepts, tools, and methods as well as the emergence of the next field of performance practice.

The development of later fields does not, however, render the earlier performance fields—or their elements—unnecessary. The earlier fields continue to serve their purpose, achieve their outcome(s), and grow and evolve through the influence of the concepts, tools, and methods that emerge in later fields. For example, the Quality Assurance standardization method has been influenced by process management (Problem Resolution), which has dictated the need to collect process and outcome data. Standardization data collection has also been influenced by managing the organization as a system (Alignment and Integration), which links these measures to organization-wide measures of performance (refer to Table 3.1). What it means to provide customer responsiveness (Quality Assurance) and customer focus (Problem Resolution) is starting to be shaped by the concept of value creation (Consumer Obsession). The true meaning of teamwork (Problem Resolution) is currently being affected by what it means to build community in the workplace (Spiritual Awakening).

The five stars of The Starburst Model™ are gravitationally bound together. Thus, deployment of tools and methods in the outer stars (fields) is influenced, at least in part, by deployment of those within the inner stars. It would, for example, be difficult to manage an organization as a system (Alignment and Integration) without having first identified and standardized the organization's work processes (Quality Assurance). It would also be difficult to identify when and where to innovate (Consumer Obsession) if the organization were not engaged in strategic planning (Alignment and Integration) and process management (Problem Resolution). In addition, organizational community building (Spiritual Awakening) is enhanced by the effective use of large group interventions (Alignment and Integration). Alternatively, the deployment of tools and methods in earlier fields can be influenced by the level of deployment of those in later fields. For example, the problem solving part of process management (Problem Resolution) can be focused

Table 3.1
The Five Fields of Performance Practice

Field of Practice / Element	Purpose	Underlying Concepts	Commonly Used Tools and Methods	Who	Desired Outcome
Quality Assurance	To ensure customers receive what they contract to receive	• Quality assurance • Customer responsiveness • Process-oriented thinking • SDCA Cycle • Discipline	• Quality system • Standardization • Basic tools of quality • The 5S's	• Management Steering Committee • Quality Department • Front-line employees	• Product and service conformance to customer requirements
Problem Resolution	To improve bottom-line performance and customer satisfaction	• PDCA Cycle • Customer focus • Variation • Teamwork	• Process management • Constraint management tools • Advanced tools • Creativity tools	• Management Steering Committee • Cross-functional (project) teams • In-function work teams	• Reduced costs • Improvements in performance • Improvements in customer satisfaction
Alignment and Integration	To ensure all organizational work contributes to achieving the organization's mission, vision, and plans	• Alignment • Integration • Organization as system • Transformation • Large-scale organizational change • Self-management	• Organizational architecture • Organizational partnerships • Managing the organization as a system • Large group interventions • Strategic planning • 7 Management and Planning Tools • Project management	• Key customers • Entire organization • Supply chain	• Improved organizational effectiveness • Elimination of barriers and unnecessary work • Improved overall customer and employee satisfaction

Consumer Obsession	To promote long-term survival of the organization	• Value creation • Organizational renewal • Mass customization • Lifetime relationships with consumers	• Innovation • Competitive intelligence • Relationship marketing • Brand management • Non-traditional market research techniques	• Current and future consumers • Entire organization • Supply chain	• Create value for consumers • Create value for employees • Create value for shareholders
Spiritual Awakening	To serve society	• Spirituality • Organization as community • Social responsibility and accountability	• New social contract for employment • Community building • Social responsibility audits • Zero-emissions systems	• All individuals in society	• The planet managed as a system • Improved life for everyone on the planet

more effectively if the organization has identified critical organizational problems to be solved through strategic planning (Alignment and Integration) and where it needs to achieve zero emissions (Spiritual Awakening). The results of social responsibility audits (Spiritual Awakening) can influence the outcomes of strategic planning (Alignment and Integration) and how a particular brand is managed (Consumer Obsession). This gravitational pull changes over time due to the maturation of each star. Therefore, an organization does not have to fully deploy all of the concepts, tools, and methods in an earlier field of performance practice in order to begin deploying elements of a later field. Concurrently, it may need to alter deployment of a specific concept, tool, or method in an earlier field because of what is learned in a later field of performance practice.

Each star is a different size. This difference reflects the growing purpose and desired outcomes of each successive field of performance practice as well as the involvement of larger parts of the organization and its marketplace (i.e., suppliers, customers, and community members). Additionally, the points of the stars extend into adjacent stars, obscuring the exact point at which one star ends and the next one begins, because the five fields of performance practice share some common tools and skill sets. For example, the basic tools of quality can be used in standardization (Quality Assurance), process management (Problem Resolution), strategic planning (Alignment and Integration), brand management (Consumer Obsession), and zero-emissions systems (Spiritual Awakening). Change management skills are also necessary in all five fields of performance practice, as is the ability to effectively coach teams and individuals.

Table 3.1 provides an overview of the five fields of performance practice. The underlying concepts and commonly used tools and methods are noted in the field where they first appear. Chapters 4 through 8 delve into each of these fields of performance practice in more detail. Chapter 12 (in Section III) discusses how to apply The Starburst Model™ to your organization.

Endnotes

1. George E. P. Box, "Some Problems of Statistics and Everyday Life," *Journal of the American Statistical Association,* Vol. 74, No. 364 (1974), 1–4.
2. Robert Naeye, *Through the Eyes of Hubble: The Birth, Life, and Violent Death of Stars* (Waukesha, WI: Kalmbach Books, 1998), 97.
3. Bernd Aschenbach, Hermann-Michael Hahn, and Joachim Trümper, *The Invisible Sky: Rosat and the Age of X-Ray Astronomy* (Secaucus, NJ: Copernicus Books, 1998), 146.
4. Naeye, *Through the Eyes of Hubble: The Birth, Life, and Violent Death of Stars,* 26.

CHAPTER 4

The Quality Assurance Field of Performance Practice

The first field of performance practice—Quality Assurance—has been evolving for thousands of years. Its purpose, as practiced today, is to ensure that customers receive what they contract to receive. Such a contract may be formal and written, but quite often is only implied by the conditions of doing business. For example, when a shopper buys a 12-ounce soft drink, the individual enters into an implied contract with the soft drink company that the can contains 12 ounces, that the ingredients listed on the can are, in fact, the ingredients in the can, and that all other information on the can accurately reflects its contents. When an individual gets a prescription filled, the person enters into an implied contract with the pharmacy that the drug in the container is the one the doctor prescribed (or an agreed-upon generic substitute) and with the pharmaceutical company that the dosage is consistent from tablet to tablet.

The desired outcome of this field of performance practice is product and service conformance to customer requirements as specified or implied by the contract. Conformance of products and services to customer requirements serves as the foundation for maintaining gains in performance and for ongoing improvement in later fields of performance practice. In a 1998 article titled "The Effects of Quality on Business Performance," Neil Hardie summarized the findings of 43 studies that looked at the correlation between quality and business performance. His analysis shows a strongly supported relationship between conformance and increased profits and market share.[1]

UNDERLYING CONCEPTS

The five concepts that underlie the Quality Assurance Field of Performance Practice focus on issues surrounding the activities necessary to achieve product and service conformance to customer requirements. Therefore, they are primarily focused on work performed at the front-line of an organization. The concepts covered in this section are quality assurance, customer responsiveness, process-oriented thinking, the SDCA Cycle, and discipline.

Quality Assurance

> ". . . [O]ne only needs to scan the daily newspapers to realize that the big stories and great issues of the day now regularly include matters of quality assurance—oil spills in the North Sea [or] product recalls. . . . There is no difficulty in concluding that in broad terms what we call quality assurance is vital to modern society."[2]
>
> —Raymond Wachniak, Manager, Central Quality Assurance, Power Generation Group, Barberton

According to Joseph Juran's research, the origins of managing for quality in the United States go back to the days of the early colonists.[3] Quality control, which had its inception in the 1930s, includes activities an organization undertakes to ensure the quality of products and services (through, for example, process design, in-process inspections, and end-of-line tests). Quality assurance, which emerged in the 1950s, is broader in scope because it adds activities that confirm that the quality control system has been effective in ensuring that products and services conform to customer requirements.

Three Manifestations of Quality Assurance

Quality assurance manifests itself in three ways. Quality of design must occur before quality of process, which must occur before quality of conformance. The design of a product or service must be such that the design, if executed correctly, meets the designated standards.[4] For example, the design for an emissions control system on an automobile has to be capable of actually achieving the necessary level of emissions; the design of a computerized hotel reservations system must allow information to be entered easily. Quality of process, as defined by its design, must be such that the process, if performed as designed, actually produces the product or service as designed.[5] Taking the two examples a step further, the design of the production processes for the emissions control system must actually produce the system as it was designed; the design of the process for using the hotel reservation system must allow reservations to be entered quickly and accurately.

There are two aspects to quality of conformance: conformance of the product or service to designated standards and conformance of the process to its design.[6] Conformance of product is the "degree to which a product's design and operating characteristics meet preestablished standards."[7] Conformance of service or process could be similarly defined as the degree to which a service's or process's design and operating characteristics meet preestablished standards. Quality of conformance assumes that the standards (often called specifications) are indicative of customer requirements, and that the customer will be satisfied if the standards are met. It is typically monitored through inspection or audit. In the emissions control system example, quality of conformance would exist if the process was followed as designed (process conformance) and the emissions control system, when tested, performed within specification limits (product conformance). In the computerized hotel reservations system example, quality of conformance would exist if the process was followed as designed (process conformance), and the reservations were entered quickly and accurately (service conformance).

> "We have come to realize the importance of planning for process capability constraints as well as conformance requirements in the design stage of new product development. Research and development can have a great new product idea, but if manufacturing cannot produce it consistently we do not have a new product to sell."
>
> —Dean A. Garner, Development Consultant, Wilson Sporting Goods

Quality Costs

Embedded within the concept of quality assurance is the quality costs concept. This concept was developed by Joseph Juran and others in the early 1950s, and was formally developed and promoted as a concept and technique by ASQ's Quality Cost Committee (formed in 1961).[8] Although this concept was originally developed for manufacturing to provide data for justifying additional expenditures on prevention, it has been expanded to include service industries. Three kinds of quality costs exist in organizations: Failure costs, appraisal costs, and prevention costs.

Failure costs are related to the failure of a product or service. These costs can be either internal or external. Internal failure costs are "associated with those defects that are found prior to transfer of the product [or service] to the customer."[9] Activities that result in internal failure costs are scrap, rework, sorting operations, and loss of throughput. External failure costs such as complaint handling, warranty charges, returned goods, and concessions made as compensation (e.g., a free meal in return for bad service) are associated with defects that are found after a product (or service) is in the hands of the customer.

A second type of cost is appraisal costs. "Appraisal costs are incurred in determining the degree of conformance to quality requirements."[10] Examples of this type of cost include inspection, testing, product or service quality audits, maintaining test equipment, and gage calibration.

The last type of costs, prevention costs, are those associated with preventing poor quality—that is, "keeping failure and appraisal costs to a minimum."[11] These include training, design reviews, and quality planning.

It is not unusual for failure and appraisal costs to decrease as prevention costs increase. Therefore, quality assurance systems need to be designed to keep total quality costs at a minimum, rather than on minimizing only one of its components.

Steps for determining and interpreting the cost of quality can be found in publications such as *Principles of Quality Costs* developed by the ASQ Quality Cost Committee (1990), *Juran's Quality Control Handbook* (1988), and *Quality Planning and Analysis* (1993).

> "Combining the concept of quality costs with process-management techniques creates a powerful quality-management tool to focus process-reengineering efforts to specific 'opportunities.' Successfully applying this tool provides an important indicator of the efficiency of a business process as measured in dollars."[12]
>
> —Jim Robison, Former Vice Chairman of the ASQ Quality Cost Committee, and COQ Advisor, The Harrington Group/QMX, and Rick Harrington, President and CEO, The Harrington Group

Customer Responsiveness

Customer responsiveness is an outgrowth of "conformance to customer requirements"—the definition of quality used in this field of performance practice. A conformance to specifications mentality is not enough. To ensure that customers receive what they contract to receive, organizations must learn more about customer needs and expectations surrounding the contract, especially when the contract is implied. They must listen to the "voice of the customer." To collect this information, many organizations have market research, customer complaints, customer questions and inquiries, warranty claims, and after-sales service call systems in place. Customer surveys can also be used to learn more about the level of—and the factors that influence—customer satisfaction and dissatisfaction. For customer responsiveness to occur, organizations must react to these data in a timely manner.

It is not unusual for organizations to use the term "customer focus" when they are actually practicing "customer responsiveness." These two terms are not synonymous. Customer responsiveness is reactive, whereas customer focus is proactive. Customer focus (as described in chapter 5) is demonstrated by working directly with customers to find better ways to meet their needs. It goes beyond the expressed needs and wants of customers to uncover the underlying purpose behind their requirements.

Process-Oriented Thinking

To respond to customers' requests, organizations must turn their attention to the processes within their organizations. A work process is a series of steps or activities that transforms inputs into outputs. A common acronym for remembering the structure of a process is SIPOC—**S**uppliers, **I**nputs, **P**rocess, **O**utputs, **C**ustomers. Process-oriented thinking, using the SIPOC model, creates processes that (when followed) produce product and service conformance to customer requirements. Achieving conformance by understanding and improving processes is superior to inspecting or sorting their output.

"At Hewlett-Packard, Dr. Deming got us thinking about all the interconnections in our circuit board assembly processes and the need to look at process data. We collected data on circuit board defects and it showed that our inspection process wasn't very effective in sorting the good from the bad. After we explained this fact to our people and reduced our reliance on inspection, our final quality got better! We also found that if we made an improvement in one part of the operation, things improved in other parts like a chain reaction, helping people to work together better."

—Tim Fuller, Partner, Fuller & Propst Associates

Process-oriented thinking recognizes that the products and services an organization provides to its customers are the result of processes linked together through inputs and outputs—often called a "chain of customers."[13] All outputs (those products, services, and by-products produced by the process) have customers (those who receive or use the outputs) and all inputs (those materials, documents, equipment, or people that are transformed or changed in some way to become the outputs) have suppliers (those who produce or supply the inputs). Even though this linkage is recognized in the Quality Assurance Field of Performance Practice, in reality most individuals consider only the next work process and ultimate end users when they talk about customers. Thus, the potential of process-oriented thinking is not fully realized until the Alignment and Integration Field of Performance Practice.

SDCA Cycle

In order to consistently meet customers' requirements, some level of standardization must exist in an organization. Standardization fosters organizational learning, provides a baseline for future improvement activities, helps employees learn new jobs more quickly, and improves the consistency of process output. Incoming materials used to produce products and services can be standardized, as well as the methods used to perform the work and the output of these processes. The requirement for standardization holds true even in organizations that make one-of-a-kind products and services. It is not unusual for organizations to achieve dramatic improvements in product and service quality as well as significant cost savings as a result of standardization activities.

> "Standardization is to quality as the foundation is to a house. Regardless of how nice a roof and interior (organizational structure and employees), without the foundation it's likely to collapse."
>
> —Duke Okes, Management Consultant, APLOMET

The **S**tandardize-**D**o-**C**heck-**A**ct (SDCA) Cycle is the thought process behind the performance of standardization activities. There are four phases to the SDCA Cycle. In the Standardize phase, a trial standard is developed based on the current best knowledge of those who do the work. Desired outcomes are also established here. In the Do phase, the trial standard is tested through use. The results of the trial are compared to the desired outcomes in the Check phase. The Act phase forces a decision to accept the standard, revise the standard, or to go through the SDCA Cycle again.

The 1986 book *Kaizen,* by Masaaki Imai, was one of the first publications to introduce the notion of the SDCA Cycle to the United States. It was stressed as both a necessary precondition (to stabilize the process) and follow-up (to standardize the process) to ongoing improvement through the use of the Plan-Do-Check-Act Cycle.

Discipline

Implementing quality assurance activities and developing and adhering to standards bring with them the need for discipline. Discipline enables organizations to ensure that their customers consistently receive what they contract to receive. Discipline is similar to self-control—there are a few overarching "rules or guidelines" governing behavior that are followed by everyone. For example, those who perform the work must have the discipline to follow the documented work instructions each time they do the job. They must also have the discipline to check the results of their work against the specified requirements. It is through this type of discipline that the practice of quality assurance becomes institutionalized, making it habitual and a part of the accepted custom within the organization.

COMMONLY USED TOOLS AND METHODS

Four sets of commonly used tools and methods are useful to organizations in the Quality Assurance Field of Performance Practice. They are a quality system, standardization, the basic tools of quality, and the 5S's. These tools and methods support the underlying concepts, help organizations ensure customers receive what they contract to receive, and facilitate product and service conformance to customer requirements.

Quality System

Most organizations approach quality assurance through the development of, and adherence to, a documented quality system. A quality system is "the collective plans, activities, and events that are provided to ensure that a product, process, or service will satisfy given needs."[14] The elements of a quality system include

a. quality planning (resulting in a document that includes both the organization's quality objectives and the methods for achieving them), the quality policy (a statement of the organization's overall approach to quality), the organizational structure for quality (the organization of the quality function and its components, and the organization of the entire enterprise for achieving quality throughout the enterprise), and the administration of quality (the structure of the quality manual, system auditing, monitoring, and review)

> "The notion that quality is everyone's job is a tenet that has long been held by those in quality. The trouble is that if it's just said, quality becomes nobody's job. Nowadays organizations document and communicate how everyone fits into the quality equation. In addition, people are encouraged to become part of the solutions by contributing to all sorts of quality-based teams."
>
> —Lowell Tomlinson, 1996–98 Chair,
> ASQ Electronics Division, American Society for Quality

b. product/service design assurance (processes that facilitate quality of design), specification development (processes that assure a link between specifications and customer requirements), and design and change control (processes that limit how and by whom designs can be changed)

c. control of purchased services, materials, and component parts (processes such as qualifying suppliers and incoming materials controls that assure the quality of purchased items and services)

d. production and delivery quality control (in-process, operational, and final product/service), including product quality audits, handling, packing, storing, and shipping

e. user contact and field performance (such as after-sales service calls and warranty claims)

f. corrective action (processes designed to respond to internal and external failures)

g. employee policy regarding quality (including management commitment to quality, quality awareness for all employees, supervisor training in quality, and recognition and rewards), training, and selection

h. product liability and user safety

i. rules for sampling and other statistical techniques [15]

If the organization has a Quality Department (or quality function), responsibility for the quality system may reside in it, with the quality manager designated as having overall responsibility. If the organization does not have a Quality Department, a member of the management team must be designated as the person with overall responsibility for the quality system.

Most current books regarding the development and implementation of quality systems are focused on the achievement of ISO 9000 or QS 9000 registration. However, there are a few books such as *The Quality System: A Sourcebook for Managers and Engineers,* by Frank Caplan, that give tips and ideas not specifically geared toward certification and registration.

Documentation

> "The existence of a functional quality system gives us stability and documentation and allows us to share lessons learned."
> —Marie Baucom Williams, President and CEO, Tennessee Quality

Quality systems must be documented in order to preserve their integrity and to facilitate communication of policies, procedures, and instructions. Usually, a quality system is documented on four levels. Occasionally, more than one level of documentation may be combined into a single manual. Today, to heighten access across the organization, these types of documents are often found in both electronic and paper formats.

The first—and most general—level of documentation describes the quality policies, the quality plan, the administration of quality, and the organization for quality, including management responsibility. The second level contains the procedures that cross work process boundaries and/or functional responsibilities (such as the procedure for document control, the procedure for control of nonconforming material, or the procedure for any of the elements listed in items b through i on page 55). The third level of documentation contains work instructions that describe in some detail the steps necessary to accomplish each work process. These instructions are a subset of the production and delivery quality control (item d on page 55). Measurement plans are also included at this level. Sometimes a fourth level of documentation is added for task instructions—specific steps for one or more activities in a work instruction where more detail is needed to fully explain how the work occurs.

Identifying the Titles of Work Processes

To create work process documentation, those who do the work have to know the titles of the work processes for which they are responsible. Many organizations select a bottom-up approach to identify work process titles by involving all work groups in this effort. Typically, each person within the group lists, at the task level, everything she or he does (based on the organization's mission statement) onto individual Post-it® Notes or cards. The information is collectively clustered by these same individuals into work processes. When the groupings are complete, titles are given to the clusters (work processes) and they are prioritized for the development of work instructions.

Several challenges must be addressed when using this approach. First, there is a tendency to end up with a large number of detailed work processes for effective standardization. In general, most work groups should have fewer than ten; some may have only one. Second, when clustering tasks, individuals tend to cluster those that appear similar but have no purposeful process relationship to each other. For example, a cluster of tasks may be titled "answering the phone" when the individual purpose of the tasks may be to answer the phone to receive customer complaints, answer the phone to give product information, and answer the phone to take orders (i.e., indicators of three separate work processes). They may also cluster according to their own personal work because it is often difficult to recognize that processes run across individual's jobs. For both of these situations, it is important to give feedback during the clustering activity. Third, because the clusters are formed within existing work groups, key processes that cross organizational boundaries may not be recognized as such. As a result, they may not be standardized properly until the organization enters the Alignment and Integration Field of Performance Practice.

All of these challenges can easily be overcome. These issues can be communicated as part of an orientation to the approach before the group starts to identify the titles of its work processes. It is also necessary to facilitate groups through each step, providing observation feedback on challenges as they arise.

> "It was amazing to us, as we began to identify our work process titles, that some of our groups had significant disagreements about what actual work was accomplished on the team. People resisted looking for processes and instead were intent to only look at particular tasks. Strong facilitation was necessary to move some groups past those problems, which we were able to finally do."
>
> —Col. Liz Anderson, 302d Support Group Commander, 302d Airlift Wing, U.S. Air Force Reserve (Any views or opinions expressed are personal to the individual and do not represent the U.S. Air Force or any other D.O.D. component official views or positions.)

Audits

Audits play a key role in the maintenance of a quality system. "A quality audit is an independent review conducted to compare some aspect of quality performance with a standard for that performance."[16] Three forms of companywide quality assurance audits can assure conformance: Quality audits, quality surveys, and product/service audits.[17] Quality audits involve periodic review of activities against some aspect of performance—such as the quality system documentation. Quality surveys (often called quality assessments or companywide audits) can be used to ascertain

- a product/service's relative standing in the marketplace (a rudimentary form of benchmarking)
- the user's situation with respect to cost, convenience, and the like over the life of the product
- opportunities to reduce the cost of poor quality
- employee perceptions of quality
- feedback to top management on policies, goals, premises, and beliefs [18]

Product/service audits are periodically performed in order to determine conformance to specified requirements. The book, *Walkthroughs, Inspections, and Technical Reviews,* by Daniel Freedman and Gerald Weinberg, published in 1990, includes how-to's, tips, worksheets, and sample reports for various types of audits.

Normally, these three types of audits occur after all regular quality control and assurance activities (e.g., inspection) have taken place. They are usually conducted by people who do not have a direct reporting relationship to the department or area being audited. Often, they are performed by outside agencies to prevent conflict of interest. The designated management representative for the organization's quality system is responsible for initiating, scheduling, and conducting these audits. Audit results can be used by leaders to make business decisions, assess risks, and identify opportunities for improvement.

> "An extra benefit of auditing is that it helps build trust. When documented policies and procedures aren't just words, but guidelines for action that are independently confirmed, it creates what I call 'organizational congruence.' Closing the gap between what is said and what is actually done satisfies a fundamental human need."
>
> —Duke Okes, Management Consultant, APLOMET

Standardization

> "If you were hired to turn a group of non-golfers into world-class golfers, would you require them to use the best-known methods: the standard equipment, a proven grip, the recommended swing and stance? Or would you let them do whatever they wanted to do?"[19]
>
> —Brian L. Joiner, author of *Fourth Generation Management: The New Business Consciousness*

To achieve consistent conformance to customer requirements, organizations can employ a structured approach to standardizing work processes that follows the SDCA Cycle. Standardization differs from problem solving and continual improvement. It involves the creation of a current reliable method (also known as a best method or current best method) both for doing the work and for monitoring its performance over time.[20] As a result, it can be carried out in the absence of existing data on the performance of the process, product, or system. Because this approach provides data on process performance that are required to initiate effective problem solving and continual improvement, it is an effective precursor to these methods.

A systematic approach, such as the one shown in Table 4.1, integrates process standardization with conformance of outputs to customer and fact-of-life (i.e., regulatory, safety, corporate, etc.) requirements. As a result, inputs and outputs as well as the process under study are standardized, thus eliminating the need to take on a separate initiative to develop standards for each of them.

Two deliverables are created during process standardization—an agreed-upon, documented way to perform the work (in accordance with customer and fact-of-life requirements) and a measurement plan. A measurement plan is for monitoring process and product/service performance over time. This plan provides an operational definition of what needs to be measured and how the measurement process will work. It typically includes

a. the step in the work process where the measurement needs to occur
b. the variable (both process and output) to be measured
c. the unit of measure
d. the measurement instrument
e. the method of measurement
f. the size of the sample
g. the frequency of sampling
h. the monitoring (or charting) tool
i. the person (designated by function or job title) responsible for performing the measurement

The data produced as a result of the plan provide assurance that the standardized work process is effective in achieving product and service conformance to customer requirements. It can also be used to pinpoint troubled processes, set priorities for resource allocation, and predict future performance.

The outcomes of standardization efforts need to be recorded using the organization's controlled document procedure (levels three and four as described earlier) to ensure that all work is documented consistently and that documentation changes systematically occur. Discipline on the part of each and every employee is required to ensure that the method for performing the work and the measurement plan are used in the course of performing daily work.

The use of a rigorous standardization methodology is recommended whenever work groups answer "no" to any of the following questions about their work processes:

- Does a documented procedure exist?
- Is the documented procedure based on customer data?
- Is there a measurement plan that is a part of the documented procedure?
- Is the documented procedure being followed by everyone who performs the work?

If done well, standardization can ensure conformance to customer requirements, improve work flow, reduce costs, and lay the foundation for future problem solving and continual improvement efforts.

> "Without work standards, there is no way to determine whether a process is effective or not. You first have to have a process to measure. Work standardization defines the process."
>
> —Duke Okes, Management Consultant, APLOMET

For some people, the term "standardization" carries with it overtones of work standardization, a derivative of the work of Frederick W. Taylor where manufacturing assembly jobs were divided into simple movements.[21] Materials were precisely positioned so that employees could work as fast as possible. Times were calculated for the performance of each task, and production standards were set

Table 4.1
A Method for Work Process Standardization*

Name of Stage	Purpose of This Stage	Reference to SDCA Cycle	Commonly Used Techniques
STAGE 1 **Frame the Work Process**	To focus the standardization effort on a specific work process that contributes to the organization's mission and vision.	Standardize	• Purpose of the work process • Work process owner • Components of the work process • Customer/output matrix
STAGE 2 **Document the Current Work Process**	To study all the ways the work process is being done today.	Standardize	• Flowchart of current procedure • Flowcharts from those who do the work
STAGE 3 **Study the Current Work Process**	To determine the starting point for the development of the trial work process based on customer and fact-of-life requirements.	Standardize	• Customer interview questions • Customer interviews • Composite importance ratings on customer requirements
STAGE 4 **Develop a Trial Work Process and Measurement Plan**	To ensure consistency in how the work is done and in how its performance is measured over time.	Standardize	• Integrated flowchart of trial work process • Task instructions • Supplier/input matrix • Measurement plan
STAGE 5 **Test the Trial Work Process and Measurement Plan**	To ensure that the trial work process and its associated measurement plan are feasible and meet all customer and fact-of-life requirements.	Do	• Data collection forms • Data collection • Improvement opportunities

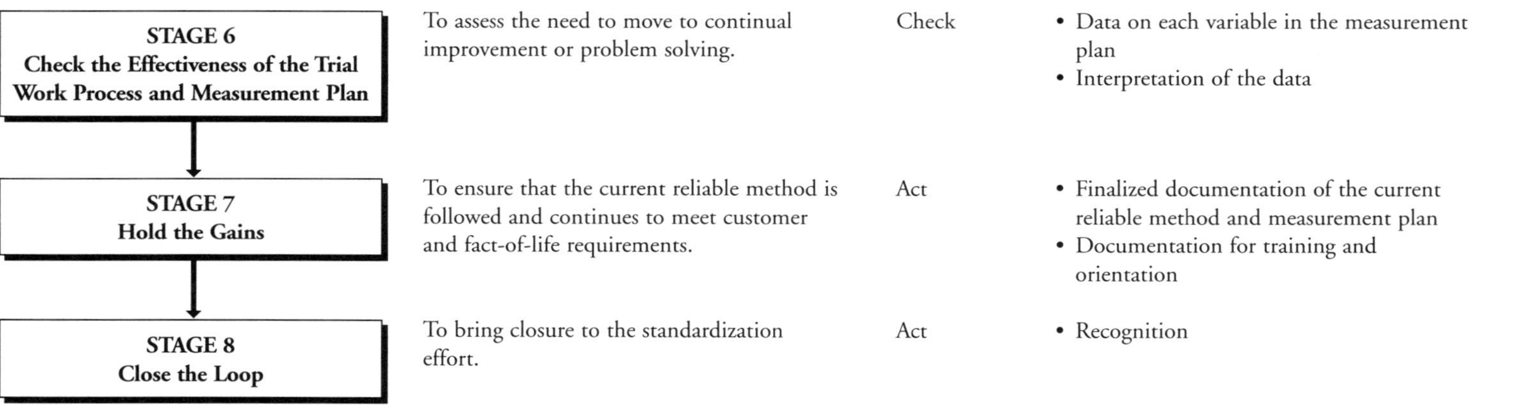

To assess the need to move to continual improvement or problem solving.	Check	• Data on each variable in the measurement plan • Interpretation of the data
To ensure that the current reliable method is followed and continues to meet customer and fact-of-life requirements.	Act	• Finalized documentation of the current reliable method and measurement plan • Documentation for training and orientation
To bring closure to the standardization effort.	Act	• Recognition

*Reprinted from Lori L. Silverman and Annabeth L. Propst. *Eight Stage Approach for Developing a Current Reliable Method* (unpublished workbook, 1995, 1997), 14–15.

for an hour's work. These standards were then used to reward "good" workers and punish "bad" workers. This is not the type or level of standardization recommended in *Critical SHIFT.* Standardization needs to occur at a level sufficient to ensure conformance of product and service to customer requirements and no more. More stringent customer requirements may require more stringent levels of standardization (e.g., washing a table in an operating room requires more stringent levels of standardization than washing a table in a restaurant). Standardization should allow for flexibility and judgment on the part of the people doing the work, and not be so restrictive that it makes people uncomfortable.

Basic Tools of Quality

The basic tools of quality are essential to an effective quality assurance system, effective standardization, and process-oriented thinking. These tools include

1. flowcharts (integrated [a.k.a. deployment] flowcharts are preferred, since they show the relationship between work activities and the person responsible for performing the activity)
2. run charts (to display data in time order as the precursor to control charts)
3. check sheets (as a tool for collecting data)
4. histograms (to show the distribution—or shape—of a set of data)
5. Pareto charts (to identify the most frequently occurring problems or causes)
6. cause and effect (a.k.a. fishbone) diagrams (a tool for identifying causes of undesirable effects)
7. scatter plots (to show the nature and strength of the relationship between two variables)
8. control charts (to identify whether the variation in the data is likely to be due to the normal functioning of a process or some special disturbance)

These tools have a variety of uses in this field of performance practice including (but not limited to) documenting a work process, monitoring the performance of a standardized work process over time, assessing the ability of the process to meet specified requirements, and displaying data to determine whether or not action needs to be taken. Their use can enhance an organization's ability to achieve product and service conformance to customer requirements.

The 5S's

Often, in pursuit of standardization, organizations recognize the need to organize the work area. A methodology known as the 5S's can be used to organize the work area in accordance with customer and fact-of-life requirements. Its use boosts efficiency, effectiveness, and comfort for the users of the work area, while promoting standardization and minimizing the opportunity for errors associated with disorganization.

The 5S's, developed in Japan in the 1980s, are the first letters of the words *seiri* (sort), *seiton* (simplify), *seiso* (sweep), *seiketsu* (standardize clean-up), and *shitsuke* (self-discipline).[22] Sorting identifies those items in the work area that are needed and removes all items no longer required. Simplification activities organize the way things are stored so that they are easy to find and convenient to the point of use. Sweeping involves cleanliness and orderliness—keeping the work area clean and keeping things in their designated places. Standardized clean-up is the systematic application of sorting, simplifying, and sweeping—doing it the same way every time. Self-discipline means following the standardized procedures for organizing the work area. Both the *5 Pillars of the Visual Workplace,* by Hiroyuki Hirano, and *The 5S's: Five Keys to a Total Quality Environment,* by Takashi Osada, provide an in-depth explanation of this approach.

Individual work groups are primarily responsible for undertaking 5S organization of their own work area. As such, each work group is responsible for decisions regarding organization and labeling. However, management may be involved in setting organization-wide standards as a way of establishing consistency throughout all areas.

> "Leadership's 5S's challenge is to attain a fundamental shift in employee attitude. This shift moves them from 'just following another management program' to embracing a new way of life for the organization. Once this happens, the organization will attain and maintain levels 4 and 5 (standardize and self-discipline) and the ongoing benefits of [the] 5S's will become apparent."
>
> —Lon L. Barrett, Auditor, Boeing,
> and 1997–98 ASQ Spokane Section Chair

WHO IS INVOLVED IN THE QUALITY ASSURANCE FIELD OF PERFORMANCE PRACTICE

Many organizations operating in the Quality Assurance Field of Performance Practice form a Management Steering Committee to direct organization-wide quality assurance efforts. The committee orchestrates the efforts of all parties involved in the development and/or maintenance of the quality system and ensures that the quality assurance activities are not in conflict with other organization-wide initiatives. In 5S initiatives, the Management Steering Committee may decide on overall standards to be used throughout the organization (e.g., colors of pipes, colors for marking aisles) that each work group must comply with for safety or environmental reasons. As preparation for standardization efforts, the Steering Committee may decide on the methods to identify work process titles, to standardize work processes, and to prioritize work processes for standardization.

If a Quality Department (or function) exists, it may assist the Management Steering Committee in tracking quality costs; managing quality system documentation; initiating, scheduling, and conducting audits; and coaching individuals and

Table 4.2

Your Organization and the Quality Assurance Field of Performance Practice

Directions: Record the activities your organization has and has not engaged in relative to the concepts, tools, and methods referenced in this field of performance practice, noting the degree of deployment of each item. Also document its future plans for deploying these concepts, tools, and methods throughout the enterprise.

Purpose: To ensure customers receive what they contract to receive		**Desired Outcome:** Product and service conformance to customer requirements		
	What Your Organization Is Doing	**What Your Organization Is Not Doing**	**Degree of Deployment***	**Plans Your Organization Has for the Future**
Underlying Concepts • Quality assurance • Customer responsiveness • Process-oriented thinking • SDCA Cycle • Discipline			 1 2 3 4 5 1 2 3 4 5 1 2 3 4 5 1 2 3 4 5 1 2 3 4 5	
Commonly Used Tools and Methods • Quality system • Standardization • Basic tools of quality • The 5S's			 1 2 3 4 5 1 2 3 4 5 1 2 3 4 5 1 2 3 4 5	

*Rating system: 1 = no systematic deployment is evident
2 = some deployment is evident with little or no results
3 = deployment is evident in several areas of the business with limited results
4 = deployment is evident in major portions of the business with measurable results
5 = full organization-wide deployment is evident with significant measurable results

Table 4.3

CHAOS and the Quality Assurance Field of Performance Practice

Directions: Note your thoughts on the future impact that the forces of **CHAOS** may have on each of the underlying concepts and the commonly used tools and methods in the Quality Assurance Field of Performance Practice.

Underlying Concepts / **CHAOS**	**Changing Definition of Work and the Workplace**	**Heightened Social Responsibility**	**Aging Baby Boomers**	**Overarching Demographic Change**	**Strategic Growth Through Technology and Innovation**
• Quality assurance					
• Customer responsiveness					
• SDCA Cycle					
• Discipline					
Commonly Used Tools and Methods					
• Quality system					
• Standardization					
• Basic tools of quality					
• The 5S's					

work groups. Front-line employees need to be actively involved in this field of performance practice. They are responsible for a wide variety of standardization and 5S activities in their respective work areas.

SHORTCOMINGS WITH THE QUALITY ASSURANCE FIELD OF PERFORMANCE PRACTICE

The purpose of the Quality Assurance Field of Performance Practice—ensuring that customers receive what they contract to receive—is fundamental. All later fields of performance practice depend on successfully achieving product and service conformance to customer requirements as a necessary antecedent to an organization's ability to stay in business.

Quality Assurance was the first field of performance practice to emerge, and for many years was enough to safeguard an organization's success. Eventually, several shortcomings became apparent. The most obvious one is that the concept of continual improvement of product, process, and service is not pervasive in this field of performance practice. Although improvement is not ignored, it tends to be limited to achieving conformance. Once conformance is achieved, no motivation for improvement exists because the desired outcome has been attained.

This field of performance practice is reactive to customer needs and expectations. It focuses on giving customers what they ask for today, within the scope of what the business has to offer. Little attention is given to determining customers' unspoken or unknown present and future needs and allowing an organization to fulfill them before they are requested.

It is evident that top management involvement is minimal in this field of performance practice. Primary responsibility for assuring conformance rests with the Quality Department and those who work on the front-line. As a result, quality may not be a strategic focus for the organization.

In general, the work in this field of performance practice does not attempt to change the existing system or constraints. As a result, it does not ensure that the work that is documented is necessary to accomplish the organization's mission or that the right products and services are being produced. It merely assures conformance with customer requirements and encourages getting the most out the existing system. It was because of these shortcomings that the second star in The Starburst Model™ emerged—the Problem Resolution Field of Performance Practice.

Endnotes

1. Neil Hardie, "The Effects of Quality on Business Performance," *Quality Management Journal,* Vol. 5, No. 3 (Summer 1998), 75.

2. Raymond Wachniak, "Ten Commandments for Quality Auditors," in *The Best on Quality, Vol. 7,* ed., John D. Hromi (Milwaukee: American Society for Quality Control, 1996), 4.
3. Joseph M. Juran, "A History of Managing for Quality, Part 1," *Quality Digest* (November 1995), 27.
4. Eugene L. Grant and Richard S. Leavenworth, *Statistical Quality Control,* 5th ed. (New York: McGraw-Hill, 1980), 338–339.
5. Joseph M. Juran and Frank M. Gryna, *Quality Planning and Analysis,* 3rd ed. (New York: McGraw-Hill, 1993), 343–360.
6. Grant and Leavenworth, *Statistical Quality Control,* 338–339.
7. David A. Garvin, *Managing Quality: The Strategic and Competitive Edge* (New York: The Free Press, 1988), 53.
8. Dean L. Bottorf, "COQ Systems: The Right Stuff," *Quality Progress* (March 1997), 33.
9. Juran and Gryna, *Quality Planning and Analysis,* 16.
10. Juran and Gryna, *Quality Planning and Analysis,* 17.
11. Juran and Gryna, *Quality Planning and Analysis,* 578–579.
12. Jim Robison and Rick Harrington, "Using Quality Costs to Drive Process Reengineering," *Quality Digest* (May 1995), 30.
13. Richard J. Schonberger, *Building a Chain of Customers* (New York: The Free Press, 1990).
14. Garvin, *Managing Quality: The Strategic and Competitive Edge,* 53.
15. Harrison M. Wadsworth, Kenneth S. Stephens, and A. Blanton Godfrey, *Modern Methods for Quality Control and Improvement* (New York: John Wiley & Sons, 1986), 36–40.
16. Juran and Gryna, *Quality Planning and Analysis,* 567.
17. Juran and Gryna, *Quality Planning and Analysis,* 565–588.
18. Juran and Gryna, *Quality Planning and Analysis,* 578–579.
19. Brian L. Joiner, "The Pros and Cons of Standardization," *Managing for Quality* (Issue 9, Fall 1993), 3.
20. Lori L. Silverman and Annabeth L. Propst, *Eight Stage Approach for Developing a Current Reliable Method* (unpublished workbook, 1995, 1997), 3.
21. Charles D. Wrege and Ronald G. Greenwood, *Frederick Taylor, The Father of Scientific Management: Myth and Reality* (Homewood, IL: Business One Irwin, 1991).
22. Hiroyuki Hirano, *5 Pillars of the Visual Workplace: The Sourcebook for 5S Implementation* (Portland, OR: Productivity Press, 1990), 20.

CHAPTER 5

The Problem Resolution Field of Performance Practice

Chapter 5 explores the Problem Resolution Field of Performance Practice—the second star in The Starburst Model™. Its purpose is to improve both bottom-line performance and customer satisfaction to ensure the organization's long-term success. Improving either one (i.e., bottom-line performance or customer satisfaction) at the expense of the other can drive an organization out of business. It is only by accomplishing both that an organization becomes healthier and more viable. The outcomes of the work in this field of practice are threefold: to reduce costs, improve performance (e.g., productivity and return on sales), and improve customer satisfaction. Many people believe that improved customer satisfaction is the inevitable result of improved performance and reduced costs. This may not be the case. Although the summary of the findings of 43 studies correlating quality with business performance suggests a possible link between improving performance and customer satisfaction, the evidence is not conclusive.[1] While some studies support the causal relationship, others do not. Therefore, it is essential to focus on all three outcomes when working in this field of performance practice.

> "There are several trends I have observed. First, in manufacturing, quality has moved from fixing defects to prevention. Second, quality applies to non-manufacturing. Third, improving quality is not a cost, it is a savings. Finally, quality is not a departmental initiative; quality is business excellence. It's managing value-added."
>
> —Richard C. Buetow, Retired Senior Vice President, Motorola, Inc., and Motorola Director of Quality

UNDERLYING CONCEPTS

The four concepts that underlie the Problem Resolution Field of Performance Practice—the PDCA Cycle, customer focus, variation, and teamwork—relate to both problem solving and continual improvement. Even though some of these concepts started to emerge in the Quality Assurance Field of Performance Practice, it was in this field of performance practice that they fully matured. For example, while teams are used in the practice of standardization, it is within the Problem Resolution field that the concept of teamwork became more fully developed, thus making its impact far more significant. Similarly, the concept of customer focus, although grounded in the earlier concept of customer responsiveness, takes on a more proactive slant.

PDCA Cycle

Fundamental to the purpose of the Problem Resolution Field of Performance Practice (improving bottom-line performance and customer satisfaction) is the concept of never-ending improvement. The **P**lan-**D**o-**C**heck-**A**ct (PDCA) cycle represents the thought process for problem solving and continual improvement much as the SDCA Cycle represents the thought process for standardization. Although the PDCA Cycle was originally popularized by Dr. Deming, he attributed it to the 1939 book, *Statistical Method from the Viewpoint of Quality Control,* by Walter Shewhart of Bell Telephone Laboratories, Inc. Consequently, it has been called the Shewhart Cycle, the Deming Cycle (in Japan), the PDCA Cycle, and within the past ten years the PDSA (**P**lan-**D**o-**S**tudy-**A**ct) Cycle.

There are four phases in the PDCA Cycle, just as there were four phases in the SDCA Cycle. The Plan phase includes identifying purpose and goals, formulating theory, defining measures of success, and planning activities based on the purpose, goals, and theory.[2] In the Do phase, the plan is tested on a limited basis—for a limited time or in a limited area. The plan is followed carefully to ensure minimal deviation from its original intent, with data being collected along the way. In the Check phase, outcomes are monitored to test the validity of initial theory and plans, results are studied for signs of progress or success or unexpected outcomes, and the search continues for new learnings and problems to solve.[3] In the Act phase, the decision is made to adopt the plan as is, to adapt the plan to take into account what has been learned in the Do and Check phases, or to abandon the plan as untenable.

> "The move from ISO 9000 to QS 9000 brought in the improvement cycle and the organization's suppliers. It focuses on the chain of processes necessary to meet customer requirements."
>
> —Marie Baucom Williams, President and CEO,
> Tennessee Quality

The PDCA Cycle, unlike the SDCA Cycle, may need to be turned several times in order to achieve the desired results. The cycle must be turned again if the original plan is abandoned in the Act phase. It is also true that if the Act phase produces the decision to adapt the plan, the adapted plan will need to be tested again before adoption, hence resulting in the need for another trip around the PDCA Cycle. What may not be apparent is that if the decision in the Act phase is to adopt the plan, the cycle must be followed one more time, since the improvement is not considered complete until its full implementation is planned, executed, and monitored.

The PDCA and SDCA Cycles are linked together. In the last turning of the PDCA Cycle, it is essential to lock the improvements in place by standardizing the materials, methods, and outcomes around the improvement through the SDCA Cycle. Similarly, in turning the SDCA Cycle, the Act phase can lead to a need for improvement—if the data indicate specific problems or opportunities for improvement—thus causing entry into the PDCA Cycle.

Customer Focus

Customer responsiveness is an underlying concept in the Quality Assurance Field of Performance Practice and is defined as giving customers what they contract to receive. Customer focus is more proactive than customer responsiveness. It involves working with customers to find better ways to meet their needs. It goes beyond the expressed needs and wants of the customer to uncover the underlying purpose driving the customer requirement. For example, if a customer asks for a specific bolt, it is important to determine if the person really needs a bolt at all, and whether the bolt needs to fit a certain hole diameter or to bear a certain amount of pressure. Sometimes the best way to serve a customer's needs is to suggest other options. It may be that some other product could serve the purpose and need equally well or even better than the originally requested item. Although some organizations are reluctant to communicate in this manner, customers almost always become more satisfied with such solicitude.

Variation

> "Variation is a fact of life, and exists in all types of processes. While this appears to be common sense, many business students are taught that actual financial figures should always equal budget, and many science students are taught that mass balances should balance exactly. . . . In our personal lives, we are often surprised when the mail does not arrive at the same time every day, complain when the weather forecast is inaccurate, and become frustrated when our plane does not leave or arrive on time. Helping people grasp this fundamental principle and 'unlearn' their deterministic view of the world is the greatest contribution the statistical profession . . . could provide to society."[4]
>
> —Galen Britz, Don Emerling, Lynne Hare, Roger Hoerl, and Janice Shade, *Statistical Thinking,* a Special Publication of the Statistics Division of ASQ

Variation exists in all things—it occurs both in processes and in data. Although the concept of variation has been understood for many centuries, Walter Shewhart was the first person to study its impact on product quality and manufacturing. His 1931 book, *Economic Control of Quality of Manufactured Product,* was the foundation of much of the later work on the topic. More recent publications on this topic include the Western Electric *Statistical Quality Control Handbook,* published in 1956, and Donald Wheeler's book, *Understanding Variation: The Key to Managing Chaos,* published in 1993. Both statistics and statistical thinking were specifically developed to deal with variation. Statistics is the science of making decisions when one is operating under conditions of uncertainty.[5] Statistics has only existed as a science since the beginning of the twentieth century, and did not become popular until the 1940s.[6] Statistical thinking adds the concept of process to statistics and incorporates elements of process-oriented thinking and continual improvement.

One of the challenges associated with achieving the outcomes of this field of performance practice (i.e., reduced costs, improved performance, and improved customer satisfaction) is the need to understand and manage variation. Understanding variation helps teams determine when the difference between two successive observations is sufficient to form the basis for action. It helps them identify where to look for the source of a problem and what kinds of action are most likely to resolve it. It also helps teams confirm or disprove the effectiveness of their actions in achieving their intended results.

Part of understanding variation involves identifying whether variation is due to common causes or special causes. Common causes of variation are built into the process or system; they are equally likely to impact all outputs. Common cause variation is predictable, yet random; that is, its average value and its boundaries can be predicted, but the actual value—variation around the average—is random. Specific causal elements of common cause variation cannot be identified. Reducing variation due to common causes requires fundamental changes to the process or system.

Special causes of variation are not built into the process or system; they are not equally likely to affect all outputs. Special cause variation is not predictable—it occurs sporadically. Therefore, specific causal elements of special cause variation can be identified, and actions that do not require fundamental changes to the process or system can be taken to remove them.

A third type of variation—structural variation[7,8]—refers to variation that exhibits a certain characteristic pattern (such as a trend or a cycle) that is predictable over time and is a fundamental outcome of the structure of the process. While some people consider structural variation a part of common cause variation, it is presented separately here. Understanding that it is distinct from common cause variation adds to process knowledge and assists in determining the level of action that is required to reduce the variation. Structural variation may be immutable (i.e., unchangeable). In many cases, even fundamental changes to the process are not sufficient to impact structural variation unless they impact the basic underlying fabric of the process or system. If the extent of structural variation is such that it is not acceptable, it may require total rejection of the existing process or system and a change to a completely different one.

One way to understand the relationship between these three types of variation is to consider Chicago weather. Over the period of a year, the daily high temperature exhibits a cycle. This cycle represents structural variation. The differences over the years between the daily highs and the average (so-called "normal") high for that day represents common cause variation. The limits on common cause variation can be calculated to identify special causes in temperature—they may not necessarily correspond to record highs. Record highs may easily be inside the limits and represent common cause variation. Special causes may be identified by a point outside the limits (e.g., a 70 degree day in January) or long runs on one side of the average (e.g., the extremely hot summer of 1995 in Chicago).

Teamwork

According to a survey published in the October 1992 issue of *TRAINING* Magazine, in organizations that identified some groups of employees as teams, the following were attributed to them:

- "76% of the respondents said that their teams have improved employee morale;
- "62% said that their teams have improved management's morale;
- "80% said that their teams have contributed to increased profits;
- "90% said that their teams have improved the quality of products or services;
- "85% said that their teams have improved the level of customer service; and
- "81% said that their teams have improved productivity."[9]

Teamwork is demonstrated through "joint action by a group of people, in which individual interests are subordinated to group unity and efficiency; coordinated effort. . . ."[10] Critical to this definition are the shared purpose and harmony that change a group into a team and instill an ongoing spirit of cooperation. This spirit of cooperation, with people working together toward common goals, is essential for improving bottom-line performance and customer satisfaction. When teamwork exists, an organization's ability to reduce costs, improve performance, and increase customer satisfaction is greatly enhanced. While teamwork can exist without formally designated teams, it is within a team context that teamwork occurs in this field of performance practice.

"Encouragement to spend time discussing group process and having the skills to do so are essential. It's frequently difficult for individuals to share directly with others how someone's behavior affects the team and its members, and to hear requests for change in one's own behavior. Being a good team member implies having done 'one's own work' and the ability to distinguish between team and personal issues. Touching on the psychological or personal makeup of people is a delicate issue for organizations."

—Lunell Haught, Ph.D., Owner, Haught Strategies

What Makes Teams Effective

"The first thing I look for in a team is a clear purpose. A team needs to start with the end in mind; charters that are lengthy or broad and unspecific may not provide a clear end point. Secondly, I look for a strong leader to keep the team on track, summarize the discussion, reach consensus, and capture action items. These few skills can make all the difference in the progress of a team. Finally, I make sure the team's purpose is connected to the organization's current strategy. Teams often lose the support they began with as the organization's priorities change. Although there are many variables that influence a team's effectiveness—these have always been critical success factors in the teams I have participated in."

—Sharon Lutz, Ph.D., Director, Integrated Analysis Team, Fairview Hospital and Healthcare Services

"[R]esearch on organizational and team effectiveness suggests that any team or group doing knowledge work needs five attributes to perform effectively: (1) knowledge, (2) information, (3) power, (4) motivation, and (5) opportunity/time."[11] These five attributes apply to this field of performance practice because problem resolution work is truly knowledge work.

Knowledge is the understanding and expertise that is held individually and collectively by the members of a group. When key people representing all interested parties are involved in addressing issues, they usually know more about the problem than any one individual in the group. Thus, the team has better information about the behavior of the problem, and a greater diversity of options to choose from in crafting a solution. Because of this, getting the right members on a team is critical.

Information refers to the facts, data, and information specific to the purpose of the team and the larger needs of the organization. The team must be provided with, or have access to, data and information about the magnitude and behavior of the issue or process on which they are working and the outcomes that need to be achieved. In addition, they also need to have information about the process itself, related processes within the organization and pertinent customers and competitors.

The team's ability to make and influence decisions determines its *power.* Its scope of decision making and its authority and goals must be well defined up front. In addition, management must be prepared to support the team's decisions. When management second-guesses teams, their power is diminished, thus causing them to make fewer risky decisions—and therefore fewer decisions overall—in the future. It is also important here to gain the commitment of other organizational members to follow through on decisions.

The amount of energy people willingly commit to the performance of the team determines their level of *motivation.* This energy expresses itself through attendance and participation at meetings as well as in the completion of prework. If organizations want individuals to perform well on teams, they cannot be demotivated through the formal structures of the organization. Reward and recognition systems must be altered so that they are no longer based solely on individual performance. This is especially true of those systems in which individual performance is used to split a fixed reward pie among employees. Conflicting goals may also hinder motivation. When individuals' personal performance, or the performance of their department, is based on objectives that are in conflict with a team's goals, the team's goals will likely suffer.

> "I found that having a clear goal is critical to team effectiveness; without it, many wallow in ambiguity and indifference. If people feel they can accomplish something that will impact the organization, members will participate and work outside the meetings."
>
> —Randy Rossi, AVP, Business Banking Manager,
> Southwest National Bank

Whether the team is allowed the physical and mental space to work in an effective manner is the subject of the fifth attribute, *opportunity/time.* Once again, organizational systems can hinder teamwork, as demonstrated by the need to achieve an individual quota even though the team is working on a much more pressing organizational issue. Allowing team members time away from regular duties, getting others to assume some of the members' daily work responsibilities, and compensating members for meeting during off-duty hours all need to be considered. Freeing up room space and providing supplies for meetings are also important.

Types of Teams

> "In healthcare, most teams are cross-functional in nature given the interdependency and need for communication across disciplines. We have found that patients are very aware of how well the staff works as a team to provide their care. Our challenge is keeping multi-disciplinary teams focused on the ultimate customer rather than on what works best for their own discipline."
>
> —Sharon Lutz, Ph.D., Director, Integrated Analysis Team,
> Fairview Hospital and Healthcare Services

Functional teams (a.k.a. natural teams or in-function work groups) and cross-functional teams are both commonly utilized in the Problem Resolution Field of Performance Practice. Functional teams typically engage in standardization, problem solving, and continual improvement work as it applies to those work processes that are directly within their control. Their purpose is enduring—they are charged with a process or set of processes, and are responsible for performing that work and producing outcomes as long as they hold a job within that area. By its very nature, membership on this type of team is mandatory.

Cross-functional teams, on the other hand, are "composed of those individuals from departments within the firm whose competencies are essential in achieving an optimal evaluation. Successful teams combine skill-sets which no single individual possesses."[12] Team members are often from different departments and perhaps different locations. There are two kinds of cross-functional teams—permanent cross-functional teams (usually designed around core competencies or systems) and temporary cross-functional teams (created to produce one-time outputs—such as a new product, or for problem-solving and improvement-oriented activities). Membership on cross-functional teams is usually voluntary. The latter type of cross-functional team is used in this field; the former is used in the Alignment and Integration Field.

> "We use several different types of teams—temporary cross-functional teams, permanent cross-functional teams, department teams, and process teams. Cross-functional teams are necessary to handle those issues that require the collective input of many functional areas while department and process teams are more task and communication focused for a specific area. Cross-functional teams give employees who have never had a chance to work together the opportunity to share ideas and learn about respective challenges. To be effective they require more orientation and team-building skills up front."
>
> —Randy Rossi, AVP, Business Banking Manager,
> Southwest National Bank

A Cautionary Note

Since the mid-1990s, questions have been raised about whether teamwork really works. An article in a 1998 issue of a leadership journal cites the results of one study showing that four out of 33 different work groups of all different kinds were actually effective teams.[13] Another article in the same issue of this journal states that "real team efforts at the top of large organizations have performance value *only* when applied to legitimate team opportunities. In other words, the senior leadership group (that is, all the CEO's direct reports) need not try to become a real team."[14] Do these articles mean that teamwork should not be pursued in the future? Some may think so. On the other hand, it is important to acknowledge the misuse of teams, the insufficiency of member development, the lack of required guidance and support, and other issues often associated with poorly performing teams. All of these issues are ripe opportunities for improvement and innovation in the field of group development.

COMMONLY USED TOOLS AND METHODS

The tools and methods described in this section include process management, constraint management tools, advanced tools, and creativity tools. They have been developed over several decades and tend to be more complex, specialized, and powerful than the tools and methods used in the Quality Assurance Field of Performance

Practice. While some of them are essential for all individuals, it is highly unlikely that any one person could be knowledgeable about or have the opportunity to use all of the advanced tools listed here.

Process Management

> "If people know what the organization is trying to achieve, they assume responsibility for process management. They map their processes and ask 'Are they effective?' and 'Where is the idle time?' They expand their views of their processes by working with customers and suppliers as part of their work teams. Teaming comes after process management."
>
> —Richard C. Buetow, Retired Senior Vice President, Motorola, Inc., and Motorola Director of Quality

Process management is an umbrella term used to describe the activities undertaken to operate and maintain processes in order for them to produce desired results for customers and the organization. The practice of process management is founded on the concepts of process-oriented thinking (described in chapter 4), customer focus, the existence of variation, and the importance of managing variation (e.g., by using the SDCA and PDCA Cycles). Process management encompasses seven activities:

1. identifying work process titles
2. creating a standard method for carrying out the work and for monitoring process performance over time
3. addressing problems that arise
4. continually improving how the work is done
5. identifying opportunities for innovation
6. sharing work process information with others
7. training members on work processes and related topics[15]

Identifying the titles of work processes, and creating a standard method for carrying out the work and monitoring process performance over time, were addressed in chapter 4. Even though these activities exist in the Quality Assurance Field of Performance Practice, their benefits cannot be fully realized until they are part of process management. The other five activities follow here.

Problem Solving

> There are two benefits to problem solving. It prevents the need to solve the same issue over and over again by validating and eliminating its root cause. It's also efficient because time is not spent changing lots of things—only those that are related to the removal of the root cause. To do it really well, problem solving needs to be a part of a larger process management system. Otherwise you can't lock in the gains."
>
> —Ellen Bovarnick, Senior Vice President, Quality, formerly of Florida Power & Light

Problem solving is defined as "action(s) taken to remove a specific, undesirable effect(s). There are two types of problems: (a) too much of something with a need to decrease or eliminate (such as expenses and customer complaints), and (b) too little of something with a need to increase (such as sales, market share, and capacity)."[16] Using a systematic problem solving methodology based on the PDCA Cycle avoids jumping to a solution without first thoroughly understanding the nature of the problem and its causes (refer to Table 5.1 for an example). Commonly used problem solving tools include control charts, Pareto charts, histograms, check sheets, scatter plots, correlation analysis, root cause analysis, and simulation. Some of these tools were described in chapter 4 under The Basic Tools of Quality; others will be described later in this chapter in the section on Advanced Tools. These tools allow teams and individuals to more fully analyze a situation and its outcomes, explore the factors that contribute to the observed outcomes, build models describing the relationship between these factors and their outcomes, and predict the effects the changes in these factors will have on the outcomes.

Continual Improvement

Continual improvement occurs when "action(s) [are] taken to optimize a specific characteristic or set of characteristics even though performance of the characteristic(s) might be acceptable to the customer."[17] The discipline of continual improvement leads organizations away from complacency when all outcomes are acceptable. It pushes organizations to continually address ways to reduce costs, and improve organizational performance and customer satisfaction. As with standardization and problem solving, utilizing a systematic approach to continual improvement based on the PDCA Cycle (such as the example shown in Table 5.1) helps teams and individuals be rigorous in their approach to continual improvement. This rigor is necessary to ensure that teams understand all aspects of the improvement opportunity and consider multiple improvement options.

> "We work with a variety of improvement methodologies: PDCA, rapid cycle improvement, reengineering, etc. The challenge comes in identifying and prioritizing improvement opportunities at various levels (department, site, system) in the organization and then selecting the appropriate improvement framework. Continual improvement is first and foremost a process of prioritizing opportunities and then allocating available resources."
>
> —Sharon Lutz, Ph.D., Director, Integrated Analysis Team,
> Fairview Hospital and Healthcare Services

The tools and approaches used in continual improvement are somewhat different than those used in problem solving. In addition to the data analysis tools used in problem solving, creativity tools, quality function deployment, and what-if analysis play a bigger role in continual improvement. Because there is no existing problem in continual improvement, it is necessary to study the customers' wants and needs in more depth in order to be able to develop improvement

Table 5.1

Methods for Problem Solving* and Continual Improvement†

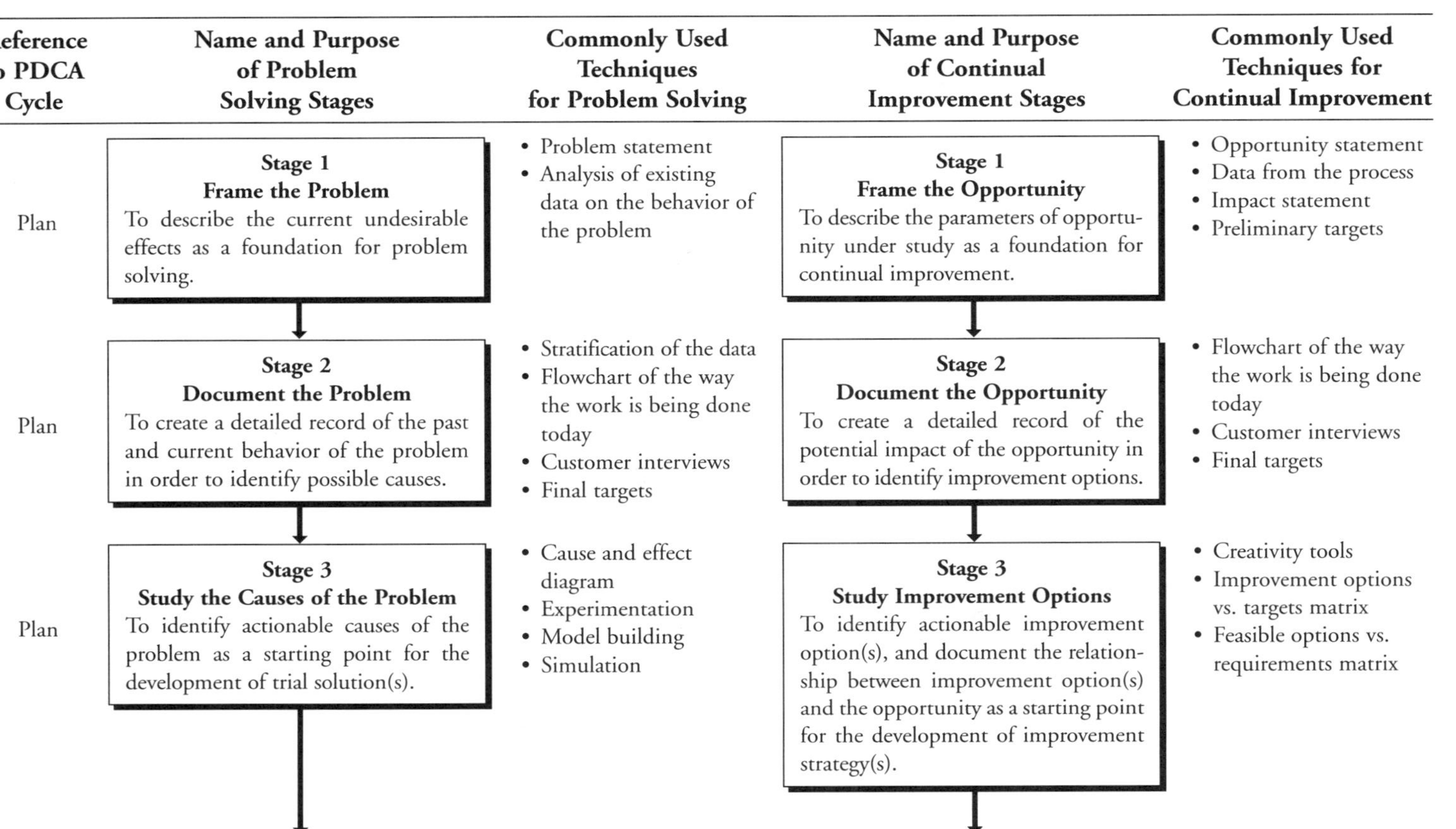

Reference to PDCA Cycle	Name and Purpose of Problem Solving Stages	Commonly Used Techniques for Problem Solving	Name and Purpose of Continual Improvement Stages	Commonly Used Techniques for Continual Improvement
Plan	**Stage 1** **Frame the Problem** To describe the current undesirable effects as a foundation for problem solving.	• Problem statement • Analysis of existing data on the behavior of the problem	**Stage 1** **Frame the Opportunity** To describe the parameters of opportunity under study as a foundation for continual improvement.	• Opportunity statement • Data from the process • Impact statement • Preliminary targets
Plan	**Stage 2** **Document the Problem** To create a detailed record of the past and current behavior of the problem in order to identify possible causes.	• Stratification of the data • Flowchart of the way the work is being done today • Customer interviews • Final targets	**Stage 2** **Document the Opportunity** To create a detailed record of the potential impact of the opportunity in order to identify improvement options.	• Flowchart of the way the work is being done today • Customer interviews • Final targets
Plan	**Stage 3** **Study the Causes of the Problem** To identify actionable causes of the problem as a starting point for the development of trial solution(s).	• Cause and effect diagram • Experimentation • Model building • Simulation	**Stage 3** **Study Improvement Options** To identify actionable improvement option(s), and document the relationship between improvement option(s) and the opportunity as a starting point for the development of improvement strategy(s).	• Creativity tools • Improvement options vs. targets matrix • Feasible options vs. requirements matrix

Table 5.1—*Continued*

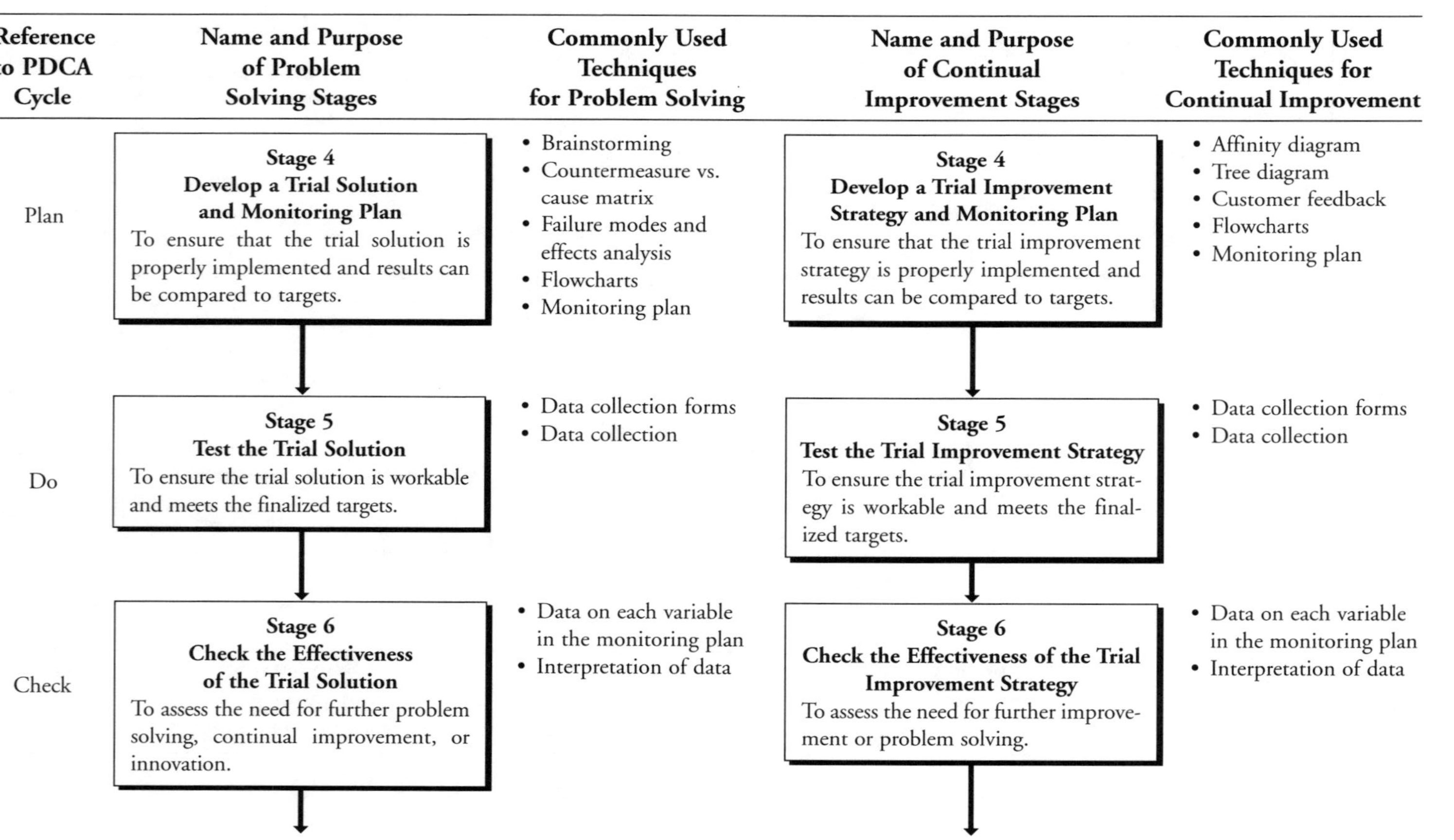

Reference to PDCA Cycle	Name and Purpose of Problem Solving Stages	Commonly Used Techniques for Problem Solving	Name and Purpose of Continual Improvement Stages	Commonly Used Techniques for Continual Improvement
Plan	**Stage 4** **Develop a Trial Solution and Monitoring Plan** To ensure that the trial solution is properly implemented and results can be compared to targets.	• Brainstorming • Countermeasure vs. cause matrix • Failure modes and effects analysis • Flowcharts • Monitoring plan	**Stage 4** **Develop a Trial Improvement Strategy and Monitoring Plan** To ensure that the trial improvement strategy is properly implemented and results can be compared to targets.	• Affinity diagram • Tree diagram • Customer feedback • Flowcharts • Monitoring plan
Do	**Stage 5** **Test the Trial Solution** To ensure the trial solution is workable and meets the finalized targets.	• Data collection forms • Data collection	**Stage 5** **Test the Trial Improvement Strategy** To ensure the trial improvement strategy is workable and meets the finalized targets.	• Data collection forms • Data collection
Check	**Stage 6** **Check the Effectiveness of the Trial Solution** To assess the need for further problem solving, continual improvement, or innovation.	• Data on each variable in the monitoring plan • Interpretation of data	**Stage 6** **Check the Effectiveness of the Trial Improvement Strategy** To assess the need for further improvement or problem solving.	• Data on each variable in the monitoring plan • Interpretation of data

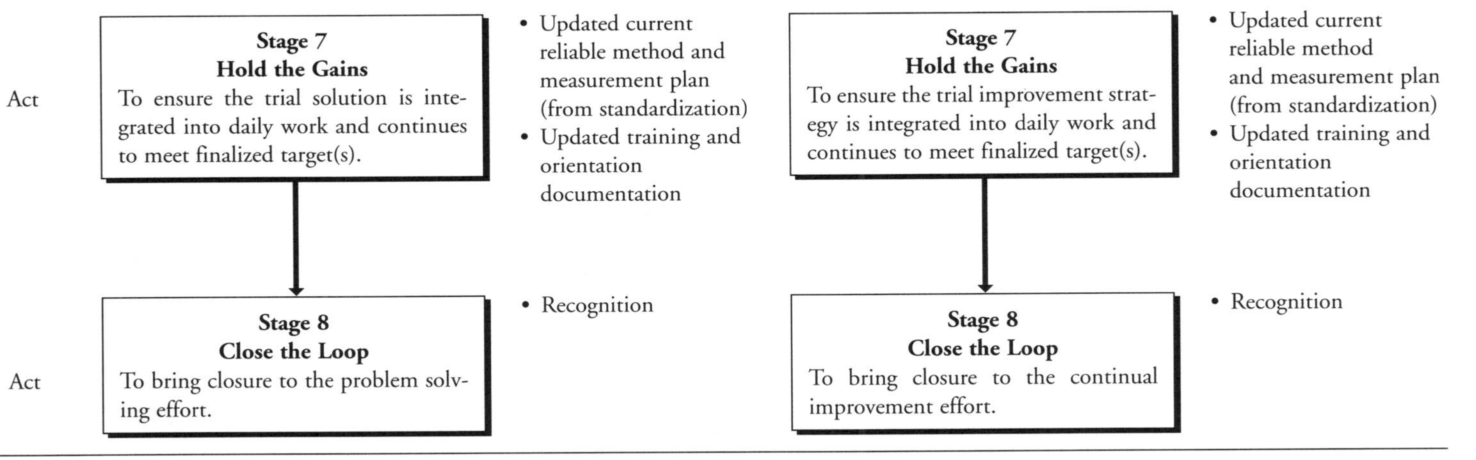

*Reprinted from Lori L. Silverman and Annabeth L. Propst, "Coaching Process Improvement Teams." Paper presented at the 1991 Fall Technical Conference, American Society for Quality Control and American Statistical Association, (October 1991), 3. Copyright © 1991 by Lori L. Silverman and Annabeth L. Propst.

†Reprinted from Lori L. Silverman and Annabeth L. Propst, *Eight Stage Approach for Continual Improvement* (unpublished workbook, 1994), 1, 2. Copyright © 1994 by Lori L. Silverman and Annabeth L. Propst.

options that effectively address them. This may demand the use of more sophisticated research approaches and the requirement to obtain additional data from customers to determine, from their perspective, the scope of the improvement.

Choosing Between Problem Solving and Continual Improvement

> "Based on my discussions with many companies, their tendency is to believe that they are working on continuous improvement when, in fact, they are truly focusing on problem solving and standardization. If organizations are not aware of the differences among these approaches, they may overestimate their current and future success."
>
> —Jill Adams-Rodeberg, Team Advisor, Midwest Express Airlines

Teams need to know when to choose between problem solving and continual improvement. The definitions given earlier provide the basis for such a decision. This decision is critical because, even though the methodologies look similar at the macro level (refer to Table 5.1), the tools and techniques used at each stage of each method are distinctly different. Figure 5.1 provides one approach for making this decision.

Some organizations elect not to make a distinction between problem solving and continual improvement. They frame issues and opportunities as problems. Other organizations believe that framing opportunities as problems is counterproductive to their culture. An organization can achieve results whether it elects to employ one or both methodologies. However, approaching an improvement situation using a problem solving methodology will likely yield different results than approaching the same situation from a continual improvement perspective.

Identify Opportunities for Innovation

Innovation (i.e., "action(s) taken to satisfy latent market wants and needs by actualizing new [i.e., not currently existing] product/service, system, or market concepts"[18]) is not, strictly speaking, a part of process management. The activity that is a part of process management is that of identifying areas where innovation is required. This is not to say that unplanned innovation does not occur as part of process management. On the contrary, innovation can occur as the result of standardization, problem solving, and continual improvement or from acting on the input to suggestion systems.

Sharing Work Process Information with Others

Teams and individuals need to disseminate information to others in order to help them address a particular problem or improvement opportunity. This sharing supports a key premise behind learning organizations—communicating lessons learned in the spirit of knowledge and practice enhancement. Some organizations set up intranet data bases for this type of communications. Others set aside special days for several work groups and cross-functional teams to explain their projects in conference settings or they may sponsor an expo in the cafeteria that showcases the work of all teams.

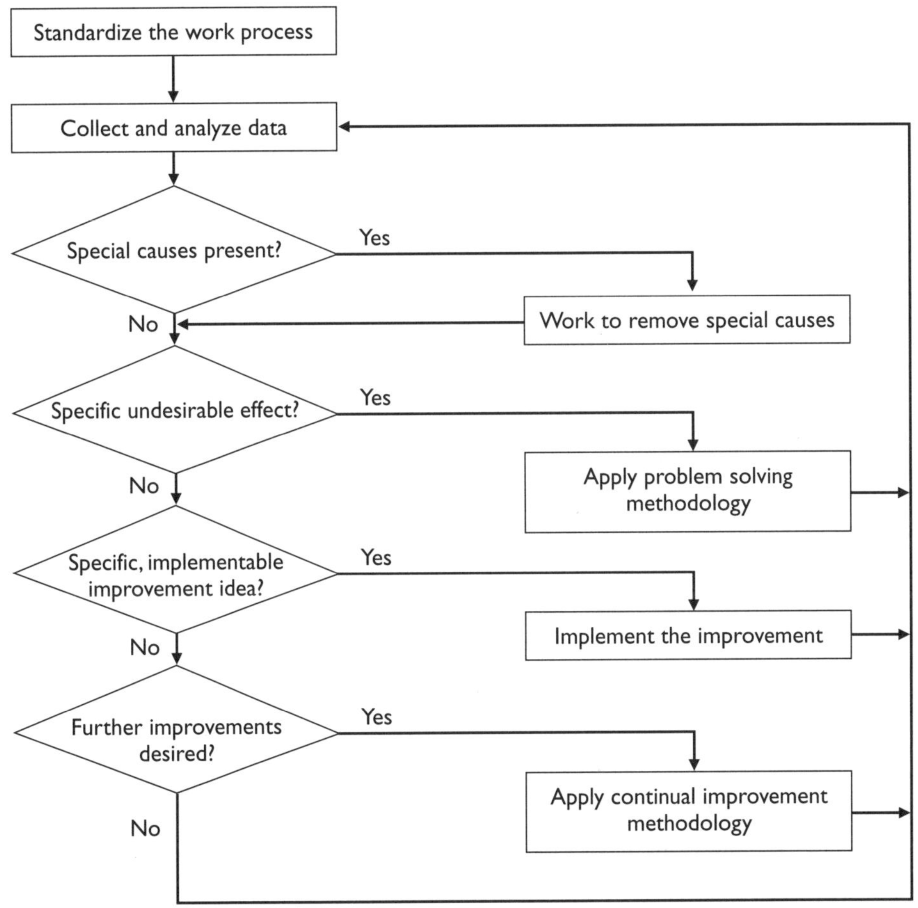

Figure 5.1
Deciding When to Use Problem Solving and Continual Improvement
Reprinted from Lori L. Silverman and Annabeth L. Propst, *Eight Stage Approach for Developing a Current Reliable Method* (unpublished workbook, 1995, 1997), 6–7. Copyright © 1995, 1997, by Lori L. Silverman and Annabeth L. Propst.

> Sharing improvement results and learning has two developmental effects. First, individuals who present their learning are more likely to internalize the process of continual improvement. Second, it helps create a common view of 'who we are and what we're about in this organization,' which can help move the company beyond previous barriers to progress."
>
> —Duke Okes, Management Consultant, APLOMET

Training Members on Work Processes and Related Topics

With the advent of process management comes the move to shift significant responsibility for job-specific training to work groups and away from training or human resources departments. Work group members may train their peers and new hires on the correct way to perform the work, how to monitor its performance, and safety procedures associated with the work using the documentation created for each process (i.e., work instructions). Included here are ongoing updates on process improvements, solutions to problems, and equipment changes. They may also be responsible for identifying the training needs that exist within the group, developing many of their own training materials, and for cross-training. In some organizations, team members educate each other on the firm's products and services as well as the improvements that are made within other parts of the organization.

Constraint Management Tools

The main thrust of constraint management is to accurately identify and properly manage an organization's constraints. A constraint is anything that prevents the organization from improving its performance. Constraints can be both physical (such as the machine with the lowest capacity) and nonphysical (including policies, reward systems, and conflicts between departments). Every organization has at least one constraint. It is either within the organization or in its marketplace.

The purpose of constraint management is to increase the throughput of the organization at a faster rate than the organization spends money on increasing capacity. This approach leads to lower costs and improved performance, and may also be a factor in customer satisfaction. Constraint management activities include identifying the constraint, getting the most out of the constraint's existing capacity (for physical constraints such as departments, functions, or equipment), keeping the constraint busy working on the right things, increasing the capacity of the constraint (for physical constraints such as machines, functions, or equipment), and breaking the constraint (for nonphysical constraints such as policies, chronic conflicts, or perceptions). The Drum-Buffer-Rope solution outlined in *The Goal* is one methodology for managing a physical constraint in a production environment.[19] The Evaporating Cloud technique presented in the book, *It's Not Luck,* can be used to resolve conflict constraints.[20]

> "Application of the Theory of Constraints (TOC) to production, distribution, and project management processes can lead to dramatic improvements in throughput, cycle time, inventory, and operating expenses. TOC is very useful to an organization's improvement efforts and provides some powerful logical problem solving tools."
>
> —Tim Fuller, Partner, Fuller & Propst Associates

Advanced Tools

In the Problem Resolution Field of Performance Practice, a need exists for tools that are more complex and specialized than the basic tools of quality introduced in the Quality Assurance Field. These advanced tools are very powerful when used in the right situation. Because they are highly specialized, there are fewer applications for any one of them. It is not necessary to be proficient in all of these advanced tools. What is important is to have a basic understanding of those that are commonly used in your industry or company, and to know whom to contact inside or outside your organization to help with the use of these tools. Below are several sets of tools that have proved valuable in this field of performance practice.

Statistical Tools

> "The use of statistically designed experiments was commonplace at our plastics technical center. In one such instance, we used a screening design to identify which processing variables affected the physical properties of extruded sheet. Later, a more specialized design enabled us to map out the response surface and find a set of robust processing conditions (i.e., those that either minimize or neutralize the effect of processing on key physical properties). We often found in such experiments that optimum conditions are very different from those recommended by the equipment manufacturer."
>
> —Nick Martino, Senior Consultant, Decision Strategies, formerly a quality engineer at a chemicals company

Included with the advanced tools are an entire collection of experimental design and analysis tools—such as fractional factorials (including Taguchi designs), mixture experiments, and central composite designs. These tools are useful in testing theories about root causes, understanding relationships between causes, and comparing the effects on the outcomes of various actions taken on the process.

Other advanced statistical tools are used for analyzing multivariate data (i.e., data from multiple items measured on a number of variables, such as evaluating many suppliers on each of several performance criteria). They include correlation analysis, regression analysis, multivariate analysis (e.g., principle components analysis), Analysis of Means, and contingency tables.

Additional graphical tools beyond the basic tools of quality exist for analyzing numerical data. Star plots (also known as radial plots or spiderweb plots) and Chernoff faces can be used to analyze multivariate data. Box plots and means plots can be used for comparing data collected on a single variable from more than one sample (e.g., fuel consumption data by aircraft) or to analyze the results of a designed experiment. Stem-and-leaf plots can be used to analyze data from a single sample or to compare data from two different samples.

Quality Function Deployment

The "house of quality," which is a central feature of Quality Function Deployment (QFD), was developed in 1972 by Mitsubishi's Kobe Shipyards and further refined by Toyota and its suppliers.[21] It was adopted by Ford Motor Company in the early 1980s and is used today by many corporations (including the service industries) to reduce new product development cycle time, improve new product launch, and clarify and prioritize customers' requirements. QFD provides a structured means to capture and respond to the "voice of the customer" in every step of product development and implementation, involving marketing, engineering, manufacturing, service, and other required departments throughout the process. Because of the involvement of these parties, the side benefits of its use include improved communications and teambuilding (less functional barriers), and more systematically based thinking.

QFD is specifically used in the Problem Resolution Field of Performance Practice for the redesign of products and/or services that are already in existence, but need to be improved. As an example, Florida Power & Light used it to improve their process for responding to customer calls. As a result, measures of customer satisfaction improved and customer complaints to the Florida Public Service Commission were reduced.[22]

The primary tool used in QFD is the matrix—a table that shows relationships between items listed on the horizontal axis (e.g., quality characteristics) and items listed on the vertical axis (e.g., customer requirements). Additions to the matrix can be used to create a "house of quality."[23] The primary addition is the "roof" that shows the interactions (positive and negative) between the elements on the horizontal axis. Other additions can include the "Quality Planning Chart" on the right-hand side of the matrix (used to develop a prioritization of the customer characteristics) and the "Quality Design Chart" at the bottom of the matrix (used to prioritize quality characteristics). The 1994 book by Shigeru Mizuno and Yoji Akao, editors, titled *QFD: The Customer-Driven Approach to Quality Planning and Deployment,* explains this approach in detail.

QFD has another use in innovation. That use of this tool is covered in the Consumer Obsession Field of Performance Practice.

Benchmarking

The purpose of benchmarking is to direct the organization to opportunities for improvement. There are three kinds: Internal benchmarking, competitive and industry benchmarking, and best-in-class benchmarking.[24]

"Internal benchmarking is the analysis of existing practice within various departments or divisions of the organization, looking for best performance as well as identifying baseline activities and drivers."[25] It is typically done as a precursor to competitive benchmarking, and may be undertaken as a stand-alone effort to improve existing performance. It can be utilized by any organization where the same task is performed in more than one location (e.g., departments, regions, shifts). The data resulting from these efforts may lead to problem solving if they uncover areas of unsatisfactory performance.

Competitive benchmarking is a technique for evaluating a firm's performance on a particular parameter or set of parameters relative to its competitors. Some refer to this tool as a competitive intelligence technique (refer to chapter 7). This technique usually involves either a market survey or an analysis of products by an independent company. For example, some organizations hire "secret shoppers" who go into both the firm's and competitors' stores to evaluate the type of service they receive and to identify areas of unsatisfactory performance based on a predetermined set of market-based criteria. The outcomes of this activity may become the basis for problem solving efforts.

Industry benchmarking is a variation of competitive benchmarking that "extends beyond the one-to-one comparison of competitive benchmarking to look for [industry] trends. . . [that] can help establish performance baselines."[26] This approach seeks out major trends across a wide spectrum of firms in related industries, instead of keying on a small number of firms who are competing head-to-head in a single well-defined market. As is the case with internal and competitive benchmarking, industry benchmarking rarely, if ever, leads to significant breakthroughs in performance gains.

Best-in-class benchmarking can be employed when an organization desires to leapfrog ahead. This type of benchmarking is discussed in the Consumer Obsession Field of Performance Practice.

Other Advanced Tools

Root cause analysis and simulation are two other advanced tools also worth noting. Root cause analysis refers to any method used to determine the root causes of a problem or undesirable condition. Two of the methods for root cause analysis are Current Reality Trees[27] (one of the Thinking Process tools utilized in Theory of Constraints) and Process Decision Program Charts[28] (one of the 7 Management and Planning Tools presented in the Alignment and Integration Field of Performance Practice).

Any method that tries to approximate the performance of a real situation by artificial means is a simulation. Many simulations are computer-based, but they do not have to be. They can be conducted through "game boards" and role play. Simulations are helpful for troubleshooting changes to the process before they are implemented (for example, building a new office building). Insights gained through this tool can prevent costly redesigns or errors, especially when the changes are difficult or they may be costly to reverse. In some cases, the entire Do phase of the PDCA Cycle can be conducted via simulation.

Creativity Tools

> "Creativity is not its own reward. It is the use of creativity to develop new ideas that leads to improvement that is meaningful."[29]
>
> —Lloyd P. Provost and Gerald J. Langley, Consultants, Associates in Process Improvement

In the pursuit of continual improvement, teams and individuals need to use a variety of creativity tools. Brainstorming is one such tool, but there are many others. The most popular creativity tools include deBono's Six Thinking Hats[30], von Oech's "Whack Pack,"[31,32] and Michalko's Thinkertoys.[33] GOAL/QPC, based in Methuen, MA, has also developed seven creativity tool boxes encompassing (1) creative problem (re)formulation—revealing structure and relationships, (2) brainstorming and its variations—generating and gathering ideas in groups, (3) brainstorming and its variations—silent, more structured brainstorming, (4) pattern breakers—dissolving existing patterns and self-projected restrictions, (5) simple analogies and associations—looking outside current knowledge fields, (6) complex analogies and associations—transferring ideas to concepts of solution, and (7) morphology—combining and interpreting options for a total solution.

Since the early 1990s, some organizations in the United States have used the TRIZ (a Russian acronym that means "the theory of the solution of inventive problems") methodology to find creative solutions to problems. Developed in 1946 by Genrikh Altshuller, he and "his associates have concluded that there are only 27 inventive principles behind all existing patents and that these principles address standard technical conflicts in design or problem solving."[34] This approach is explained in Altshuller's 1984 book, *Creativity as an Exacting Science: The Theory of the Solution of Inventive Problems,* and H. Altov's 1994 book, *The Art of Inventing: And Suddenly the Inventor Appeared.*

WHO IS INVOLVED IN THE PROBLEM RESOLUTION FIELD OF PERFORMANCE PRACTICE

The Management Steering Committee, cross-functional teams, and in-function work groups are involved in Problem Resolution efforts. The Steering Committee is responsible for chartering cross-functional teams to tackle a specific issue—one of an immediate and temporary nature. The charter provides the team with its purpose, membership (i.e., leader, management liaison, members), desired outcomes, and deadline date, as well as background information on the issue. Normally the team is provided with training on a specific methodology (usually problem solving; sometimes continual improvement), the concept of variation, tools appropriate to the methodology it will be using, and the fundamentals of teamwork. The team might even be provided with a coach who helps facilitate it. The Management Steering Committee reviews the team's work on an ongoing basis, providing support and critical resources.

There are several facets to the Steering Committee's role with in-function work groups. It must create a system for monitoring the performance of in-function work groups that includes periodic work review and progress in process management. This monitoring information is needed for the committee to make organizational decisions on resource allocation and the performance of operating plans.

The system needs to support work groups by expediting communications, upholding their decisions, and taking actions that encourage work in this field of performance practice, in addition to providing them with the resources they need to perform their roles in the enterprise, including training and coaching. In order for work groups to meet organizational expectations, the committee must provide an overall plan that allows them to prioritize their efforts in concert with organizational strategies and objectives.

SHORTCOMINGS WITH THE PROBLEM RESOLUTION FIELD OF PERFORMANCE PRACTICE

The Problem Resolution Field of Performance Practice emerged to address the shortcomings that arose in the Quality Assurance Field. These shortcomings were (1) lack of pervasive application of a continual improvement mindset, (2) not anticipating customers' needs and expectations before they expressed them, (3) limited management responsibility for quality, and (4) little (if any) attempt to change the existing system or constraints. In Problem Resolution, the use of the PDCA Cycle and process management brings the continual improvement mindset to the forefront. Customer focus—working with the customers to find better ways to meet their needs—is also stressed throughout process management. Additionally, organizational productivity and performance constraints begin to be addressed through problem solving efforts. Management takes on more responsibility for quality and performance by creating systems in which cross-functional and natural work teams can achieve their goals.

Even though this field of performance practice has improved customer satisfaction, reduced costs, and improved performance as its desired outcomes, organizations do not always realize gains in these areas. The link between a customer-focused approach to business and actual improvements in customer satisfaction and costs is not strongly supported by research in the field.[35] This may be due to the shortcomings that still exist in this field of performance practice. They include (a) working on well-defined individual problems that unsuspectingly result in a zero or negative impact on the performance of the organization as a whole; (b) the inability to guarantee the linkage of customer requirements, and problem solving and continual improvement efforts to overall market strategy, key organizational systems, daily work processes, supplier requirements, organizational structure and culture, and employee well-being and satisfaction; (c) the potential conflict between multiple improvement and problem-focused initiatives; and (d) the lack of a systematic approach to innovation.

In addition, this field of performance practice does not focus on the organization's cultural elements—its assumptions, values, and guiding principles—and

Table 5.2

Your Organization and the Problem Resolution Field of Performance Practice

Directions: Record the activities your organization has and has not engaged in relative to the concepts, tools, and methods referenced in this field of performance practice, noting the degree of deployment of each item. Also document its future plans for deploying these concepts, tools, and methods throughout the enterprise.

Purpose: To improve bottom-line performance and customer satisfaction		**Desired Outcomes:** • Reduced costs • Improvements in performance • Improvements in customer satisfaction		
	What Your Organization Is Doing	**What Your Organization Is Not Doing**	**Degree of Deployment***	**Plans Your Organization Has for the Future**
Underlying Concepts • PDCA Cycle • Customer focus • Variation • Teamwork			 1 2 3 4 5 1 2 3 4 5 1 2 3 4 5 1 2 3 4 5	
Commonly Used Tools and Methods • Process management • Constraint management tools • Advanced tools • Creativity tools			 1 2 3 4 5 1 2 3 4 5 1 2 3 4 5 1 2 3 4 5	

*Rating system: 1 = no systematic deployment is evident
2 = some deployment is evident with little or no results
3 = deployment is evident in several areas of the business with limited results
4 = deployment is evident in major portions of the business with measurable results
5 = full organization-wide deployment is evident with significant measurable results

Table 5.3

CHAOS and the Problem Resolution Field of Performance Practice

Directions: Note your thoughts on the future impact that the forces of **CHAOS** may have on each of the underlying concepts and the commonly used tools and methods in the Problem Resolution Field of Performance Practice.

CHAOS / **Underlying Concepts**	**Changing Definition of Work and the Workplace**	**Heightened Social Responsibility**	**Aging Baby Boomers**	**Overarching Demographic Change**	**Strategic Growth Through Technology and Innovation**
• PDCA Cycle					
• Customer focus					
• Variation					
• Teamwork					
Commonly Used Tools and Methods					
• Process management					
• Constraint management tools					
• Advanced tools					
• Creativity tools					

how they intertwine with the more strategic and operational aspects of the business. As these and other challenges became apparent, so did the need to develop another field of performance practice—Alignment and Integration—the third star in The Starburst Model™.

Endnotes

1. Neil Hardie, "The Effects of Quality on Business Performance," *Quality Management Journal,* Vol. 5, No. 3 (Summer 1998), 65–83.
2. Peter R. Scholtes, *The Leader's Handbook* (New York: McGraw-Hill, 1998), 34.
3. Scholtes, *The Leader's Handbook,* 34.
4. Galen Britz, Don Emerling, Lynne Hare, Roger Hoerl, and Janice Shade, *Statistical Thinking,* a Special Publication of the Statistics Division of ASQ (Spring 1996), 6.
5. John A. Ingram, *Introductory Statistics* (Menlo Park, CA: Cummings Publishing Company, 1974), 5.
6. Ingram, *Introductory Statistics,* 3.
7. Steven P. Bailey and W. H. Fellner, "Some Useful Aids for Understanding and Quantifying Process Control and Improvement Opportunities," Paper presented at the 1993 ASQC/ASA Fall Technical Conference.
8. Brian L. Joiner, *Fourth Generation Management—The New Business Consciousness* (New York: McGraw-Hill, 1994), 115–116.
9. Jack Gordon, "Work Teams: How Far Have They Come?" *TRAINING* (October 1992), 64.
10. *Webster's New World Dictionary—Third College Edition* (New York: Macmillan, 1994), 137.
11. Susan Albers Mohrman et al., *Tomorrow's Organization: Crafting Winning Capabilities in a Dynamic World* (San Francisco: Jossey-Bass Inc., Publishers, 1998), 29.
12. M. F. Doyle, "Cross-Functional Implementation Teams," *Purchasing World* (February 1991), 20.
13. J. Richard. Hackman, "Why Teams Don't Work," *Leader to Leader* (Winter 1998), 25.
14. Jon R. Katzenbach, "Making Teams Work at the Top," *Leader to Leader* (Winter 1998), 32.
15. Lori L. Silverman and Annabeth L. Propst, "Ensuring Success: A Model for Self-Managed Teams" (unpublished paper, 1996), 7.
16. Lori L. Silverman and Annabeth L. Propst, "Coaching Process Improvement Teams." Paper presented at the 1991 ASQC/ASA Fall Technical Conference (October 1991).
17. Silverman and Propst, "Coaching Process Improvement Teams."
18. Lori L. Silverman, Annabeth L. Propst, and Steven N. Silverman, "Eight Stage Approach for Innovation" (unpublished workbook, 1995).
19. Elihayu M. Goldratt, *The Goal* (Croton-on-Hudson, NY: North River Press, 1984).
20. Elihayu M. Goldratt, *It's Not Luck* (Croton-on-Hudson, NY: North River Press, 1994).
21. John R. Hauser and Don Clausing, "The House of Quality," *Harvard Business Review* (May–June 1988), 63.

22. Hauser and Clausing, "The House of Quality," 65–68.

23. Kurt R. Hofmeister, "QFD in the Services Environment," *The ASI Journal,* Vol. 3, No. 2 (Fall 1990), H-13.

24. Kathleen H. J. Leibfried and C. J. McNair, CMA, *Benchmarking: A Tool For Continuous Improvement* (New York: HarperBusiness, 1992), 28.

25. Leibfried and McNair, *Benchmarking: A Tool For Continuous Improvement,* 28.

26. Leibfried and McNair, *Benchmarking: A Tool For Continuous Improvement,* 28–29.

27. Goldratt, *It's Not Luck.*

28. Shigeru Mizuno, *Management for Quality Improvement: The Seven New QC Tools* (Cambridge, MA: Productivity Press, 1988), 227.

29. Lloyd P. Provost and Gerald J. Langley, "The Importance of Concepts in Creativity and Improvement," *Quality Progress* (March 1998), 37.

30. Edward de Bono, *Six Thinking Hats* (New York: Little Brown and Company, 1986).

31. Roger von Oech, *A Whack on the Side of the Head* (New York: Warner Books Inc., 1983).

32. Roger von Oech, *A Kick in the Seat of the Pants* (New York: Harper Perennial, 1986).

33. Michael Michalko, *Thinkertoys* (Berkeley, CA: Ten Speed Press, 1991).

34. Provost and Langley, "The Importance of Concepts in Creativity and Improvement," 36–37.

35. Hardie, "The Effects of Quality on Business Performance," 65–83.

CHAPTER 6

The Alignment and Integration Field of Performance Practice

Chapter 6 covers the third star in The Starburst Model™—the Alignment and Integration Field of Performance Practice. The purpose of this field is to ensure that all organizational work contributes to achieving the organization's mission, vision, and plans; it is assumed throughout this chapter that they are appropriate for the organization. Through its alignment and integration efforts, the enterprise can realize (a) improved organizational effectiveness, (b) elimination of barriers and unnecessary work, and (c) improved overall customer and employee satisfaction. Many organizations use the Malcolm Baldrige National Quality Award Criteria for Performance Excellence and other state award criteria to assess their efforts in this field of performance practice and the two that precede it (i.e., Quality Assurance and Problem Resolution).

UNDERLYING CONCEPTS

The underlying concepts in the Alignment and Integration Field of Performance Practice—alignment and integration, organization as system, transformation, large-scale organizational change, and self-management—are the first to address the organization as a whole. Previous fields of performance practice focused on fulfilling a specific need—such as conformance to customer requirements—or a specific problem. In this field, the concepts also speak to ongoing, enterprise-wide change and taking responsibility for self.

Three paradoxes emerge from the concepts covered in this field. The first one covers meeting the needs of the entire organization at the same time that individual employee needs are being met. The second paradox has to do with providing security in the midst of constant change. The last paradox speaks to meeting customers' needs and wants at the same time that the organization (and its shareholders) achieves its needs and wants (e.g., financial performance). It is not a matter of selecting and following one alternative in a paradox. Because a paradox is a contradiction and, thus, cannot be solved, both alternatives must be considered as reality and actively managed on an ongoing basis.

Alignment and Integration

> "Alignment can be thought of as both a noun and a verb. Alignment as a noun refers to the integration of key systems and processes and responses to changes in the external environment. But no organization can stay in alignment very long, since almost every business lives in an environment of constant change. We think the real power of alignment comes when we view it as a set of actions—as a verb."[1]
>
> —Dr. George H. Labovitz, Chairman, and Victor Rosansky, Executive Vice President, Organizational Dynamics, Inc.

Alignment is both vertical and horizontal. Horizontal alignment connects work processes in an unbroken chain. The first link of the chain is the point at which customer needs or wants enter the organization. The last link is the point at which products and services are used by the customer. The chain is joined together by feedback on how well the products and services meet the customers' requirements. It is also joined by actions that translate customer requirements into supplier requirements and, ultimately, outputs that are moved through the system to become products and services. Since the early 1990s, some organizations have strived to create alignment around a process orientation to the business. While they may be effective in directing the core of the business in this manner, they often neglect to similarly refocus their support functions and their culture, causing a disconnect in approach.

Vertical alignment flows from overall business strategy through strategic plans, through annual plans, through daily operational plans, through key organizational systems, through daily work processes to tasks and activities necessary to accomplish them. Since vertical and horizontal alignment occur simultaneously in the real world, the elements of both must also be compatible with each other.

One challenge of alignment is to provide organizational focus on the most critical items, while at the same time getting enterprise members to realize the interdependencies among all aspects of the organizational system. Another challenge is to align organizational structure and culture, and employee well-being and satisfaction, with the elements of both vertical and horizontal alignment. Alignment is beneficial because it makes an organization more agile in times of change.

> "Alignment is more than integration. It also connotes a directional sense to key stakeholders such as employees, customers, and shareholders."
>
> —Dr. George H. Labovitz, Chairman, Organizational Dynamics, Inc.

Integration is the deployment of company ideology (i.e., vision, mission, values, and guiding principles) and quality-based philosophies, strategies, goals and objectives across and throughout the organization's work processes and people. It is within this field of performance practice that quality concepts, tools, and methods begin to integrate into the ongoing management of the enterprise. Consequently, it is typical for organizations who are at this point in their development to move away from the phrase "total quality management" as the backdrop for their improvement initiatives. However, this departure does not mean that quality concepts, tools, and methods have been abandoned. Instead, they are being embedded into the organization's overall business philosophy, the performance of all operating systems, and each employees' day-to-day work. It is at this point that "quality" moves into the realm of "management."

Organization as System

The concept of "organization as system" is in the Alignment and Integration Field of Performance Practice because alignment and integration cannot effectively take place without attention to the whole—the marketplace within which the organization operates and its customers, suppliers, systems, processes, and people. Concurrently, the outer boundary of the system provides the frame within which alignment and integration occur.

Systems function according to a set of principles, one of which is adaptation. If the organization does not adapt to ongoing shifts in marketplace forces (e.g., competitor strategies, customer wants and needs, and currency valuations), it can die. In order to understand the type of performance that is required by the organization to adapt to these forces, the enterprise must be clear on its customers' wants and needs. It must know how to translate the wants and needs into viable products and services and articulate the flow of work required to bring them to market.

In addition to adaptation, several other systems principles exist that are equally as important. First, in order to achieve overall system optimization, all efforts within the enterprise need to be aligned around the same vision, mission, initiatives, plans, and targets. Second, because of the interdependencies that exist within the overall system, a change in one part will influence other parts, even though these relationships may not appear obvious and the effects are delayed over time. Finally, when individuals, even star performers, are asked to perform in broken parts of the system, the system will win almost every time.

> "Using systems thinking concepts has helped me develop interventions that are more sustainable. For example, seeing the whole picture and demonstrating the interdependencies between different parts of the organization helps me to coach leaders and internal consultants. They can see their impact on the whole of the organization and align their behaviors with their belief systems. Consequently, they are able to think and act differently, and maintain this behavior change over time."
>
> —William H. Braswell, Jr., Vice President,
> Quality Resources, Premera Blue Cross

Transformation

> "As an organization transforms so must its people. Senior leaders and the organization are challenged to support transformation behaviors that demonstrate authenticity, lack of defensiveness, self-reflection, and the ability to give and receive useful feedback. Our culture seems to identify change as a sign that we've been doing something 'wrong' instead of as a reasonable response to a changing environment. It is remarkable how fragile and vulnerable even the most powerful are."
>
> —Lunell Haught, Owner, Haught Strategies

Transformation is "the radical shift from one state of being to another, where the new state is uncertain until it emerges and, by definition, is better able to meet the more sophisticated demands of the environment than the old 'tried and true' state. Transformation usually results from radical marketplace or environmental changes coupled with the organization's inability to handle current and future requirements using its existing mindset, resources, skills, structures, and practices."[2] Organizational leaders may or may not hear the "call to action" that is stimulated by the resulting tension between the organization and its environment. As a result, there are two kinds of transformation—conscious transformational change and reactive transformational change.[3] Conscious transformational change results when leaders heed, or even anticipate, this "call" and proactively involve themselves in addressing it. Reactive transformation, on the other hand, as demonstrated by the need to downsize significantly in a short period of time or drastically reduce costs overnight, occurs when leaders ignore warning signals.

> "We are feeling change fatigue and reorganization fatigue. We will no longer continue to do things just to do them. We will look at why we are doing them and their payoff."
>
> —Jack Gordon, Editor, *TRAINING* Magazine

Transformation is an underlying concept in the Alignment and Integration Field because the push to align and integrate may be an appropriate response to a marketplace pressure, and as such, require significant alterations within the organization. Often the need to improve effectiveness within and between various operations speaks to the need for transformation through the alignment of processes and the integration of organizational ideology (e.g., values and guiding principles) and quality practices throughout the work. Additionally, alignment may be disrupted as a result of the implementation of internal product, service, and process innovation efforts. To continue to satisfy customers, transformation may be needed to bring various parts of the organization back into alignment.

Methods for achieving transformation range from creating a learning organization, to implementing a quality initiative, to reengineering systems, to closing down specific operations. Each transformational method has its own benefits and drawbacks, some more serious than others. When selecting an approach, it is important to address both its short- and long-term implications as well as its relationship to the organization's business philosophy, values, and guiding principles.

> "Real Time Strategic Change, a type of large group intervention, differs from other change interventions in many important ways. One clearly defining aspect is the process of bringing key stakeholders, often numbering in the hundreds, together at the same time. In this way, organizations can and do effect long-lasting and sustainable change in that very room. It's exciting to experience in real-time an aligned, empowered, and informed workplace."
>
> —Carrie Hays, training and organizational development consultant, Yountville, CA

Large-Scale Organizational Change

The topic of large-scale organizational change was first fully described in the 1989 book, *Large-Scale Organizational Change.*[4] Up until that time, little had been written about this phenomenon. Thus, it is not surprising that organizations are just beginning to learn about what it is and how to effectively make it happen.

Large-scale organizational change is "a lasting change in the character of the organization that significantly alters its performance."[5] The term "large-scale" can refer to the size of the organization (i.e., big and complex), to the depth of the change, or to the relationship between the change and the organization (i.e., the pervasiveness of the change).[6] Two types of change can occur—change in "character" and change in "performance." The outcome of these two types of change is that the organization becomes fundamentally different (character) and is able to produce fundamentally different results (performance). In order for large-scale organizational change to have occurred, these changes must be sustained over time.

It is important that the approach used to effect large-scale change is in concert with research results on large-scale change. For example, having a Steering Committee for quality or change management that is not identical to the group that leads the organization creates a parallel structure. As such, it is not an effective way to promote large-scale change. "Unless the organization's management style and its design both change significantly, the work of the parallel organization is often disregarded, the bureaucracy is impervious to efforts to change it, and the parallel structure itself withers away."[7]

> "When will companies realize that they may not have the vehicle to run in a certain direction or to change directions in economically dangerous times?"
>
> —Howard Gitlow, Ph.D., Professor of Management Science, School of Business Administration, University of Miami

Research conducted through the Center for Effective Organizations at the University of Southern California shows that success in organizational change correlates to the following:

- It must be guided by a mission and values statement as well as a clearly stated business strategy and set of beliefs about what makes an organization effective.
- It must be integrated companywide and led by top management.
- It must be based on a three or more year plan.[8]

Change driven from the bottom up is not correlated with success. Unfortunately, many change initiatives do not take into account these correlations. Consequently, to successfully effect large-scale change it is important to review research and literature in the fields of organizational behavior and organizational development. Specifically, research needs to include transformational change; organizational learning; organizational structure and job design; interpersonal, group, and intergroup relations; and culture.

> "In order to have effective organization-wide initiatives, you have to put your advice in such a way that it sounds as if it comes from the organization's leaders. Find out what these leaders want to do and why. Show the links between what you are doing and what they want to do. If necessary, tailor what you are doing to fit. The problem with this is that the leaders may want something that you do not believe is good or right."
>
> —Heero Hacquebord, President,
> Consulting in Continual Improvement

Many large-scale change approaches (in addition to small group and individual change approaches) are based on Lewin's three-step "unfreezing-movement-refreezing" model of change.[9] There are several problems with Lewin's model and the approaches that are based on it. The types of changes being faced by organizations today—transformational and discontinuous—are different than those experienced when the model was published in 1951. Lewin's model also emphasizes the creation of change instead of its ongoing, continual nature. It assumes that there may be no difference between individual "espoused" values (what one verbally says are values) and "theory-in-use" values (the values demonstrated through one's behaviors), and that people are aware of the need to develop new behaviors and skills.

The works emerging out of chaos theory—Confucian/East Asian views of change, Prigogine and Jantsch's work on evolution and disequilibrium, and Capra's work on probability waves, are causing some practitioners to create approaches to large-scale organizational change that are fundamentally different than those espoused by organizational development practitioners of the past.[10,11] These approaches begin to address the limitations in Lewin's model. They assume that change is constant and cyclical with no end to be achieved, that it moves from one form or state to another, and that it is to be expected since everything is normally in dynamic fluctuation. This emerging work suggests that, while striving for equilibrium may be safe and comforting (e.g., let's build a more collaborative workplace), it may also bring an organization closer to stagnation.

Self-Management

Self-management speaks to self-control (or what some might call empowerment). It assumes each individual has the skills, knowledge, information, and data required to do a job, to make decisions about changes related to it, and to serve customers' needs. Because there is an acknowledgment that organizations are systems and that individual actions can, and will, impact others, the individual also receives ongoing information about the surrounding environment (both internal and external). In order for self-management to occur, work needs to be defined in terms of outcomes (i.e., expected results). Expectations about the person's role in achieving these outcomes must be clearly communicated, and the person must receive ongoing direct feedback.[12]

> "Self-management requires increased individual accountability—a fact that has caused many an employee to shy away from the idea. In order for self-management to become a part of the organization's culture, the culture itself must change. Individual employees must want the increased responsibilities and the accountabilities. Risk taking must be encouraged and rewarded. Communication must be *truly* open and feedback must be continual and developmental."
>
> —Linda Ernst, President, Training Resource

Self-management assumes that each person can learn and demonstrate leadership behaviors when needed. Thus, supervision in the traditional sense is no longer viable or necessary. This change has stimulated new definitions and roles for leadership. Some organizations use self-managed teams to implement the concept of self-management. Although the potential value of self-managed teams has been recognized, self-management is not an appropriate objective for all groups in all organizations. Self-managed teams are well suited to those situations in which tasks are routine, team members can easily understand major pieces of each others' work, and team members can freely share knowledge with each other.[13] It may be difficult to fully utilize self-managed teams in situations where the nature of the work is continually changing or there are barriers to communication. Therefore, temporary teams, committees, or task forces that come together briefly to address a specific issue, problem or challenge are not well suited for self-management.

COMMONLY USED TOOLS AND METHODS

Commonly used tools and methods in the Alignment and Integration Field of Performance Practice help the organization to address the system as a "whole" rather than its individual parts (i.e., departments, functions, or units). They also promote alignment and integration, large-scale transformational change, and self-management. These tools and methods are organizational architecture, organizational partnerships, managing the organization as a system, large group interventions, strategic planning, the 7 Management and Planning Tools, and project management.

Organizational Architecture

The term, "organizational architecture" appeared in a 1992 book titled *Organizational Architecture: Designs for Changing Organizations*[14] and in a 1992 *Harvard Business Review* article titled, "The CEO as Organization Architect: An Interview with Xerox's Paul Allaire."[15] Organizational architecture involves "the creation and ongoing management of an organizational framework that encompasses *all* formal and informal systems and structures as well as their inherent interactions."[16] Because no framework is ever perfect, it requires continual adaptation and change based on new marketplace forces and learned experiences from the current architecture.

When asked how well each and every element in their organization fits together (i.e., whether the parts fit together as well as pieces of a jigsaw puzzle) individuals from a variety of organizations typically say "not very well." Most architectures that exist today have been unconsciously put together over the lifespan of the organization. While some of the elements within these architectures may fit together well, others may be at odds with each other in terms of goals and priorities. Conflicts may arise over finite resources, or at worst, they may cancel out the benefits that each element brings to the table.

The following organizational architecture elements provide one approach to achieving enterprise-wide alignment. They also serve as vehicles for integrating quality and corporate ideology throughout the organization. These elements include

1. organizational assumptions (fundamental truths about people and the world)
2. organizational values (fundamental ideals that define the boundaries of acceptable behaviors and decisions) and guiding principles (a set of beliefs that orient conduct)

   > "It is critical that an organization's values be aligned with its strategic objectives. This ensures that action necessary to carry out these objectives will be supported. I am fortunate to work at an organization whose values were created at its inception. These values are a filter for how the organization does business. They are so important that a two-day orientation program has been built around them to ensure they are upheld by everyone."
   >
   > —Jill Adams-Rodeberg, Team Advisor, Midwest Express Airlines

3. organizational mission (what the organization is collectively paid to do today and for whom) and vision statements (from a consumer perspective, what the organization needs to become in the future)
4. overall market strategy (separate from specific breakthrough strategies that result from strategic planning, organizations may have one overall market strategy such as being the low-cost provider, or each brand may have its own strategy, as exemplified by a "healthy" cereal)
5. the processes and systems that are integral to helping the enterprise achieve its mission and work towards its vision, including the work that needs to occur for the organization to manage itself as a system
6. infrastructure design principles for the enterprise (e.g., form follows function, minimize the number of levels in the organization, every organizational member will be on a team, etc.)

7. the infrastructure design itself (e.g., degree of decentralization, how and where teams will be used, and the number and placement of formal leaders) [17]

It is imperative that human resource systems, such as those associated with compensation, rewards and recognition, training and development, career planning and placement, and performance, be aligned with all aspects of the organization's architecture. They also need to be consonant with a process-oriented approach to business. It is not uncommon for organizations to structure themselves organizationally around key processes and to have human resource systems (e.g. competencies) structured around individual jobs. Because of the nature of human resource systems, they may need to be altered early on in this approach (i.e., after step 4). In the authors' experiences, not enough attention is paid to their central role in the ongoing performance of the enterprise and their effect on transformation initiatives.

> "Many people were surprised with regard to the depth of detail that organizational architecture encompassed. We expected the discussions on values, guiding principles, and assumptions. What we didn't expect were the necessary discussions about how reward systems, performance appraisals, and other human resource issues must be brought into alignment with our new architecture."
>
> —Col. Liz Anderson, 302d Support Group Commander, 302d Airlift Wing, U.S. Air Force Reserve (Any views or opinions expressed are personal to the individual and do not represent the U.S. Air Force Reserve or any other D.O.D. component official views or positions.)

If an organization has not previously articulated these organizational architecture elements, it will want to start at the top and work its way down through the list. This approach will ensure optimal alignment and integration since the outputs of each element feed into the next (i.e., Edgar Schein's work on culture suggests that an organization's assumptions give rise to its values and beliefs, and that these, in turn, give rise to its artifacts—structure, policies, procedures, and other visible organizational symbols[18]). Organizations that need to rework one or more of these elements may also want to start at the top of the list even though the element they want to alter (e.g., infrastructure design) is at the end of the list. However, they do not need to spend a great deal of time reviewing the earlier elements. Those enterprises that have articulated all of the elements of organizational architecture, but have not done so in the order shown here, may want to revisit them. Reviews of this type can uncover conflicting assumptions, misaligned values and guiding principles, and unintended infrastructure design principles.

Organizational Partnerships

To achieve increased efficiencies and marketplace presence, enterprises are using various forms of organizational partnerships, such as strategic alliances, joint ventures and collaborations. These partnerships involve two or more organizations coming together to accomplish a task, function, or project that aligns with the aims of all of the involved organizations, but cannot be performed by any of them individually. These partnerships can help bring differing and complementary expertise together. An example is GM's joint venture with Isuzu to build new generation diesel engines for GM trucks—further strengthening their ongoing partnership. Partnerships can also support the need for technology breakthroughs and/or standardization. A consortium called The Virtual Socket Interface Alliance is an example. The consortium creates mix-and-match standards for its intellectual-property semiconductor firm members, a.k.a. chip-less chip companies. In addition, partnerships strengthen marketing efforts. Disney's exclusive relationship with McDonald's for the promotion of its movies through items such as Happy Meals is a prime example. These relationships can also ease the stress of downsizing (i.e., outsourcing a particular function), create the opportunity to enter new markets (especially in countries such as China), provide working capital, and accomplish other strategic objectives.

It is not unusual for these partnerships to require a particular set of behaviors in its member organizations. For example, each firm might need to employ the Six Sigma approach to quality (a type of integration) or use practices based on an agreed-upon set of international standards. Many of these types of agreements also necessitate the alignment of both core business processes and those that support their accomplishment.

Managing the Organization as a System

What does it mean to manage an organization as a system? In order to manage a system, one must first understand it. According to Russell Ackoff, the only way to understand a system is through synthesis.[19] The first step is figuring out how that thing works as part of a larger whole, the function it performs in the larger whole, and how it interacts within the whole. For example, to understand the Earth as a system, it is necessary to understand how it operates as part of the solar system, the function it performs in the solar system, and how the Earth interacts with other objects (planets, moons, comets) that are part of the solar system. The next steps in understanding a system through synthesis are to describe the functions of, and the interactions between, the components of the system and their links within the larger whole. In the Earth as a system example, this includes getting a sense of how the various components of the Earth interact with each other, the effects the oceans have on the weather (and vice versa), the effects the weather has on the polar ice cap, the effects of sun spots on the Earth, and how the interactions between the earth and the moon or other planets affect these interactions.

> "There has been an evolutionary trend over the past 20 years from Quality Control to Quality Assurance to Total Quality Management (mid- to late 1980s) to overall performance excellence (within the last five years). Overall performance excellence looks at the system as a whole. It moves from improvement to breakthrough—

quality of management of the overall enterprise. Overall performance excellence aligns strategy to key processes to human resources to business results with a balanced set of measures."

—Harry Hertz, Director, National Quality Program, National Institute of Standards and Technology

There are three synthesis techniques that can help an organization to manage itself as a system—systems mapping, systems diagram, and systems walk-through. These techniques assist the enterprise in creating horizontal and vertical alignment. In addition, they help the organization to integrate quality concepts into the fabric of its work.

A systems map (also referred to as a process tree) is a diagram that displays the linkages and the flow of work between all work processes within the enterprise. It can be used to manage the hand-off approaches between work processes, assess whether work can occur in parallel rather than sequentially, and determine whether constraints exist in the system. Once a systems map is in place, some organizations assign process owners to individual work processes as a point of contact for process management activities. After work processes are documented in a systems map they can be aggregated into macro processes (i.e., subsystems). These macro processes can be used to communicate organization-wide work process flow to employees, to reorganize the enterprise from a process-oriented perspective, and to monitor process management activities and results.

A systems diagram can be used to illustrate the relationships between macro processes and external entities that are impacted by, and have an impact on, the organization (i.e., customers, suppliers, distributors, partners). The first step in developing these diagrams is to list all of the external entities in detail and to note the nature of their relationship to the organization (e.g., Job Service supplies us with potential hires; Mangrove Village does not want toxic discharges put into the sewer system). The second step is to link these entities with the macro processes through the use of arrows (note: arrow heads can go both directions). The last step is to write the nature of the impact on the appropriate arrow. This type of diagram can be used to assess the potential impact of internal changes on the various external constituencies and to learn about the function that the organization plays in the community at large.

"People are beginning to understand the complexity and interconnectedness within their organizations. They see the need to manage the organization as a whole instead of isolated components, but have no idea how to get started. It is at this point that a systems diagram is most helpful. When individuals participate in the development of the diagram, they gain an understanding of what the 'whole' looks like—grasping the linkages between processes and the inter-relationships between groups of people, as well as the cause and effect relationships that exist.

"Recently, I worked with an HR department in a large financial institution. Prior to developing a systems diagram, groups were blaming each other for high error rates, high overtime, long cycle time, and high turnover, but did not know where to focus. In one day of work on a systems diagram to describe the current HR organization, the department began to see and articulate:

- How problems and errors upstream create problems downstream.
- How groups are dependent on each other, and that blame may not be appropriate.
- How complex the environment is.
- Where to focus improvement efforts to eliminate errors throughout the flow of work.

"I have used the systems diagram to describe both current and future environments. Using the diagram to describe the current environment generally creates new awareness of how the organization works as a whole. Using the diagram to describe the future environment has provided less 'aha' experiences, but can help to define where the organization needs to develop itself."

—Dana Ginn, Consultant, Cambridge Management Consulting

A systems walk-through is a method for following the flow of work from the customer's needs through the organization back to the customer. If a systems walk-through follows the creation of a systems map, a walk-through can verify the linkages between work processes based on actual inputs and outputs and discover additional linkages not noted on the systems map. A walk-through can also uncover unnecessary work (e.g., duplicated efforts) and disconnects between the actual work flow and the documented systems map.

The tools in the systems thinking toolbox are also useful in describing an entire system (such as the marketplace forces that impact a specific product) and the interactions between its various parts. These tools include

- dynamic thinking tools (causal loop diagrams, behavior over time diagrams, and systems archetypes)
- structural thinking tools (graphical function diagrams, structure-behavior pairs, and policy structure diagrams)
- computer-based tools (computer modeling, management flight simulator, and learning laboratories) [20]

They complement the three techniques described earlier and can provide richer information when making systemwide decisions.

Lean Production

Lean production is another approach to managing the organization as a system that is gaining in popularity. It is also referred to as lean manufacturing and lean thinking. Lean production simply means running an organization without waste. The concept of eliminating non–value-added waste such as wait time, inventory, movement, and defective product originated with Henry Ford and was modernized by Taiichi Ohno and Toyota. Lean manufacturing "provides a way to specify value, line up value-creating actions in the best sequence, conduct these activities without interruption whenever someone requests them, and perform them more and more effectively. . . . it is *lean* because it provides a way to do more with less."[21] Proponents of lean production do not believe in eliminating jobs to reduce costs. Instead, they focus on ways to create work by enhancing value.

> "Lean manufacturing concepts translate into improved processes and higher quality products at lower costs. This translates into competitiveness in the marketplace, which ultimately results in long-term survival and prosperity."
>
> —Lon L. Barrett, Auditor, Boeing,
> and 1997–98 ASQ Spokane Section Chair

Lean production defines value as the "capability provided to a customer at the right time at an appropriate price, as defined in each case by the [ultimate] customer."[22] Once value has been defined for a specific product or service, the next step is to map its value stream. "The *value stream* is the set of all the specific actions required to bring a specific product [and/or service] through the three critical management tasks of any business: the *problem-solving task* running from concept through detailed design and engineering to production launch, the *information management task* running from order-taking through detailed scheduling to delivery, and the *physical transformation task* proceeding from raw materials to a finished product in the hands of the customer."[23] A value stream map (which is similar to a systems map) can help identify all of the steps required to design, order, make, and deliver a product. These steps are then categorized as (1) creating value as perceived by the customer; (2) creating no value for the customer but are required by the current system and, therefore, cannot be eliminated immediately; or (3) creating no value for the customer and are able to be eliminated immediately.[24] All steps in Category 3 are discontinued at once, while efforts are taken to eliminate steps in Category 2.

One way to eliminate non–value-added steps is to understand how the product or service flows through the organization—including where wait time occurs, what is done at each step, and where scrap is created. Boundaries within the organizational structure, such as departments, functions, and jobs, and a batch processing mentality (performing each step separately and cueing work in batches for the next operation) typically serve as barriers to flow. Using the concept of continuous flow throughout the *entire* value stream can significantly reduce cycle time and increase efficiency. Lean production also adds the concept of pull—"nothing is produced by the upstream supplier until the downstream customer signals a need"[25]—to these other concepts (value, value stream, and flow) thus initiating the never-ending pursuit of perfection.

Organization-Wide Measurement Systems

Earlier, the Earth was used to describe what it means to manage something as a system. Organizations as systems have an advantage over this example. Their members can impact the results that do not satisfy them, or create the results they desire by altering how the organization functions within its larger system. At some level, they can influence the interactions between the organization and its environment, as well as the interactions between the components of the organization.

In order to alter how the organization functions in an informed manner, an enterprise must develop a measurement system that measures the performance of the whole system, not just the performance of its individual parts. Here, performance means performance against the aim (i.e., mission and vision) of the system. For example, if the aim of the system is to disseminate knowledge, the rate at which knowledge is disseminated and the level of dissemination should be measured. (These measures are not the same as measuring the number of training events that took place.) If the aim of the system is to solve the problems that small business owners have, there should be measures of the rate at which their problems are solved, or how their businesses have become "better." (These measures are not the same as the number of new services that are introduced in a year, or how well these services are performed.)

The first set of steps in developing an organization-wide measurement system include stating the aim of the organization (its mission and vision; also a part of organizational architecture), articulating measures that are good indicators of performance against this aim, creating a measurement plan around these indicators, and measuring progress against them. Once these overall measures are in place, they can be deployed through the organization's subsystems and work processes. This deployment ensures overall alignment between organization-wide measures and key data collected within individual work processes.

A second set of steps involves adding and/or deleting measures from the organization-wide measurement plan. Measures that can be added include those that track the performance of subsystems and the interactions between these subsystems. These additional measures must be linked to measures of the overall system. Once the measurement plan has been functioning for several cycles, decisions can be made to delete measures that are not informative and to search for others that may yield the desired information.

There are several models for structuring an organization-wide measurement system—the balanced scorecard,[26] the dashboard,[27] and the instrument panel (Tableau de Bord)[28] The skills involved in creating any type of organization-wide measurement system are similar to, but more complex and broader in scope, than those required to develop measurement plans in the Quality Assurance Field of Performance Practice.

Data from the measurement system can be used in concert with a systems map, a systems diagram, and a systems walk-through to monitor the overall performance of the system, the performance of its components, and the interactions between components. The organization-wide measurement system itself impacts methods in earlier fields of performance practice. For example, data can be fed back into process management activities to focus them on areas where the organization is feeling pain. The data can also be used during strategic planning to help assess the effectiveness of the last strategic planning cycle, including its deployment, and to drive changes in this cycle. In order to continue to provide valid information, an organization-wide measurement system must be updated each strategic planning cycle and when the mission of the organization shifts in focus.

> "We need to build an infrastructure to manage the business on a daily basis to accomplish its strategic objectives. There are three main components to this infrastructure. The first is top level indicators. The second is to build a process management system (quality in daily work). The third is to use problem solving and redesign technology to move the processes to close the gaps. Once this management system is in place, you need to integrate it with the organization's strategic plans. The next level for quality is to merge our processes with those of our customers and suppliers. One result of using this management system is that cultural issues will stick out like a sore thumb. About half of them will self-correct; the other half must be dealt with."
>
> —Ellen Bovarnick, Senior Vice President, Quality, formerly of Florida Power & Light

A Note on Reengineering

In the early 1990s, the term *reengineering* was introduced to describe a systematic approach to redesigning processes or organizations. Many reengineering activities involved improving the use of computer systems in large organizations. Reengineering became popular overnight because its introduction occurred at the same time that many large organizations were trying to figure out how to make their investments in computerization pay off.

Reengineering attempts to build on the concepts of process-oriented thinking, alignment, and organization as system by focusing on the processes that transform inputs into outputs, aligning all process activities within a single enterprise unit to eliminate the impact of conflicting organizational goals on their performance. This work often resulted in a restructuring of the firm and, in all too many cases, turned out to be nothing more than a short-term cost-cutting initiative. Even though reengineering has achieved its intended results in some situations, many times it has not. "Recent reports, supported with viewpoints expressed by the founders of the reengineering movement, claim that more than 70 percent of reengineering efforts have failed to achieve their purposes."[29] It is not surprising that reengineering has acquired an unsavory reputation.

Large Group Interventions

Over the past decade a number of large group intervention techniques have emerged that more quickly effect large-scale change. Some of these intervention techniques include: Future Search conferences, Real Time Strategic Change, ICA (Institute of Cultural Affairs) Strategic Planning Process, the Conference Model®, Fast Cycle Full Participation Work Design, Real Time Work Design, Participative

Design, Simu-Real, Work-Outs, and Open Space technology.[30] These approaches, as summarized in the book, *Large Group Interventions,* by Barbara Benedict Bunker and Billie Alban, allow organizations to involve hundreds, if not thousands, of individuals to work together to accomplish a common outcome. In the process, the organization can more quickly achieve what Kathleen Dannemiller has coined "one heart and one mind"[31]—a key factor in alignment and integration.

Large group interventions are grounded in large group theory. Small group theory and large group theory are not the same—they are based on different psychological processes and have different issues attached to them. There are four dynamics of large group interventions that can arise

1. the dilemma of voice (amount of individual airtime and the feeling of being heard)
2. the dilemma of structure (amount needed to manage anxiety in the room and active individual participation)
3. the egocentric dilemma (each person acting as though his or her reality is the only true reality)
4. affect contagion (experiencing and expressing feelings because one feels them vicariously in others) [32]

It is critical to become knowledgeable in large group theory, the unique dynamics of large groups, and the specific steps behind the intervention, before using the methods listed above.

These approaches have a variety of uses. They can help an organization to create its preferred future, to receive the input and feedback of all employees in the strategic planning process, and to redesign subsystems and processes. In addition, they can be used in lieu of classroom training programs and traditional large group meetings. Large group interventions have been used successfully in diverse industries, including transportation (Amtrak, United Airlines), hospitality (Marriott), automotive (Ford Motor Company), financial services (World Bank, Bank of Montreal), health care (Inova Health System), and chemicals (DuPont).

> "I have designed and facilitated over 30 large group interventions using Real Time Strategic Change. Individuals from all levels, disciplines, and perspectives, listen, learn, and work together to define and shape the current and future direction of their organization. People who participate are moved—sometimes to tears, sometimes to laughter, but always to enthusiasm at having been heard, and at having the opportunity to contribute to the success of their organization in a meaningful way. Energy is unleashed in these events . . . and leads from commitment and ownership to the success of the organization. It's not about change directed from the top-down or change initiated exclusively bottom-up. It's about building community through empowerment and inclusion."
>
> —Carrie Hays, training and organizational development consultant, Yountville, CA

Strategic Planning

It is not enough for an organization to attend to its immediate needs—it must also attend to its future. The process of strategic planning is essential to vertical alignment. There are five phases to strategic planning: (1) assessing the environment; (2) developing the long-range plan; (3) developing the annual plan; (4) deploying, finalizing, and implementing the plans; and (5) performing ongoing reviews.[33] The information displayed in Table 6.1 is a starting point for moving forward with strategic planning and incorporates elements from other fields of performance practice. These five steps follow the PDCA Cycle; however, they start with the "Check" phase.

> "People who are true to quality have made it a part of their business. For them, it evolved into a more sophisticated strategic planning approach that included organizational and process capacity. They have integrated quality into their life, and their way of doing business. As a result, these organizations will blow their competition away. The future for quality will be to link customers directly to organizational capacity and to package all of this in a rigorous planning approach."
>
> —Nancy M. Johnson, Ph.D., Vice President, Corporate Research and Development, American Family Insurance

Phase 1, Assessing the Environment, has both an internal and an external focus. Internal scanning replaces gut feel by providing both qualitative and quantitative data on the health of the organization. Internal scan data are provided by the measurement plans developed as part of standardization in the Quality Assurance Field of Performance Practice and the organization-wide measurement system, covered earlier in this chapter. Through the synthesis of external scanning information (from sources such as competitors, social trends, economic forces, and customers' future wants and needs), the organization can determine its overall market strategy (also a part of organizational architecture presented earlier in this chapter) and create/refine its mission and vision statements (also a part of organizational architecture).

In Phase 2, Developing the Long-Range Plan, no more than three organizational breakthrough strategies, and their associated multi-year objectives, are determined for the planning cycle (typically five years in length). A breakthrough strategy is something that has not been done before, an existing process/subsystem that is broken and cannot be fixed, or a dramatic improvement in capability to provide existing products/services. It is at this point in the strategic planning process that measures are determined for each of the breakthrough strategies and incorporated into the enterprise's organization-wide measurement plan.

The outcome of Phase 3, Developing the Annual Plan, is the annual objectives that will be undertaken in the coming year in pursuit of the breakthrough strategies. At this point, the enterprise also creates measures around these objectives and adds them to the organization-wide measurement system.

Table 6.1
Strategic Planning: Core Elements and Enhancements

Phase	**Core Elements**	**Specific Phase Enhancements***
Assessing the Environment	1. Collect information/data (both external and internal) a. External: Customers, competitors, economic trends, societal trends, government/legislation, technology, industry trends, etc. b. Internal: Existing organization-wide data, people—staffing and capabilities, equipment and facilities 2. Synthesize external and internal information/data a. Identify strengths, weaknesses, opportunities, and threats (SWOT analysis) b. Identify themes and their impact on the organization 3. Create/revise organization-wide market strategy, and mission and vision statements	1. Use competitive intelligence data 2. Assess latent market wants and needs in addition to current customer requirements 3. Develop scenarios 15 to 25 years into the future 4. Identify existing core competencies and those needed to fulfill the vision 5. Involve customers and suppliers in meetings 6. Use organization-wide measurement system data as part of external and internal assessments 7. Use organization-wide systems map and systems diagram as well as work process capability data to help determine internal capabilities
Developing the Long-Range Plan	1. Determine possible breakthrough strategies 2. Select no more than three breakthrough strategies 3. Identify multi-year objectives for each breakthrough strategy 4. Determine what needs to occur to minimize impact of threats on breakthrough strategies, multi-year objectives, and the entire long-range plan 5. Develop a measurement plan that includes each breakthrough strategy and multi-year objective 6. Create long-range financial, human resource, and marketing forecasts	1. Use core competency development as a breakthrough strategy 2. Link breakthrough strategies and multi-year objectives to organization-wide systems map and systems diagram

Developing the Annual Plan	1. Determine which multi-year objectives will be pursued in the annual plan 2. Create annual objectives for each multi-year objective that will be pursued in the coming year (can be done organization-wide, by business unit, or by brand) 3. Develop measures for each annual objective	1. Link annual objectives to organization-wide systems map and systems diagram
Deploying, Finalizing, and Implementing the Plans	1. Each accountable group develops targets and activities for those annual objectives that apply to it, including budget and human resource needs. This can be done (a) by business unit or brand, (b) by work group, or (c) by project team assigned to a specific breakthrough strategy 2. Consolidate plans, budgets, and marketing and human resource needs for the entire organization 3. Review consolidated plans, budgets, and marketing, and human resource needs to ensure that the organization can achieve its annual and multi-year objectives 4. Communicate finalized annual plan to all employees 5. Each accountable group develops implementation plans for its targets and activities 6. Finalize all plans, budgets, etc. 7. Execute the long-range and the annual plans	1. Use targets/activities for "catchball" with employees 2. Use software for communications and data analysis
Performing Ongoing Reviews of All Plans and Plan Implementation	1. Review targets and activities (monthly) 2. Review annual objectives (quarterly) 3. Review multi-year objectives and breakthrough strategies (yearly) 4. Update external and internal environmental assessments on an ongoing basis	1. Use the basic quality tools (e.g., run charts, control charts, Pareto charts, etc.) and graphical display of data 2. Use information and knowledge from reviews to improve performance and enhance the long-range and the annual plans

*The 7 Management and Planning Tools and large group interventions are enhancements that apply to all five phases.

Chart adapted from Lori L. Silverman and Dona Hotopp, "Strategic Planning: Core Elements and Enhancements," 1996.

The first step in Phase 4, Deploying, Finalizing, and Implementing the Plans, includes having each part of the organization determine the activities and targets necessary for it to contribute to the annual objectives and the breakthrough strategies. Once these activities and targets are finalized, they are consolidated across the organization, checked again for consistency, and implemented by the appropriate groups. Implementation is one of the key challenges in planning. The best-made plans that sit on the shelf collecting dust are no more effective than those that were never created.

It is during Phase 5, Performing Ongoing Reviews of all Plans and Plan Implementation, that the PDCA Cycle is fully incorporated into the planning process. Strategic planning must be iterative in nature. Each cycle of strategic planning must build on previous learnings and feed into future cycles. Flowcharting the process of strategic planning encourages standardization and the opportunity for ongoing improvement and innovation in the planning process, in addition to promoting ongoing planning efforts.

In industries where the future is unpredictable and ever-changing, scenario development is a means of grasping the implications of uncertainties and wildcards on the organization's future. When used as a part of strategic planning, scenario development facilitates the creation of long-term strategies that are "breakthrough" in orientation. Thus, organizations move away from strategies that are "more of the same." This approach can be used effectively in industries, such as high technology, where the dynamics of the industry may cause it to alter its plans frequently and on short notice, making strategic planning a difficult method to embrace. As Gary Hamel's quote stated in chapter 1, what is truly needed is a "radical new look at the process of developing strategic plans"[34] in order for organizations to be able to quickly and effectively create breakthrough value-creating strategies.

> "The challenges we face in helping our organization include how to respond to changes in the environment or in strategy quickly enough."
>
> —Vice President, Quality, Financial Services

7 Management and Planning Tools

The 7 Management and Planning Tools were announced as a result of the research conducted by The Committee for Developing QC Tools, a part of the Union of Japanese Scientists and Engineers, in January 1977. The seven tools are affinity diagrams (useful in synthesizing information), interrelationship diagraphs, tree diagrams, matrices, Process Decision Program Charts (PDPC), matrix data analysis (the one quantitative tool), and arrow diagrams.[35]

Four of these tools—affinity diagrams, interrelationship diagraphs, matrices, and tree diagrams—are frequently used in strategic planning efforts. However, they have many other uses including the collection and interpretation of market research information, new product development, and the planning of one-time projects (such as a move from one facility to another). Six of these tools are specifically designed to analyze qualitative data (i.e., words, ideas, comments). Their use can foster vertical alignment (their role in strategic planning), and guide the synthesis of seemingly inconsistent qualitative information into its inherent patterns (noting the latent, and potentially causal, relationships among them) and the planning of future actions. Books such as *Planning for Quality, Productivity, and Competitive Position,* by Howard Gitlow and Process Management International, Inc. (1990), *The Memory Jogger Plus+*™, by Michael Brassard (1989), and *The Seven New QC Tools: Practical Applications for Managers,* by Yoshinobu Nayatani and others (1984) describe how to construct each tool and their applications in a business environment.

Project Management

"Dr. Joseph Juran defines a project as a problem scheduled for solution. . . . Project management is the planning, scheduling, and controlling of project activities to meet project objectives."[36] Project management is a method of problem solving wherein the problem is the completion of a project in a manner that meets the needs of its customers. Projects can range from implementing a specific change (e.g., technology) to the creation of a structure (e.g., a new plant or warehouse), to the implementation of strategic planning activities.

> "In the area of project management I see a greater role for internal quality consultants as project leaders, rather than just facilitators."
>
> —Nancy M. Johnson, Ph.D., Vice President, Corporate Research and Development, American Family Insurance

There are numerous steps involved in the planning, scheduling, and controlling of the project and many technical approaches to undertaking project management. In addition to the 7 Management and Planning tools (primarily arrow diagrams), Gantt charts (bar charts), PERT (Performance Evaluation and Review Technique) charts, and the CPM (Critical Path Method) can be used for project scheduling. These techniques can be found as part of college and university courses on operations management. A recent development in the project management arena is Critical Chain scheduling, an application of the Theory of Constraints to project management. The data from Critical Chain implementations suggest that significant breakthroughs in project performance (i.e., time to complete) can be achieved within the budgetary and scope objectives of a project.

Project management is a part of the Alignment and Integration Field of Performance Practice because it can be used to align all resources deployed to a project around the goal for the project. Quality-related concepts, such as the PDCA Cycle, work as a process, and information-based decision making, are integral to approaches in use today.

WHO IS INVOLVED IN THE ALIGNMENT AND INTEGRATION FIELD OF PERFORMANCE PRACTICE

This is the first field of performance practice in which the involvement of each and every organizational member is crucial to the organization's ability to achieve the outcomes associated with the field. These include improved organizational effectiveness, elimination of barriers and unnecessary work, and improved overall customer and employee satisfaction. The benefits of horizontal and vertical alignment cannot be realized without the entire enterprise as the frame of reference. For many enterprises, this alignment includes their key customers (80/20 rule) and members of their supply chain (including organizational partnerships covered earlier in the chapter). An organization's supply chain includes both forward integration from the enterprise to the consumer and backward integration to raw material suppliers, as required. In order to be effective, integration—the deployment of company ideology (i.e., vision, mission, values, and guiding principles) and quality-based philosophies, strategies, goals, and objectives across and throughout the organization's work processes and people—must also involve these same stakeholders.

SHORTCOMINGS WITH THE ALIGNMENT AND INTEGRATION FIELD OF PERFORMANCE PRACTICE

The Alignment and Integration Field of Performance Practice is strategic in nature, and as such, heavily involves management. Effort is put forth to change the existing system through alignment and to eliminate constraints through the integration of ideology and quality-based practices. Both of these shortcomings arose in Quality Assurance and continued through the Problem Resolution Field of Performance Practice. Alignment and Integration also addresses the linkage of problem resolution efforts and customer requirements to all facets of the business, including its many initiatives, in addition to its focus on organizational culture (all issues in Problem Resolution).

Even though many organizations are currently enamored with this field of performance practice, we recognize that it also holds some shortcomings. These shortcomings include a predisposition to attend to internal issues even though it continues the concept of customer focus from the Problem Resolution Field, continued lack of a systematic approach to innovation, and the inability to anticipate market trends based on unknown customer wants and needs. It is because of these shortcomings that the fourth star in The Starburst Model™ began to emerge—the Consumer Obsession Field of Performance Practice.

Table 6.2

Your Organization and the Alignment and Integration Field of Performance Practice

Directions: Record the activities your organization has and has not engaged in relative to the concepts, tools, and methods referenced in this field of performance practice, noting the degree of deployment of each item. Also document its future plans for deploying these concepts, tools, and methods throughout the enterprise.

Purpose: To ensure all organizational work contributes to achieving the organization's mission, vision, and plans		**Desired Outcomes:** • Improved organizational effectiveness • Elimination of barriers and unnecessary work • Improved overall customer and employee satisfaction		
	What Your Organization Is Doing	**What Your Organization Is Not Doing**	**Degree of Deployment***	**Plans Your Organization Has for the Future**
Underlying Concepts • Alignment • Integration • Organization as system • Transformation • Large-scale organizational change • Self-management			 1 2 3 4 5 1 2 3 4 5 1 2 3 4 5 1 2 3 4 5 1 2 3 4 5 1 2 3 4 5	
Commonly Used Tools and Methods • Organizational architecture • Organizational partnerships • Managing the organization as a system • Large group interventions • Strategic planning • 7 Management and Planning Tools • Project management			 1 2 3 4 5 1 2 3 4 5 1 2 3 4 5 1 2 3 4 5 1 2 3 4 5 1 2 3 4 5 1 2 3 4 5	

* Rating system:
1 = no systematic deployment is evident
2 = some deployment is evident with little or no results
3 = deployment is evident in several areas of the business with limited results
4 = deployment is evident in major portions of the business with measurable results
5 = full organization-wide deployment is evident with significant measurable results

Table 6.3

CHAOS and the Alignment and Integration Field of Performance Practice

Directions: Note your thoughts on the future impact that the forces of **CHAOS** may have on each of the underlying concepts and the commonly used tools and methods in the Alignment and Integration Field of Performance Practice.

CHAOS / Underlying Concepts	Changing Definition of Work and the Workplace	Heightened Social Responsibility	Aging Baby Boomers	Overarching Demographic Change	Strategic Growth Through Technology and Innovation
• Alignment					
• Integration					
• Organization as system					
• Transformation					
• Large-scale organizational change					
• Self-management					
Commonly Used Tools and Methods					
• Organizational architecture					
• Organizational partnerships					
• Managing the organization as a system					
• Large group interventions					
• Strategic planning					
• 7 Management and Planning Tools					
• Project management					

Endnotes

1. George Labovitz and Victor Rosansky, *The Power of Alignment* (New York: John Wiley & Sons, Inc., 1997), 5.
2. Linda Ackerman Anderson, with Dean Anderson and Martin Marquardt, "Development, Transition or Transformation: Bringing Change Leadership Into the 21st Century," *OD Practitioner,* Vol. 28, No. 4 (1997), 8–9.
3. Anderson, with Anderson and Marquardt. "Development, Transition or Transformation: Bringing Change Leadership Into the 21st Century," 5–16.
4. Allan M. Mohrman, Jr. et al., *Large-Scale Organizational Change* (San Francisco: Jossey-Bass Inc., Publishers, 1989).
5. Mohrman, Jr. et al., *Large-Scale Organizational Change,* 2.
6. Mohrman, Jr. et al, *Large-Scale Organizational Change,* 10–11.
7. Mohrman, Jr. et al., *Large-Scale Organizational Change,* 275.
8. Edward E. Lawler, "Organizational Capabilities: The Ultimate Competitive Advantage," presentation given at the Strategic Leadership Forum (New York, NY, April 21, 1998).
9. W. Warner Burke, *Organizational Development: A Process of Learning and Changing* (Reading, MA: Addison-Wesley Publishing Company), 55–56.
10. Burke, *Organizational Development: A Process of Learning and Changing,* 87–90.
11. Robert J. Marshak, "Lewin Meets Confucius: A Re-View of the OD Model of Change," *Journal of Applied Behavioral Science* (December 1993), 400–403.
12. Robert M. Tomasko, *Rethinking the Corporation: The Architecture of Change* (New York: American Management Association, 1993), 86–88.
13. W. A. Pasmore, *Designing Effective Organizations: The Sociotechnical Systems Perspective* (New York: John Wiley & Sons, Inc., 1988), 33.
14. David A. Nadler et al., *Organizational Architecture: Designs for Changing Organizations* (San Francisco: Jossey-Bass Inc., Publishers, 1992).
15. Robert Howard, "The CEO as Organizational Architect: An Interview with Xerox's Paul Allaire," *Harvard Business Review* (September–October 1992), 107–121.
16. Lori L. Silverman, "Organizational Architecture: A Framework for Successful Transformation" (unpublished paper, May 1997), 1.
17. Silverman, "Organizational Architecture: A Framework for Successful Transformation," 3.
18. Edgar H. Schein, *Organizational Culture and Leadership* (San Francisco: Jossey-Bass Inc., Publishers, 1992), 16–27.
19. Russell Ackoff, keynote presentation given at the Upsizing the Organization Conference sponsored by the Indiana Quality and Productivity Improvement Council (September 1997).
20. Daniel H. Kim, *Systems Thinking Tools: A User's Reference Guide* (Cambridge, MA: Pegasus Communications, Inc., 1994), 11.
21. James P. Womack and Daniel T. Jones, *Lean Thinking: Banish Waste and Create Wealth in Your Corporation* (New York: Simon & Schuster, 1996), 15.
22. Womack and Jones, *Lean Thinking: Banish Waste and Create Wealth in Your Corporation,* 311.
23. Womack and Jones, *Lean Thinking: Banish Waste and Create Wealth in Your Corporation,* 19.

24. Womack and Jones, *Lean Thinking: Banish Waste and Create Wealth in Your Corporation,* 38.

25. Womack and Jones, *Lean Thinking: Banish Waste and Create Wealth in Your Corporation,* 309.

26. Robert S. Kaplan and David P. Norton, *Balanced Scorecard* (Boston: Harvard Business School Press, 1996).

27. Christopher Meyer, "How the Right Measures Help Teams Excel," *Harvard Business Review* (May–June 1994), 95–103.

28. E. Chiapello and M. Lebas, "The Tableau de Bord, A French Approach to Management Information," European Accounting Association (Bergen, Norway, May 2–4, 1996).

29. Susan Albers Mohrman et al., *Tomorrow's Organization: Crafting Winning Capabilities in a Dynamic World* (San Francisco: Jossey-Bass Inc., Publishers, 1998), 205.

30. Barbara Benedict Bunker and Billie Alban, *Large Group Interventions* (San Francisco: Jossey-Bass Inc., Publishers, 1997).

31. Bunker and Alban, *Large Group Interventions,* 70.

32. Bunker and Alban, *Large Group Interventions,* 201–209.

33. Lori L. Silverman and Dona Hotopp, "Strategic Planning: Core Elements and Enhancements" (unpublished chart, 1996, 1997).

34. Gary Hamel, "Strategy Innovation and the Quest for Value," *Sloan Management Review* (Winter 1998), 10.

35. Howard S. Gitlow and Process Management International, Inc., *Planning for Quality, Productivity, and Competitive Position* (Homewood, IL: Dow Jones-Irwin, 1990), 54.

36. James P. Lewis, *Fundamentals of Project Management* (New York: American Management Association, 1995), 1.

C H A P T E R

7

The Consumer Obsession Field of Performance Practice

Chapter 7 introduces the fourth star in The Starburst Model™—the Consumer Obsession Field of Performance Practice. The term *consumer,* rather than *customer,* is used in the title of this field because the word *consumer* focuses on the end user (i.e., individual, organization) of a product and/or service (what marketers call an "offering," since products and services in today's world are bundled together by the time the end user receives them). This label does not imply that employees or shareholders are no longer important. It suggests that all members of "the system" need to be fixated on end users and providing offerings that create value. When the word *customer* is used in this chapter it is used in reference to intermediate customers as well as end users.

The term *obsession* describes the third shift in practice toward customers. The Quality Assurance Field of Performance Practice speaks to customer responsiveness—being reactive to customers' requirements (primarily customers of the next work process or the end users of the specific outputs of the work process under study). Work within this field is directed toward product and service conformance to customers' requirements. The Problem Resolution and Alignment and Integration Fields of Performance Practice attend to customer focus—being proactive to customers' requirements—by finding better ways to meet their needs by going beyond expressed needs and wants to uncover the underlying purpose behind their requirements. In the Consumer Obsession Field, being obsessed implies being out in front of the marketplace—anticipating what will bring value to customers (some of whom may not even be known today) by uncovering latent (i.e., hidden) market wants and needs—and translating these latent wants and needs into offerings that will bring them value. Thus, this field of performance practice comes after, rather than before, alignment and integration because internal organizational alignment based on a customer-focus approach is a necessary precursor to value creation.

> "Arnie Weimerskirch, VP Quality, Honeywell, says that the Baldrige criteria always need to represent the leading edge of validated (proven) management practice. I believe the criteria need to drive organizations to achieve their full competitive advantage in the marketplace. Both of these items, requirements for competitiveness and validated management practice, will continue to be inputs to evolving the Baldrige criteria. The criteria will also be tightened around alignment and integration. In the future, organizations will need to have a better understanding of supply and value chains and how to integrate them into management systems. They will have to figure out how value to customers, people, and assets fit together into an overall value equation."
>
> —Harry Hertz, Director, National Quality Program, National Institute of Standards and Technology

The purpose of the Consumer Obsession Field of Performance Practice is to promote the long-term survival of the organization. This field of practice has been emerging over the past 100 years—with brand management leading the way. Many of the other tools and methods, and their associated underlying concepts, have appeared only within the past two decades. Because of this slow emergence, some individuals do not separate value creation from alignment and integration. Here, consumer obsession is treated as a separate field of performance practice because its purpose and outcomes are significantly different than those associated with the Alignment and Integration Field. Even though the Alignment and Integration Field attends to external entities, it still has an inward-focused perspective attached to it (e.g., managing the organization as a system in order to reap additional financial benefits).

The outcome of this field supports the concurrent creation of value for consumers, employees, and shareholders. A cycle is created when value is simultaneously provided to these parties. "Shareholders provide things of value (paychecks, bricks and mortar, capital equipment, training) to employees, who in turn provide things of value (products, services, applications support) to customers, who in turn provide things of value (dollar bills) to shareholders."[1] This cycle and what one perceives as value can change daily, leading to ongoing organizational learning and improvement. The previous three fields of performance practice had quality-based field of performance outcomes (e.g., elimination of unnecessary work, reduced costs, conformance to customer requirements). The Consumer Obsession Field of Performance Practice does not. This shift does not imply that quality is no longer important. On the contrary, it suggests that quality is fundamental to value creation. This mindset will be explored more in the section called Value Creation.

UNDERLYING CONCEPTS

The underlying concepts in this chapter arise out of the **CHAOS** described in chapter 1. These concepts are value creation, organizational renewal, mass customization, and lifetime relationships with consumers. Consumers are becoming

CHAOS

- [C]hanging definition of work and the workplace
- [H]eightened social responsibility
- [A]ging baby boomers
- [O]verarching demographic change
- [S]trategic growth through technology and innovation

more sophisticated, and the demands of the marketplace are changing more rapidly and more radically than ever before. In addition, technology allows for the production of lot sizes of one. It is very likely that additional concepts in this field of performance practice will emerge as the workplace forces of the future continue to play out.

Value Creation

> "Quality should not be your objective. That quality is limited becomes a problem only if, for some inexplicable reason, you have a need to make it your primary corporate objective and focus. It shouldn't be. Creating value should. And before you think I am consigning quality to a position of minor importance, consider this metaphor: Quality is the foundation on which to build value. Structurally speaking, what is the most critical element of any building? Its foundation. But the foundation isn't the essence of a building any more than quality is—or should be—the essence of a business."[2]
>
> —John Guaspari, author of *I Know It When I See It* and *It's About Time*

The desired outcome of the Consumer Obsession Field of Practice is to create value for consumers, employees, and shareholders. But, what does the word *value* mean in this context? Value is "the perception of the resources received minus the resources given up in a marketplace exchange in comparison with a referent alternative . . . [where resources] are represented by love, status, information, money, problem solutions, time, and sensory gratification."[3] A marketplace exchange is any transaction between two or more parties (each referred to as an exchange partner) independent of whether they are internal or external to the organization. Because value is always relative or comparative (which means it is never an absolute nor does it belong to something in and of itself), it must be judged in comparison to something else—a referent alternative.

A referent alternative may be a direct competitor (such as Kellogg's versus Post's raisin bran cereal), the same brand the last time the person used it, a substitute product that accomplishes the same objective (e.g., personal development gained through an Outward Bound experience or an executive development program), or a completely different alternative (e.g., buying a car versus purchasing an extravagant vacation package). Consciously or unconsciously, these referent alternatives are selected by each exchange partner, and may be influenced by advertising and promotional efforts.

Benefits (a resource received that leaves an individual with more of the resource than the person had before) and costs (a resource given up that leaves an individual with less of the resource than the person had before) are relative to the current amount of resources held by an exchange partner. For example, all things being equal, if the fast-food restaurant an individual frequents (which is currently 12 minutes from home) opens a new location that is three minutes from where the person lives, the individual has accrued a *benefit* relative to the resource of time. This is true even though the person is still giving up three minutes of travel time (what some might perceive as a *cost*). On the other hand, consider that the person's favorite fast-food restaurant (which is three minutes from home) closes down because another location opened up 12 minutes away. This new location has a playland for children (a sensory gratification resource for the person's kids, which the old location and referents do not offer). Even though the individual has accrued more cost on the time resource, the person may still elect to travel 12 minutes because of the accrued benefits on the sensory gratification resource. Thus, it is the perception, not the actual level, of resources received minus those given up that the exchange partner compares to the referent alternative(s).

Each exchange partner will have a different view of benefits and costs as well as the resources received and given up in the exchange. In the earlier example, the fast-food restaurant's new location receives money (which is an increased benefit of the money resource) and has to manage new processes to maintain the playland (may cost money and time—both of which are resources). These resources differ from those described in relationship to the consumer's experiences in this same example.

> "In order to add value to organizations, there needs to be (1) a much tighter line between quality and marketing activities, (2) an understanding of the role of employee satisfaction and its relation to customer satisfaction and quality, and (3) fast-cycle learning of people within the organization to deliver high quality output to customers (knowledge management)."
>
> —Vice President, Quality, Financial Services

How does this definition of value influence the behavior of the organization relative to its quality and performance practices? First, it suggests that the language of customer and supplier may be limiting. All customers are, by definition, both customers and suppliers; the same is true for suppliers. Hence, when speaking about value, the term *exchange partners* can be used to describe all of the involved parties. Second, there are customer processes as well as organizational processes. The organization is responsible for helping customers within distribution channels, as well as those who are end users, identify and improve these processes. This work is similar to the work that is occurring in supply chain management. Third, benchmarking assumes that all customers and/or competitors are using the same referent alternatives. The value creation perspective presented here suggests that this may not be the case. Finally, what someone considers to be a benefit or a cost is situational. This implies that requirements are continually changing at the individual level even though they may stay the same at the market segment level. Therefore, processes will need to be flexible and adjustable by all exchange partners at the point of use or consumption (e.g., pay-per-view and video-on-demand television features).

In order to assess the value of an offering to consumers, it is important to clarify the organization's definition of the term *value.* Once the term is understood by everyone, the enterprise can develop and test methods for assessing value. Only recently have efforts been undertaken to determine how to measure and manage value creation, given the definition presented here. There are a number of composite measures such as "economic value added" and "shareholder value added" that use the term *value.* Increased attention is also being given to what has been defined as "the value chain" (popularized by Michael Porter in his 1985 book, *Competitive Advantage: Creating and Sustaining Superior Performance*) and "the value stream" in lean production (as described in the Alignment and Integration Field and discussed by James Womack and Daniel Jones in the books, *The Machine That Changed the World* and *Lean Thinking*). Even though these approaches use the word *value,* they differ from what is being suggested in this chapter. Attention needs to be given to what it means to provide more resources for an offering in a marketplace exchange than customers currently receive when compared with referent alternatives.

> "At Lipton, the emphasis was on quality, mostly under the assumption that value creation would come as a result. Had we earlier had the wisdom gained over the last few years regarding emphasis on the value creation advantages of a focus on quality, we might have saved Unilever's jeweled crown a severe tarnishing."
>
> —Lynne B. Hare, Director,
> Applied Statistics, Nabisco, Inc.

Organizational Renewal

> "We respect all of the other things people say about leadership—that you've got to inspire, you've got to cause followership, you've got [to] make a good impression, you've got to represent the company—but they are givens. The real pivotal thing is to take the institution elsewhere. That's the renewal. . . . We won't be what we need to be if we don't do that renewing."[4]
>
> —Bob Galvin, Chairman of the Executive
> Committee, Motorola, Inc.

Organizations cannot ignore that they are now operating in extremely complex, chaotic environments and that their long-term survival depends on their ability to anticipate what their customers may want and need. As a result, enterprises must be able to engage in perpetual self-renewal in order to provide ongoing value to all of their constituents. Renewal goes beyond organizational transformation. "Continuous self-renewal is built on the tension that develops between two symbiotic forces—the need for ongoing improvement in operational performance as provided by continuous rationalization, and the need for growth and expansion as generated by continuous revitalization. [Whereas] the rationalization process focuses on resource productivity . . . and a process of continuous refinement of ongoing activities [to] ensure that current assets and resources are used effectively . . . revitalization focuses on challenging and changing the existing rules . . . [in order to create] new competencies and businesses."[5]

This type of renewal presents an ongoing paradox—both forces must be managed simultaneously. The resulting tension can increase over time, especially when organizations find themselves in the throes of "substantial upheaval and disequilibrium, generally precipitated by a destabilizing event or series of events . . . such [as] the emergence of a new technology, major judicial or legislative action, or the appearance of a new player who somehow alters the basis of competition. . . . These periods of upheaval require . . . discontinuous change in an organization—a step-function change that affects practically every major variable in the equation of an enterprise. This form of change responds to environmental discontinuity through a carefully designed, deliberately led period of organizational discontinuity."[6] As a result, mechanisms that help the enterprise to recognize environmental discontinuity and trigger organizational discontinuity need to be put in place. The organizational architecture methodology described in the Alignment and Integration Field of Performance Practice can be employed to assist in this period of organizational discontinuity.

> "Six years ago our marketing group planned for a new product introduction every two to three years. With the increase in demand, as well as the desire to grow the business, this cycle was shortened to a year, and now to six months."
>
> —Dean A. Garner, Development Consultant, Wilson Sporting Goods

Mass Customization

Mass customization is an outgrowth of technological advances and the desire to be flexible enough to meet the wants and needs of individual customers. This concept was originally put forward by Stanley Davis in 1987, with researchers at IBM leading the development of a framework for thinking about the shift from mass production to mass customization.[7] Mass customization is a logical extension of the realization that every exchange partner approaches a transaction with a different perspective (as explained earlier in the section Value Creation). To date, four different approaches to mass customization have been put forth. They are collaborative, adaptive, cosmetic, and transparent.

1. "Collaborative customizers conduct a dialogue with individual customers to help them articulate their needs, to identify the precise offering that fulfills those needs, and to make customized products for them. [This approach] is appropriate for businesses whose customers cannot easily articulate what they want and grow frustrated when forced to select from a plethora of options.
2. "Adaptive customizers offer one standard, but customizable, product that is designed so that users can alter it themselves. [This approach] is appropriate

for businesses whose customers want the product to perform in different ways on different occasions, and available technology makes it possible for them to customize the product easily on their own.

3. "Cosmetic customizers present a standard product differently to different customers. [This approach] is appropriate when customers use a product the same way and differ only in how they want it presented.
4. "Transparent customizers provide individual customers with unique goods or services without letting them know explicitly that those products and services have been customized for them. [This approach] is appropriate when customers' specific needs are predictable or can easily be deduced, and especially when customers do not want to state their needs repeatedly."[8]

For some, mass customization is easier to understand from a services perspective, where the consumer regularly participates as a just-in-time cocreator of the offering. For example, when ordering fast food at a restaurant or making travel reservations, the consumer is able to define what is needed and desired at the point of contact with the supplier.

Hewlett Packard suggests that the key to mass customization in manufacturing environments is "postponing the task of differentiating a product for a specific customer until the latest possible point in the supply network (a company's supply, manufacturing, and distribution chain)."[9] It has found that products and manufacturing processes need to be designed in independent modules so they can be rearranged easily and inexpensively, and that an organization's supply network must be agile enough to help the organization deliver customized goods in a cost-effective manner.

More profound is the understanding that each individual consumer is composed of many market segments depending upon the time of day, the day of the week, and the location of the individual. Mass customization does not necessarily mean that an organization needs to provide unique offerings for each individual or organization it serves. What it implies is that the organization needs to understand consumers' needs and wants as individuals (i.e., "market segments of one") rather than as part of the mass marketplace, and that codevelopment and cocreation between suppliers and consumers need to become the norm.

> "In this new marketing concept, this knowledge, understanding, and commitment is not the social province of the marketing department. Rather it is shared throughout the organization. In the words of B. Joseph Pine, mass customization represents 'the death of the marketing function . . . the triumph of the marketing discipline.' Marketing becomes part of the organizational culture and the knowledge systems that guide decision making at all levels."[10]
>
> —Frederick E. Webster, Jr., Ph.D., Charles Henry Jones Third Century Professor of Management, Amos Tuck School of Business Administration, Dartmouth College

Lifetime Relationships with Consumers

"I feel that developing lifetime relationships with customers is truly the key to commerce in the 21st Century. We have tracked customers over their life points as a means of targeting the products and services needed at certain times i.e., home equity loans as children approach college age, investment products during peak earning years, etc. It is statistically proven the more products and services our customers hold, the better the likelihood they will stay with us."

—Randy Rossi, AVP, Business Banking Manager,
Southwest National Bank

If an organization elects to create value for its consumers, employees, and shareholders, it must develop close relationships with its consumers, as opposed to focusing on "making a sale." In order to develop these types of relationships, high levels of interdependence and collaboration are required between customers and suppliers (i.e., all exchange partners).[11] A high degree of trust is also a necessity.[12] As a result, transactions cannot be managed as separate discrete occurrences. Nor can they occur without a degree of loyalty among all involved parties.

Loyalty has three components to it. The first component is the loyalty that consumers have to supplier organizations. The second component is the loyalty the supplier organization has to its consumers. The final component is the resulting interaction between these two sets of loyalty behaviors. As practiced today, most marketing efforts tend to ignore the last two parts of the equation, resulting once again in a focus on the organization rather than the end user. To embrace a "customer loyalty" perspective, marketing efforts must shift away from a focus on "brand loyalty."

It would be impossible for organizations to develop deep, intimate relationships with every consumer they serve.[13] And the opposite is also true. Given that there are only 24 hours in a day and seven days in a week, consumers do not have the time or the energy to devote to numerous, time-consuming relationships. However, this implies that organizations need to cultivate lifetime relationships with those consumers who desire to enter into this type of relationship.

COMMONLY USED TOOLS AND METHODS

Some of the tools and methods needed to effect consumer obsession are only now in the process of being created and used in organizational settings. The authors of this book strongly disagree with those who suggest that current approaches are sufficient to simultaneously create value for consumers, employees, and shareholders and that it is just a matter of expanding the scope of quality and performance improvement initiatives to include value creation. The tools and methods covered in this section include innovation, competitive intelligence, relationship marketing, brand management, and non-traditional market research techniques.

Innovation

"A quality phrase that was very popular and still is very popular is 'listen to your customer.' That statement is not good enough . . . to compete in the world any longer. It might be good enough, in the short term, to make the customer happy but in the long term, it won't. . . . By the time your customer has told you what he wants, he has also told every one of your competitors. To a large extent, the customer, by the time they tell you what they want, isn't anticipating how far you have progressed in your capabilities to give them something that would put them far in front of their competitors. . . . Anticipating the needs of the end users is what that's all about. Let's go look at what people who actually use these products would do with this electronic capability and go provide that capability to our customers even before they have asked for it. Let's get that to them in a very, very fast period of time, and allow them to get a competitive advantage in the marketplace. Then customers not only are happy, they are almost in love with you. It generates relationships that are really partnerships, and not just coincidences that we're doing business together."[14]

—Thomas J. Engibous, President and CEO,
Texas Instruments Incorporated

How can organizations anticipate future consumer wants and needs? To involve the entire organization, marketing and research and development activities need to move out of the marketing/research and development functions and be integrated into the activities of all individuals who work for the enterprise. The organization also needs to employ a systematic, step-by-step approach to ferret out potential product/service, process, and/or system innovation opportunities, assess their potential, and ensure their development, as appropriate. Table 7.1 presents an overview of one approach to innovation inspired by the work of Dr. Noriaki Kano, Science University of Tokyo. This approach can be utilized by any group of employees within an organization.

Here, innovation is defined as "actions taken to satisfy latent (i.e., hidden) market wants and needs by actualizing new (i.e., not currently existing) product/service, system, or market options (i.e., using an existing product/service or system in a manner that is fundamentally different from what exists today)."[15] Employees do not need to be geniuses or innately creative to exhibit innovative behaviors. What is required is an organizational culture that expects, recognizes, and rewards, rather than punishes, assumption-breaking behaviors and a systematic approach to innovation.

Conduct Best-In-Class Benchmarking Studies

"Leveraging what others have learned means you don't have to reinvent the wheel. Some people opt for 'industrial tourism' instead of rigor. Consequently, they only get a small portion of the value."

—Ellen Bovarnick, Senior Vice President, Quality,
formerly of Florida Power & Light

Table 7.1

A Method for Innovation*

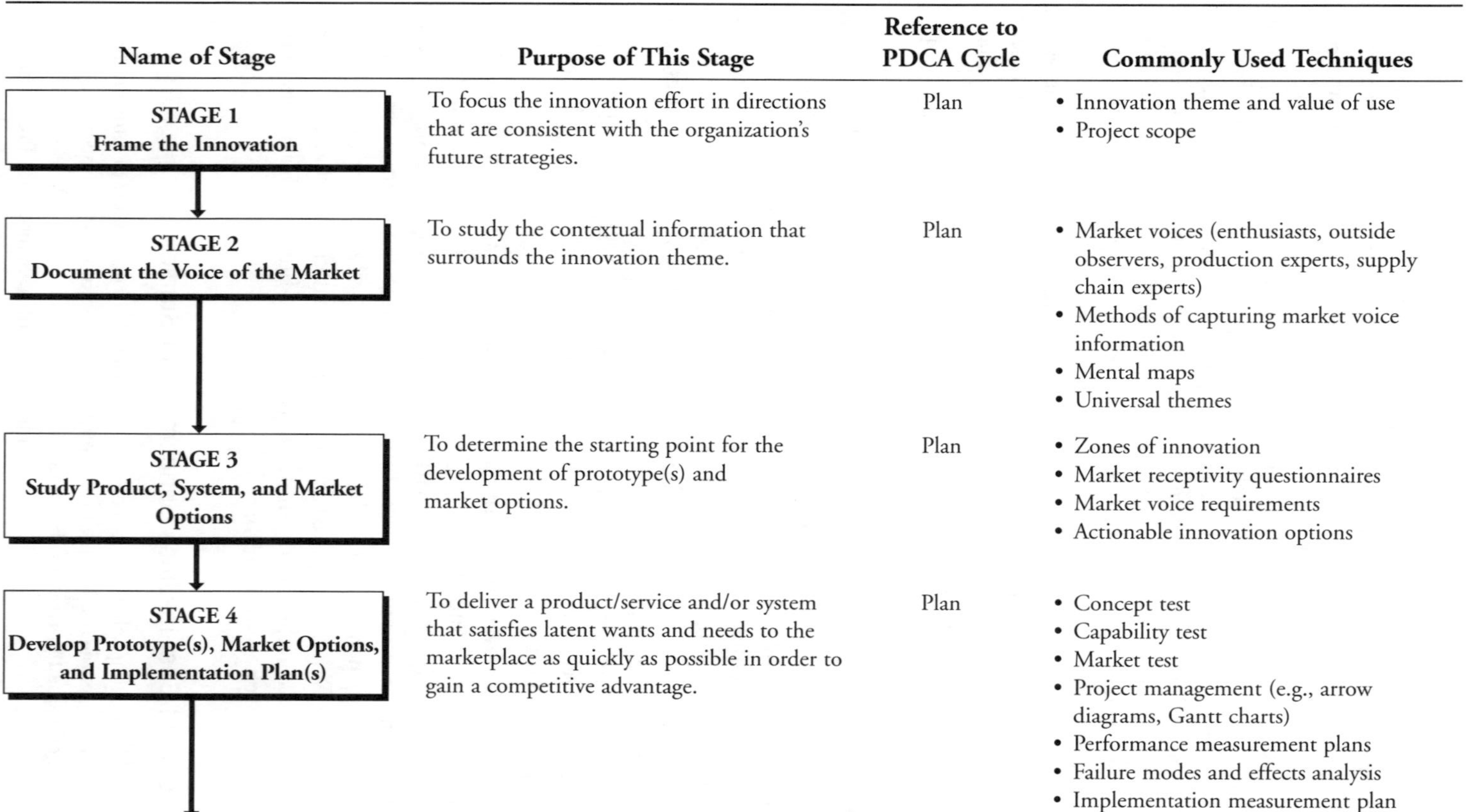

Name of Stage	Purpose of This Stage	Reference to PDCA Cycle	Commonly Used Techniques
STAGE 1 **Frame the Innovation**	To focus the innovation effort in directions that are consistent with the organization's future strategies.	Plan	• Innovation theme and value of use • Project scope
STAGE 2 **Document the Voice of the Market**	To study the contextual information that surrounds the innovation theme.	Plan	• Market voices (enthusiasts, outside observers, production experts, supply chain experts) • Methods of capturing market voice information • Mental maps • Universal themes
STAGE 3 **Study Product, System, and Market Options**	To determine the starting point for the development of prototype(s) and market options.	Plan	• Zones of innovation • Market receptivity questionnaires • Market voice requirements • Actionable innovation options
STAGE 4 **Develop Prototype(s), Market Options, and Implementation Plan(s)**	To deliver a product/service and/or system that satisfies latent wants and needs to the marketplace as quickly as possible in order to gain a competitive advantage.	Plan	• Concept test • Capability test • Market test • Project management (e.g., arrow diagrams, Gantt charts) • Performance measurement plans • Failure modes and effects analysis • Implementation measurement plan

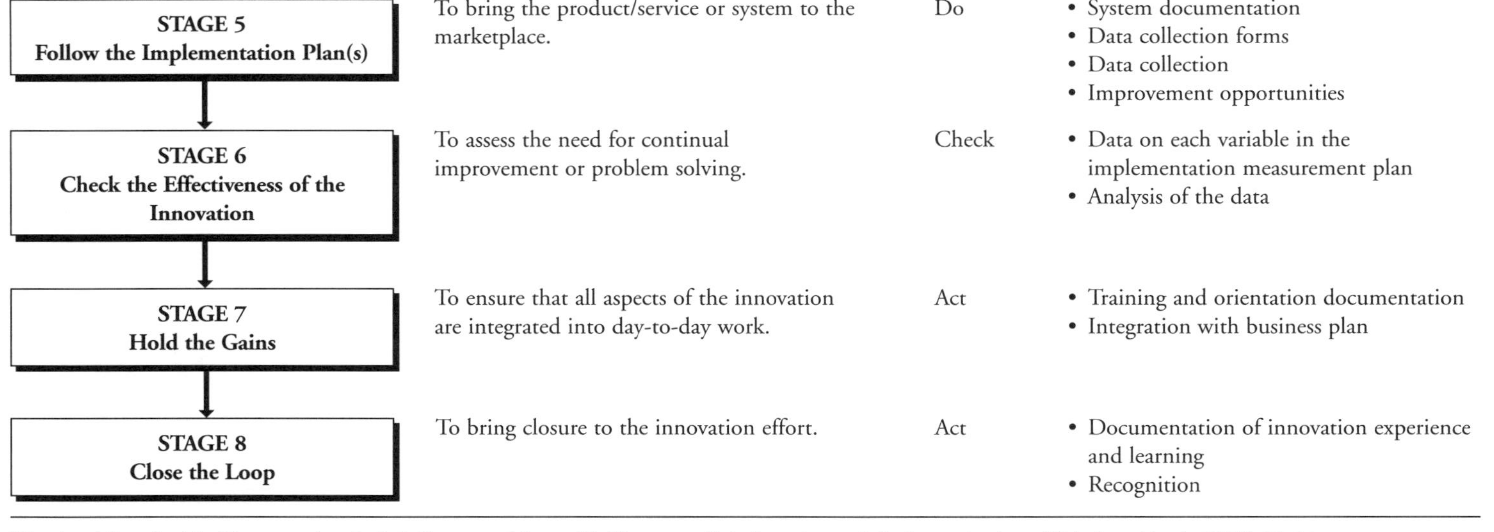

Stage	Purpose	PDCA	Outputs
STAGE 5 **Follow the Implementation Plan(s)**	To bring the product/service or system to the marketplace.	Do	• System documentation • Data collection forms • Data collection • Improvement opportunities
STAGE 6 **Check the Effectiveness of the Innovation**	To assess the need for continual improvement or problem solving.	Check	• Data on each variable in the implementation measurement plan • Analysis of the data
STAGE 7 **Hold the Gains**	To ensure that all aspects of the innovation are integrated into day-to-day work.	Act	• Training and orientation documentation • Integration with business plan
STAGE 8 **Close the Loop**	To bring closure to the innovation effort.	Act	• Documentation of innovation experience and learning • Recognition

*Reprinted from Lori L. Silverman, Annabeth L. Propst, and Steven N. Silverman, *Eight Stage Approach for Innovation* (unpublished workbook, 1995), 10–11.

Best-in-class benchmarking "looks across multiple industries in search of new, innovative practices, no matter what their source."[16] This approach identifies the best organization in a particular resource category (see Value Creation for a listing of resource categories), and studies not only its results (to get an indication of how good performance can be in that resource category) but also its methods (not for the purposes of copying them but in order to extract those ideas that might be applied or modified to fit with a firm's processes). For example, for a number of years, organizations benchmarked L. L. Bean's order fulfillment process because it could fill and ship all orders in less than 24 hours. This level of performance impacted two of the value creation resource areas—time (number of hours between the order and the receipt of the item) and problem solution (the need to wear a particular jacket on vacation). Once those who visited L. L. Bean returned to their work sites, the challenge became one of extracting principles and approaches to apply to the organization's processes that actually increased value for the organization, its customers, and its employees.

What is considered best in class today may not be tomorrow. Best-in-class benchmarking assumes that what is a latent want and need to an organization is something that is being done by another organization (albeit one that may be in a completely different industry). It also assumes that applying these ideas to another organization would provide increased value to that organization's consumers. This may not be the case.

Quality Function Deployment

As mentioned in chapter 5, Quality Function Deployment (QFD) has a role in the redesign of products and/or services that are already in existence, but need to be improved. It can also be practiced in innovation, for new product development, as demonstrated by companies such as Kodak and 3M. In the software industry, QFD has been used for new product development by AT&T, Digital Equipment Corporation, and Hewlett-Packard, and has led to shorter development times, better requirements, greater customer satisfaction, and improved designs.[17] Hughes Aircraft employed QFD in another innovation application—process and system innovation—developing a plan for creating a "factory of the future," a manufacturing facility to build microwave modules.[18]

Competitive Intelligence

"Competitive intelligence is a systematic program for gathering and analyzing information about your competitors' activities and general business trends to further your own company's goals."[19] From a value creation perspective, "competitors" are not just those firms that are in the same industry as your organization; they also include the referent alternatives used by the organization's consumers.

Although these types of systems are relatively new in the United States (i.e., less than 7 percent of large companies have a special division, with 80 percent less than five years old) Japanese firms have had them in place since World War II; they are used by government agencies in Europe (e.g., state-run German banks use them to protect assets); and emerging economies such as China, Vietnam, Korea, and Thailand view them as a means of winning economic wars against industrialized nations.[20] There are a number of reasons organizations are embracing competitive intelligence systems. They include the reduction in product cycles, the rapid pace and global nature of business, technology innovations, government and political changes, and the increased entry of new competitors into existing markets.

Where can competitive intelligence information be found? Information can be gained on the Web through home pages, help-wanted ads posted on sites such as CareerPath.com and the Monster Board, and information sources such as CEO Express (a comprehensive directory of links to major newspapers and trade magazines, customer news feeds, government agencies, and IPO alerts) and Deja News (a Web-based search engine that monitors Usenet discussion forums, tracking more than 50,000 different newsgroups).[21] Because this information is secondhand, it is available to everyone and may not be focused enough for an organization's specific purposes. Some of the best information is gained through conversation—by using one's personal network and by aggregating the knowledge of people in the organization (e.g., having them compare notes after a trade show or convention), checking local sources (e.g., through the community newspaper in the city where a firm is headquartered), and acquisition from fee-based proprietary information services (to increase the reliability of the information).

The raw data gained from these sources are not competitive intelligence. It is the synthesis and analysis of this information that turns it from data into usable information that can be used in strategic planning, innovation, and new product/service development.

Relationship Marketing

> "Home Depot stores . . . have determined that while a shopper spends only $38 on a single visit, the typical shopper visits the store 30 times a year. Throughout a lifetime, that typical customer will spend $25,000. The flip side of this equation is that alienating a Home Depot customer on his or her first visit would cost the store not $38, but $25,000."[22]

Relationship marketing is not a tool to employ as a means of attracting and retaining customers—what some call customer loyalty. It is an emerging strategy in the field of marketing that moves away from the transactional marketing paradigm (i.e., discrete, ad-hoc interactions) toward ongoing, long-term relationship exchange.[23,24] As a newly emerging marketing and business strategy, concepts and research on relationship marketing have only recently emerged—even though the term itself has been a part of the marketing academic literature since the early 1980s.

As a strategy, relationship marketing requires attention to a number of processes whose purpose is to attract and retain customers, and manage their expectations. These processes fall under the categories of business bonding, value bonding, and structural bonding.

- "Business bonding processes [are concerned with] quality (doing it right the first time), responsiveness (both speed and courtesy) to contacts and requests, and the competence and professionalism of those who directly or indirectly serve customers.
- "Value bonding processes [speak to those surrounding] mass customization, target costing (improving the price value to customers by reducing the cost of doing business), and proactive innovation.
- "Structural bonding processes [have to do with] front-line information systems (deployment of on-line information systems for front-line customer interface), [design of a] customer-oriented organization (teams and functions organized around customers and/or markets), customer-generated marketing (active involvement of customers in word of mouth, product design, and process improvement), and a customer retention culture (reward and recognition systems are anchored to customer retention and loyalty)."[25]

"Ironically, the very things that marketers are doing to build relationships are often the things that are destroying those relationships."[26] Some of these behaviors were covered in the Lifetime Relationships with Consumers section of this chapter and include consumers having to maintain numerous one-to-one relationships (e.g., frequent buyer programs), forgetting two parts of the loyalty equation (supplier loyalty to consumers and the interaction effect between loyalty to and from consumers), being preoccupied with "best" customers (i.e., those who spend the most dollars with the firm), and offering so many variations on a product that consumers are confused about what to purchase (e.g., toothpaste—whitening, fluoride, sensitive teeth, with baking soda, speckles that don't do anything, flavors, etc.). To obtain the full benefits of this approach, companies need to reflect more on how they are using relationship marketing, fully understand the theory underlying its practice (i.e., loyalty, trust, interdependence, and cooperation), and employ these principles in their push to cultivate more intimate customer relationships.

> "[A] close look suggests that relationships between companies and consumers are troubled at best. When we talk to people about their lives as consumers . . . we hear about the confusing, stressful, insensitive, and manipulative marketplace in which they feel trapped and victimized. Companies may delight in learning more about their customers than ever before and in providing features and services to please every palate. But customers delight in neither. . . . They tolerate sales clerks who hound them with questions every time they buy a battery. . . . They deal with the glut of new features in their computers and cameras. They juggle the flood of invitations to participate in frequent-buyer award programs. Customer satisfaction rates in the United States are at an all-time low, while com-

plaints, boycotts, and other expressions of consumer discontent rise. This mounting wave of unhappiness has yet to reach the bottom line. Sooner or later, however, corporate performance will suffer unless relationship marketing becomes what it is supposed to be: the epitome of customer orientation."[27]

—Susan Fournier, Ph.D., Assistant Professor, Harvard Business School; Susan Dobscha, Ph.D., Assistant Professor, Bentley College; David Glen Mick, Ph.D., Associate Professor, University of Wisconsin–Madison

Brand Management

"The average American supermarket is stuffed with 30,000 different items. Since 1980, the number of products launched each year has tripled; in 1996 alone, companies introduced some 17,000 new products. For sellers, this reality is daunting: How do I stand out?"[28]

Brand management has been around for more than 100 years. It encompasses broad topics such as brand equity, brand meaning, brand marketing, and brand strategy. As consumers become more sophisticated and organizational growth becomes more difficult, organizations cannot ignore that brand management can bring a distinct, long-term competitive advantage in all marketplaces (including high-tech firms). However, the challenge in this work is that the focus of all activities must remain on the consumer, not the brand. "The truth is, what makes a brand powerful is the emotional involvement of customers."[29] This level of emotional involvement, developed through a history of brand interactions, includes a strong expression of emotional attachment to, and the feeling that one is vested personally in, the brand's success.

Brand audits are one method for uncovering the range of emotions and images consumers associate with brands.[30] These audits should be conducted with organizational leadership as well as with consumers in order for informed, brand-related decision making to occur. Techniques such as those mentioned in the Non-Traditional Market Research Techniques section found later in this chapter are also being used to measure the feelings and beliefs associated with a particular brand. As the marketplace continues to change more rapidly each day, the outcomes of this type of research will be important to innovation initiatives and the repositioning of current offerings.

"We did a study in conjunction with our local newspaper about first name recognition. A marketing firm contacted the total circulation, which covers over 50% of the residents in our market area. The results showed that a high percentage gave our name when asked to cite the first bank they thought of. That was a good indication of how our image/name faired in the minds of the general public. The questions that followed were critical. If recognition is so strong, why isn't our market share higher? How do you leverage the data into a powerful marketing strategy? Is there something that prevents people from banking with us?"

—Randy Rossi, AVP, Business Banking Manager, Southwest National Bank

Brand Meaning

If one assumes that a brand is a bundle of jointly created and jointly held meaning, then it becomes imperative to create a language surrounding the brand that is well-formulated, shared, and understood from the perspectives of both the organization and the consumer.[31] This suggests that the symbolic nature of language is a critical issue for managers and those who provide offerings directly to consumers. However, consumers are becoming more pessimistic and confused as the perceived uncertainty and risk associated with the purchase process and the number of purchase choices increase for a specific offering. These consumer trends will make it difficult for organizations to entice consumers to give over the cognitive resources necessary to learn about the languages and symbols they associate with a variety of brands. Yet without this information, organizations will not be able to develop unique brand positioning, or what some call "brand culture"[32] to ensure growth and competitive advantage for the future.

> "There is a movement under way to develop a 'Quality-Brand India' so that anyone will immediately recognize products made in India."
>
> —Navin S. Dedhia, Chair, International Chapter, American Society for Quality

Non-Traditional Market Research Techniques

> "Let's face it: problem-focused research studies and runaway numbers crunching are misleading. They are not designed to reveal . . . consumer discontent . . . and in fact, they may get in the way of such insights. Isolated readings of the sugar content in cereal or the readability of digital displays tell us nothing about despairing customers and the role that marketing policies play in exacerbating their discontent. To get inside people's heads, marketers need to turn to the tools of ethnography and phenomenology: qualitative social-science methods dedicated to richly describing and interpreting people's lives."[33]
>
> —Susan Fournier, Ph.D., Assistant Professor, Harvard Business School;
> Susan Dobscha, Ph.D., Assistant Professor, Bentley College;
> David Glen Mick, Ph.D., Associate Professor,
> University of Wisconsin–Madison

Traditional marketing research methodologies, such as surveys, sampling techniques, and field and laboratory designs need to be fundamentally rethought because they do not unveil the depth of consumer experience necessary for innovative product and service design.[34,35] These methodologies often permit researchers to be way too conspicuous in the research process and do not allow them to get inside the heads and hearts of consumers to figure out how what the organization provides to them intertwines with and adds to consumers' overall life satisfaction.

What types of techniques would allow organizations to gain the required level of understanding? The techniques being put forth (some as early as the 1950s) come out of the fields of sociology and anthropology. They include storytelling, photography, videotaping, metaphors through visual imagery (e.g., Zaltman Metaphor Elicitation Technique[36,37]), personal life histories, case studies, and other observational and interpretive techniques. The use of these techniques forces employees to observe how their firms' consumers interact with what is provided to them and to participate with consumers in daily activities where they use the firms' offerings. As importantly, these non-traditional market research techniques acknowledge that thoughts arise from images, not words; that most communication is nonverbal; that the use of metaphor is effective at revealing thoughts and feelings; that emotion and reason are equally important in decision making; that most thought, emotion, and learning occur unconsciously; and that mental models significantly impact an individual's thought processes.[38]

Simply using these non-traditional techniques is not enough because organizations can fall into the same dilemma that is occurring today with relationship marketing. Organizational members and their leaders need to be familiar with the theories that underlie these techniques—theories that come out of the fields of psychology, communications, philosophy, and other disciplines in the social sciences. In addition, employing these non-traditional techniques does not erase the need to more fully utilize existing sources of internal and third-party-generated (e.g., demographics, Internet chat groups, etc.) consumer data as a means of anticipating future customer wants and needs.

WHO IS INVOLVED IN THE CONSUMER OBSESSION FIELD OF PERFORMANCE PRACTICE

In the Consumer Obsession Field of Performance Practice, every member of the organization has a role in anticipating the future wants and needs of the organization's current and future consumers. This role is in addition to the members' role in continually clarifying the wants and needs that exist for those consumers who already have a relationship with the enterprise. Members of the organization's supply chain also have a responsibility to collect, synthesize, analyze, and report customer-related information to the organization as a means of benefiting all involved parties. Because relationships are two-way streets, all exchange partners have some level of obligation to each other, if they desire to engage in an intimate, long-term relationship.

SHORTCOMINGS WITH THE CONSUMER OBSESSION FIELD OF PERFORMANCE PRACTICE

One major contribution of the Consumer Obsession Field of Performance Practice is the need to anticipate what will bring value to consumers (some of whom may not even be known today) by uncovering latent (i.e., hidden) market wants and

Table 7.2

Your Organization and the Consumer Obsession Field of Performance Practice

Directions: Record the activities your organization has and has not engaged in relative to the concepts, tools, and methods referenced in this field of performance practice, noting the degree of deployment of each item. Also document its future plans for deploying these concepts, tools, and methods throughout the enterprise.

Purpose: To promote long-term survival of the organization		**Desired Outcomes:** • Create value for consumers • Create value for employees • Create value for shareholders		
	What Your Organization Is Doing	**What Your Organization Is Not Doing**	**Degree of Deployment***	**Plans Your Organization Has for the Future**
Underlying Concepts • Value creation • Organizational renewal • Mass customization • Lifetime relationships with consumers			 1 2 3 4 5 1 2 3 4 5 1 2 3 4 5 1 2 3 4 5	
Commonly Used Tools and Methods • Innovation • Competitive intelligence • Relationship marketing • Brand management • Non-traditional market research techniques			 1 2 3 4 5 1 2 3 4 5 1 2 3 4 5 1 2 3 4 5 1 2 3 4 5	

* Rating system: 1 = no systematic deployment is evident
2 = some deployment is evident with little or no results
3 = deployment is evident in several areas of the business with limited results
4 = deployment is evident in major portions of the business with measurable results
5 = full organization-wide deployment is evident with significant measurable results

Table 7.3

CHAOS and the Consumer Obsession Field of Performance Practice

Directions: Note your thoughts on the future impact that the forces of **CHAOS** may have on each of the underlying concepts and the commonly used tools and methods in the Consumer Obsession Field of Performance Practice.

CHAOS / **Underlying Concepts**	**Changing Definition of Work and the Workplace**	**Heightened Social Responsibility**	**Aging Baby Boomers**	**Overarching Demographic Change**	**Strategic Growth Through Technology and Innovation**
• Value creation					
• Organizational renewal					
• Mass customization					
• Lifetime relationships with consumers					
Commonly Used Tools and Methods					
• Innovation					
• Competitive intelligence					
• Relationship marketing					
• Brand management					
• Non-traditional market research techniques					

needs—and translating these latent wants and needs into offerings that will bring value to them. This is a significant move beyond customer responsiveness (Quality Assurance) and customer focus (Problem Resolution, and Alignment and Integration). Because of its external focus—its introduction of a systematic approach to innovation, and its emphasis on latent market wants and needs—this field addresses the shortcomings that arose from the Alignment and Integration Field of Performance Practice. It broadens the scope of the integration definition provided in chapter 6 by suggesting that value creation–based philosophies, concepts, tools, methods, and strategies also need to be deployed across and throughout the organization's work processes and employees' behaviors.

Because this field of practice is still emerging, it is difficult to determine what might be its potential limitations. There are, however, a number of issues that still need to be resolved. Foremost, the required techniques are not fully fleshed out. In some cases they are rudimentary or even nonexistent. Perhaps because of this, in practice, individuals and their organizations are skimming over the concepts, tools, and methods and not recognizing "consumer obsession" as different from "customer focus." They think they are already doing "it," so the various aspects of Consumer Obsession (i.e., relationship marketing, mass customization, and innovation) are not given the depth of attention they merit. In this performance practice, an "either/or" mindset still predominates over a "both/and" mindset. Managing paradoxes as commonplace events is still not fully grasped by all employees and thus limits the choices available to enterprises when they engage in ongoing renewal. While externally focused, this field lacks an appreciation for and understanding of the connectedness between all living things. It is this last issue—one of many catalysts—that is spurring the emergence of the fifth star in The Starburst Model™, the Spiritual Awakening Field of Performance Practice.

Endnotes

1. John Guaspari, "The Next Big Thing," *Across the Board* (March 1998), 20.
2. John Guaspari, "Quality Is Not a Way of Life," *Across the Board* (November–December 1997), 46.
3. C. Whan Park, Deborah MacInnis, Steven Silverman, and Bernard Jaworski, "A Value-Based Conceptual Framework Linking the Marketing Mix and Marketplace Exchange" (unpublished working paper, January 1998), 4, 7.
4. Bob Galvin as quoted in Bill Ginnodo, "Leading Change: A Conversation with Motorola's Bob Galvin," *Quality Digest* (November 1997), 34.
5. Sumantra Ghoshal and Christopher A. Bartlett, *The Individualized Corporation: A Fundamentally New Approach to Management* (New York: HarperCollins, 1997), 134–135.
6. Donald C. Hambrick, David A. Nadler, and Michael L. Tushman, *Navigating Change: How CEOs, Top Teams, and Boards Steer Transformation* (Boston: Harvard Business School Press, 1998), 7–8.

7. Frederick E. Webster, Jr., *Market-Driven Management: Using the New Marketing Concept to Create a Customer-Oriented Company* (New York: John Wiley & Sons, Inc., 1994), 259.

8. James H. Gilmore and B. Joseph Pine II, "The Four Faces of Mass Customization," *Harvard Business Review"* (January–February 1997), 92–94.

9. Edward Feitzinger and Hau L. Lee, "Mass Customization at Hewlett-Packard: The Power of Postponement," *Harvard Business Review* (January–February 1997), 116.

10. Webster, Jr., *Market-Driven Management: Using the New Marketing Concept to Create a Customer-Oriented Company,* 263.

11. Jagdish N. Sheth, "Relationship Marketing: A New School of Marketing Thought" (presentation handouts, University of Pittsburgh, April 1994), 3.

12. Leonard L. Berry, "Relationship Marketing of Services—Growing Interest, Emerging Perspective," *Journal of the Academy of Marketing Science,* Vol. 23, No. 4 (1995), 242.

13. Susan Fournier, Susan Dobscha, and David Glen Mick, "Preventing the Premature Death of Relationship Marketing," *Harvard Business Review* (January–February 1998), 49.

14. Brad Stratton, "TI Has Eye on Alignment," *Quality Progress* (October 1997), 28.

15. Lori L. Silverman, Annabeth L. Propst, and Steven N. Silverman, *Eight Stage Approach for Innovation* (unpublished workbook, 1995), 3.

16. Kathleen H. J. Leibfried and C. J. McNair, CMA, *Benchmarking: A Tool for Continuous Improvement* (New York: HarperCollins Publishers, Inc., 1992), 30.

17. Richard E. Zultner, "Software Quality Function Deployment: The First Five Years—Lessons Learned," *Proceedings of the 48th Annual Quality Congress* (Milwaukee: American Society for Quality Control, May 1994), 783.

18. Peter L. Bersbach and Philip R. Wahl, "QFD on a Defense Contract," *Proceedings of the 44th Annual Quality Congress* (Milwaukee: American Society for Quality Control, May 1990), 413.

19. Larry Kahaner, *Competitive Intelligence: How to Gather, Analyze, and Use Information to Move Your Business to the Top* (New York: Simon & Schuster, 1996), 16.

20. Kahaner, *Competitive Intelligence: How to Gather, Analyze, and Use Information to Move Your Business to the Top,* 16–17.

21. Chris Pyle, "Competitive Intelligence—Get Smart!" *Fast Company* (April–May 1998), 268–279.

22. Gilbert A. Churchill, Jr., and J. Paul Peter, *Marketing: Creating Value for Customers* (Burr Ridge, IL: Richard D. Irwin, Inc., 1995), 389.

23. Barnett A. Greenberg and Fuan Li, "Relationship Marketing: A Tactic, a Strategic Choice, or a Paradigm," *1998 AMA Winter Educators' Conference Proceedings,* Volume 9 (Chicago: American Marketing Association, 1998), 211.

24. Ravindranath Madhavan, Reshma H. Shah, and Rajiv Grover, "Motivations for and Theoretical Foundations of Relationship Marketing," *1994 AMA Winter Educators' Conference Proceedings,* Volume 5 (Chicago: American Marketing Association, 1994), 183.

25. Sheth, "Relationship Marketing: A New School of Marketing Thought," 17–19.

26. Fournier, Dobscha, and Mick, "Preventing the Premature Death of Relationship Marketing," 44.

27. Fournier, Dobscha, and Mick, "Preventing the Premature Death of Relationship Marketing," 43–44.
28. Daniel H. Pink, "Metaphor Marketing," *Fast Company* (April–May 1998), 216.
29. Charlotte Beers, "Building Brands Worthy of Devotion," *Leader to Leader* (Winter 1998), 39.
30. Beers, "Building Brands Worthy of Devotion," 29.
31. Steven N. Silverman and David E. Sprott, "Brands and Consumer Experience: A Multi-Method Approach for Studying Consumer-Based Brand Meaning" (unpublished working paper, October 1997), 2.
32. Jean-Marie Dru and Robin Lemberg, "Disrupt Your Business," *Journal of Business Strategy* (May–June 1997), 24.
33. Fournier, Dobscha, and Mick, "Preventing the Premature Death of Relationship Marketing," 44.
34. Gerald Zaltman, "Rethinking Market Research: Putting People Back In," *Journal of Marketing Research* (November 1997), 424.
35. Fournier, Dobscha, and Mick, "Preventing the Premature Death of Relationship Marketing," 50.
36. Gerald Zaltman and Robin A. Higie, "Seeing the Voice of the Customer: The Zaltman Metaphor Elicitation Technique," Working Paper (Report No. 93-114) (Cambridge, MA: Marketing Science Institute, 1993).
37. Zaltman, "Rethinking Market Research: Putting People Back In," 428–432.
38. Zaltman, "Rethinking Market Research: Putting People Back In," 424–428.

CHAPTER 8

The Spiritual Awakening Field of Performance Practice

This chapter overviews the fifth star in The Starburst Model™, the Spiritual Awakening Field of Performance Practice. In this field, the word *spiritual* means "the greater self and all-that-is are blended into a balanced whole, and in this way the concept of being that is the fundamental and sacred spring of life is given voice and being for all."[1] This use of the word *spiritual* comes from American Indian literature and is not synonymous with "religion." If, as the American Indian people believe, breath is life, then the purpose of a good life is the intermingling of all breaths within the universe—a profound recognition of universal interdependency. The achievement of harmony and balance, a keen awareness that all of life is living and imbued with spirit, and an acknowledgment that all things are sacred and of equal value are all principles inherent in this definition.

The challenge the use of the term *spiritual* brings forth is the relationship between both individual and organizational spirit and improved organizational performance. It has been only since the late 1980s that a few organizations in the United States have become aware of the need to allow spirit to be recognized in the workplace. Some enterprises in other countries moved to this level of consciousness sooner because of their cultures and belief systems. Thus, the use of the word *awakening* implies a level of activity that is a step or more above slumber.

How did this field of performance practice come to be included in a book on the future of quality in organizational performance? Go back to chapter 1, Living in the Workplace of the Future. In this chapter, it was suggested that the Knowledge Economy (or Information Age) is giving way to the Dream Society (or Existential Era), where it is suggested that intellectual capital will be replaced as the currency of the future by the ability to tell stories that produce "dreams" for public consumption.[2] Add to this the changing nature of work and the workplace—new employment contracts, a new definition of work, more inclusive organizational designs, a heightened push for organizations to be socially responsible and accountable, and changing demographics (i.e., aging baby boomers, increasing numbers of women and minorities in the workforce)—bringing about a different set of personal values and principles. These changes suggest that a fundamental transformation, albeit unspoken, may be taking place in what is truly important to individuals and to organizations. For individuals, this shift is visible today with the proliferation of self-improvement and self-actualization books and courses, and the attention being paid to the importance of self assessment and reflection. For organizations, this shift is embodied in the move to align their strategies, work, and people with broad-based corporate values. It is also displayed in the media attention given to unethical business practices and the public backlash against environmentally unfriendly behaviors.

> "With the 40-something generation searching for soul, self, and meaning wherever it can find them, the workplace is not out of bounds. Connecticut psychiatrist M. Scott Peck, author of *The Road Less Traveled* and *A World Waiting to be Born,* sees no reason why a spiritual rebirth couldn't or shouldn't happen in the workplace as easily as the church. It is, after all, where most people spend most of their time."[3]

The purpose of the Spiritual Awakening Field of Performance Practice is service to society. This change in focus is significant. Until this point, the earlier fields concentrated on a portion of the enterprise (Quality Assurance and Problem Resolution), or the entire organization, including its customers and its supply chain (Alignment and Integration and Consumer Obsession). Here, the purpose focuses on a higher-order value. The outcomes of this field of performance practice are to improve life for everyone on the planet and to manage the planet as a system. They are much broader in scope than those in the previous fields of performance practice and are an extension of a whole systems or living systems perspective, where everything is seen as interconnected. As such, these outcomes also have a purpose. This purpose serves as the umbrella under which the purposes and outcomes of the previous four fields need to be achieved.

The World Business Academy, developed out of work begun in the 1970s at the Stanford Research Institute, was "founded with the conviction that business, the most powerful institution in our culture today, must 'assume responsibility for the whole.'"[4] In 1998, it consisted of nearly 50 Fellows and 500 members from companies throughout the world, and communicates its message through conferences and the journal, *Perspectives on Business and Global Change* (published through Berrett-Koehler). Richard Barrett, president of Richard Barrett and Associates and formerly the values coordinator at the World Bank in Washington, D.C., suggests that three crises are driving this revolution to higher values: (1) the ecological and environmental destruction of the planet, (2) the growing inequalities between the rich and poor nations, and (3) the rising tide of the unemployed, the combined effect of which will be "a growing recognition that corporations exist to serve society, and not the other way round. . . . We will see that we are totally interconnected and that the planet is our precious life support system."[5]

Not many organizations are fully convinced that it makes good business sense to attend to the needs of society as a whole and those of the planet at large. Some go so far as to suggest that no organization does anything without its self-interest as the primary concern. The three organizations discussed in the Heightened Social Responsibility section of chapter 1—Tom's of Maine, Ben & Jerry's, and The Body Shop—are examples of firms who put societal needs and issues at the forefront of their businesses because it is "the right thing to do." While the bulk of organizations have yet to accept this more lofty ideal, a few have embraced it fully, finding that success lies not in serving investors alone, but also in providing for the needs of employees, customers, the environment, and the communities within which they do business.

> "When I was named head coach of the Chicago Bulls in 1989, my dream was not just to win championships, but to do it in a way that wove together my two greatest passions: Basketball and spiritual exploration. On the surface this may sound like a crazy idea, but intuitively I sensed that there was a link between spirit and sport. . . . The day I took over the Bulls, I vowed to create an environment based on the principles of selflessness and compassion I'd learned as a Christian in my parents' home; sitting on a cushion practicing Zen; and studying the teachings of the Lakota Sioux. . . . [W]orking with the Bulls I've learned that the most effective way to forge a winning team is to call on the players' need to connect with something larger than themselves. Even for those who don't consider themselves 'spiritual' in a conventional sense, creating a successful team—whether it's an NBA champion or a record-setting sales force—is essentially a spiritual act. It requires the individuals involved to surrender their self-interest for the greater good so that the whole adds up to more than the sum of its parts."[6]
>
> —Phil Jackson and Hugh Delehanty, authors of *Sacred Hoops: Spiritual Lessons of a Hardwood Warrior*

The purpose and outcomes of this field suggest that, for organizations to be truly productive, they have to create within themselves a sense of spirit and commitment to something greater. Does this imply that attention to profitability, value, and quality become unimportant? Not at all. The implication is that by attending first to a higher-order good—service to society—organizations will be able to reap additional benefits. This thinking is no different than that offered by Dr. Deming in the 1980s when he suggested that, by addressing product and service quality, organizations could attain higher levels of profitability. If one projects forward, assuming that a number of organizations within an industry are fully using the first four fields of performance practice, then the question arises of how to differentiate an organization from its competitors in the eyes of its customers. Perhaps this field of performance practice provides the answer.

The purpose and outcomes also suggest that individually, people can bring their bodies, minds, hearts, and souls—their entire self—into the workplace. For organizations, this hints that they, too, may have bodies (e.g., their structure), minds (e.g., their work processes and systems), hearts (e.g., the relationships developed and nurtured internally and externally), and souls (e.g., their higher-order purpose, and overarching values and principles). This sort of contemplation is awkward for organizations because it brings with it a fear of the unknown and a need to converse about topics that are currently taboo.

UNDERLYING CONCEPTS

Given what is known today, the concepts that underlie The Spiritual Awakening Field of Performance Practice are spirituality, organization as community, and social responsibility and accountability. Two of these concepts—organization as community, and social responsibility and accountability—are also explored in chapter 1, Living in the Workplace of the Future.

Spirituality

> "The most important impact quality can make is on the restoration of the individual through his/her own hands—through a deep-seated theory of life. We need to make people better people to be better employees."
>
> —Howard Gitlow, Ph.D., Professor of Management Science, School of Business Administration, University of Miami

Think back to high school or college. Hear the school song being played and sung. Remember what it was like to participate in a pep rally. Visualize the school's insignia, its colors, and its mascot. Recall what you wore to social and sporting events. For many, high school was their first experience of "spirit" and its resulting sense of enthusiasm and oneness. School spirit often extends beyond the boundaries of the organization to include the community at large. Thus, the energy created at the school's epicenter is perpetuated through its influence on others.

Is this same sense of spirit appropriate in the workplace? What about the definition of *spiritual* provided earlier? It suggests that because everything in the universe is "blended together into a balanced whole," each person has an obligation to attend to a higher-order purpose in life. For some, this is not a matter of whether it is applicable to organizational performance. Rather, it is a question of how it influences performance. Since the early 1990s, several books have been written about the influence of the spiritual on leadership practices and organizational performance. Within the context of business, these books also collectively engage in discussions about the meaning of life, and the role of the soul and spirituality in the workplace. They include those written by Lee G. Bolman and Terrence E. Deal (*Leading with Soul: An Uncommon Journey of Spirit*), Allan Briskin (*The Stirring of Soul in the Workplace*), James Autry (*Life and Work: A Manager's Search for Meaning*), Michael Novak (*Business as a Calling: Work and the Examined Life*), Thomas

H. Naylor (*The Search for Meaning in the Workplace*), and David Whyte (*The Heart Aroused: Poetry and the Preservation of the Soul in Corporate America*).

Stop for a minute and ponder some of the ways in which leading organizations have introduced spirit into their work environment. Since the early 1990s, organizations such as AT&T, Shell Oil, Deloitte & Touche, and Boeing have employed poet David Whyte. At Boeing, 500 top managers listened to Whyte three days a month for a year to help them think more creatively about the company and their lives.[7] The World Bank has a Spiritual Unfoldment Society started by Richard Barrett in 1993. The society meets weekly to discuss spiritual topics, drawing upwards of several hundred people from the organization and from nearby companies.[8] Craig and Patricia Neal run the Heartland Institute and the Conscious Business Alliance, both of which help individuals (from firms such as Chevron, Levi Strauss, 3M, Pitney Bowes, and Pillsbury) and companies discover purpose and meaning in the workplace.[9] Dave Hanson, vice president of Land O'Lakes Fluid Dairy Division, used the theme "We Care" while managing the Food Ingredient Division to help it become the company's most profitable; he now frequently meets with other departments that share spiritual values, or at least care about people and finding meaning in work.[10] Max DePree, chairman of Herman Miller, has embraced the leader as servant model, originally put forth by Robert Greenleaf, whereby a leader exists only to serve his or her followers (refer to chapter 11 for an explanation of this approach).[11] Perhaps these individuals and organizations see a link between spirituality and organizational performance.

> "The team room at the Sheri L. Berto Center is . . . a sacred space adorned with Native American totems and other symbolic objects. . . . On one wall hangs a wooden arrow with a tobacco pouch tied to it—the Lakota Sioux symbol of prayer—and on another a bear claw necklace, which, I'm told, conveys power and wisdom upon its beholder. The room also contains the middle feather of an owl (for balance and harmony); a painting that tells the story of the great mystical warrior, Crazy Horse; and photos of a white buffalo calf born in Wisconsin. To the Sioux, the white buffalo is the most sacred of animals, a symbol of prosperity and fortune. . . . This is the room where the spirit of the team takes form."[12]
>
> —Phil Jackson and Hugh Delehanty, authors of
> *Sacred Hoops: Spiritual Lessons of a Hardwood Warrior*

As an organizing principle, Diana Whitney, founder of The Taos Institute, asserts that spirit and its relationship to business, our work lives, and organizational development can be clustered into four areas: Spirit as energy, spirit as meaning, spirit as sacred, and spirit as epistemology.[13] Spirit as energy encompasses the "energy" or "feel" of the workplace. Think about what feelings are engendered as a result of walking into an unfamiliar organization. It is not unusual to get a sense of the enterprise—its level of stress and tension, its level of warmth and receptivity, its overall mood. Spirit as energy also acknowledges the circular nature of life and work. Additionally, it addresses forms of enterprise-wide transformation that focus on removing the blocks to high performance and the flow of energy in the organization. This type of energy, or spirit, at work can result from celebrations, such as promotions and team accomplishments; events that include play, such as birthday parties, picnics, and training sessions; spontaneous humor and laughter; and the appropriate urgency to accomplish critical tasks and objectives. It can also arise when people are allowed to release their personal energy to fully apply what they know, suggesting the importance of job fit and personal development.

Spirit as meaning speaks to those elements of ideology (shared vision and values) that provide the catalyst for change. Within this context, leaders must inspire their workforce to engage in transformation through stories that provide symbolic meaning for organizational members. Speeches and presentations become defining moments for those leaders who give them. In addition, employees are more apt to change if they are provided with meaningful work that engages their mind, body, heart, and soul. Spirit as meaning is also displayed through strategic planning activities and use of the organization's corporate identity (i.e., logo, tag line, image) on items such as mugs, T-shirts, jackets, newsletters, and reports.

Spirit as sacred implies that all of life is permeated with a divine spiritual presence—one that is integral to the quality of all beings—and that there is a connection and interdependence between all life and all forms of energy—the notion of wholeness. This type of spirit is a common part of Native American and Buddhist belief systems. However, because of its reference to the divine, it can be a particularly uncomfortable topic to speak about in organizational settings, yet its presence is real. It displays itself through the belief that relationships are the center of social organization—and as such, they must be honored and people must be treated as sacred. Thus, it becomes necessary for leaders to demonstrate respect by fully sharing information. Doing so allows people and the situation to stay or become whole, rather than fragmented or disconnected. This is also true of improvement feedback that is not given or given in a disrespectful manner. In addition, the tension that results from moving from the "old way" to the "new way" of doing things (i.e., procedures, policies) often touches at what is considered sacred.

Spirit as epistemology recognizes the existence of spirit(s) beyond the three-dimensional world, which are invited to communicate through rituals and ceremonies. Here it is acknowledged that knowledge can be gained through spiritual relationships and intuition. This type of spirit attends to cooperation with the forces of nature and encourages communities and organizations to be constructed in harmony with spirit. Individuals who have knowledge of the founder(s) of the organization, acts of heroism, and critical parts of an organization's history provide the touchstones for this to occur. Some leaders and/or consultants who are hired to "heal" the organization (e.g., bring it back from the brink of moral or financial bankruptcy) often play the role described here. Those whose advice is most sought within the organization, independent of their formal roles, are also key to spirit as epistemology.

> "Get used to it. Spirituality is creeping into the office. Having survived downsizing and reengineering, overworked employees are stealing a moment and ask-

ing: 'What does all this mean? Why do I feel so unfulfilled?' And companies are turning inward in search of a 'soul' as a way to foster creativity and motivate leaders. . . . It's not about bringing religion into the office or requiring that employees chant mantras at their workstations. Rather the spirituality movement in the corporation is an attempt to create a sense of meaning and purpose at work and a connection between the company and its people."[14]

The key question that continues to arise from the application of these four spirituality areas to organizational life is, "What do they have to do with improving organizational performance?" Imagine an organization that does not demonstrate the behaviors outlined above. What would it be like to work in such an environment over an extended period of time? How effective would people be at getting the work done, at engaging in meaningful interactions with each other, or at creating value for the organization's consumers? Do your responses touch on the absence of productivity, creativity, or other aspects of performance? If so, then the key question has been answered.

The concept of spirituality provides the impetus for an organization and its members to serve society (the overall purpose of this field) and the rationale for attending to the larger whole—society at large and the Earth as a planet. An in-depth understanding of and appreciation for this concept and each of its four facets can serve as a guide for the tools and methods used in all five fields of performance practice to achieve their respective outcomes.

"[Richard] Barrett is preaching the gospel of spirituality in the workplace—but with a difference. Where others earnestly emphasize the human element in work, Barrett speaks the language of pragmatism: He offers a quantifiable approach to measuring the alignment between organizational and individual beliefs. His premise is simple: People and companies do well, financially and otherwise, to the degree that their interests match their values. To create that alignment, you have to see it. And to see it, you have to find a way to measure it. Barrett has a way to measure that alignment—and a vision for improving it."[15]

Organization as Community

"Instead of merely giving students a place to live, Chadbourne [Residential College, a residence hall on the University of Wisconsin–Madison campus] gives them a place . . . to form a *community.* 'What are you interested in?' it asks. . . . And 'Would you like to help with this?' . . . Bill Cronon '76, the faculty director . . . thinks the most important thing about Chadbourne is '. . . what it's like to live in a community, and what it's like to lead—to have an idea, to imagine what it would be like to realize that idea, and to persuade other people to join you in it.' . . . The fall semester of 1997 saw 238 activities attended by 10,563 students. Faculty or staff visits numbered 361."[16]

Chapter 1 introduced the concept of community as one type of organizational structure. Before exploring how it might play out in organizational settings, it is important to define it as a general concept. In researching material for their book, *Creating Community Anywhere: Finding Support and Connections in a Fragmented World,* Carolyn Schaffer and Kristin Anundsen discovered that "[c]ommunity is a dynamic whole that emerges when a group of people

- "participate in common practices;
- "depend on one another;
- "make decisions together;
- "identify themselves as part of something larger than the sum of their individual relationships; and
- "commit themselves for the long term to their own, one another's, and the group's well-being."[17]

This definition does not identify the scope of community by geography, duration, or relationship structure, suggesting, instead, a more robust definition.

> "If the 'soul' (i.e., the new trend in business) blossoms in community, and the current nature of organizations is not to hang on to people, do we redefine community as something that is neither geography or time bound? Or do we say we can't really have community because no one has security or commitment? Or, as the literature on professionals indicates, that our allegiance needs to be to our profession (i.e., engineering, consulting, quality, training, etc.) so it doesn't matter what organization we work in? Perhaps we believe that because we have eliminated geography as a qualifier (as in cyber-community), we can now use intensity of feeling as a qualifier. So a recovering cancer patient group becomes a community, Alcoholics Anonymous becomes a community, e-mail skin head folks become a community because of their intense feelings. The real issue is what actually constitutes 'belonging'?"
>
> —Lunell Haught, Ph.D., Owner, Haught Strategies

Many communities of the future will be characterized as communities of choice, where members can elect to come and go on short notice. Examples today include geographic communities, religious communities, volunteer service, special interests (such as those that form through Internet usage), businesses in the Silicon Valley of California, and cultural communities.[18] What are the implications of this choice to organizations? It means that organizations will have to determine how to attract and retain talent, since people will see nothing wrong with moving between organizations at a faster rate than they do today when their needs are not met. It means that alignment and integration will be more difficult to achieve. It also suggests that standardization and work process documentation may become more critical. On the other hand, new ideas may be more quickly inserted into the system and it may be easier to engage in ongoing renewal.

There are several purposes for invoking community in the workplace. It could exist as a vehicle for learning—learning through practice (see Communities of Practice described in chapter 9) and/or learning as knowledge acquisition. It might be fostered to gain commitment to action, such as that required to carry out daily work and the organization's strategic plan, or to engender alignment by promoting and sustaining a set of beliefs (e.g., values).

Within an organization, multiple communities can exist at any one time, and membership may regularly change. Communities can form around life passages (e.g., those who were hired and/or promoted at the same time, individuals who attended a series of leadership development workshops together, or those who have young children). They may also arise for physical well-being (e.g., participants in an aerobics class) or spiritual healing (e.g., a group of health care professionals who continually treat terminally ill patients).

Given the earlier definition, several additional factors often help characterize community in the workplace. First, the community has a reason for being (as described earlier), which, along with a few key principles, allows it to be self-organizing. All members participate to the extent that they choose to do so, with everyone sharing in the responsibility for decision making and the community's development. Second, relationships are authentic, with the community's principles guiding the behaviors that are demonstrated. Last, leadership may be situational, with individuals rising to the occasion based on the task at hand and their skills, abilities, and interests.

While some suggest, as noted in chapter 1, that organizationally based communities are highly evolved, self-managed teams, they appear to go a step beyond this definition. If organizational community is defined in terms of place or geography, then it might have a constitution that outlines the rights and responsibilities of its constituents (a more specific form of the "few key principles") and a method of governance that upholds it. Employees would be recognized as citizens, its supply chain and customers as partners, and owners as investors.

> "Community is nurtured when people know each other's stories (their hopes, their fears, their goals for work life). Community is fostered when feedback is truly inherent in the corporate culture, when we tell each other, with compassion, what must be known if we are to mature and grow. Community profoundly influences performance when truth is spoken without fear and the whole organization moves forward as a result."[19]
>
> —Eric Klein and John B. Izzo, Ph.D., authors of *Awakening Corporate Soul: Four Paths to Unleash the Power of People at Work*

Social Responsibility and Accountability

> ". . . [Nike's] 'brand soul' has been especially hurt by the spate of negative stories about its overseas labor practices and defensive posture. 'What's happening to Nike is extremely dangerous for any brand,' says John Bowen, a New York consultant and writer on brand resonance. 'Consumers today are more concerned about the culture of the organization behind the brand. They want to feel good about the company they are buying from.' "[20]

Organizations are socially responsible and accountable to both the planet and society, above and beyond their financial commitments to shareholders. This obligation implies a responsibility to themselves, including their shareholders, employees, customers, and suppliers in areas such as working conditions, work standards, and treatment of employees. The 1998 Criteria for Performance Excellence from the Malcolm Baldrige National Quality Award speaks to social responsibility under the company responsibility and citizenship portion of the leadership category. Thirty out of 1000 points are devoted to societal responsibilities—"how the company addresses the current and potential impacts on society of its products, services, and operations"—and support of key communities—"how the company, its senior leaders, and its employees support and strengthen their key communities."[21] The criteria state that "fulfilling societal responsibilities means not only meeting all local, state, and federal laws and regulatory requirements, but also treating these and related requirements as areas for improvement 'beyond mere compliance.' "[22]

Duane Elgin and Coleen LeDrew suggest, under the umbrella of social responsibility, that there are three major ecologies that need to be integrated and sustained simultaneously: (1) a physical ecology (the way current generations live cannot jeopardize the Earth's ability to uphold future generations), (2) a social ecology (that values all types of relationships), and (3) a spiritual ecology (explored earlier in this chapter).[23] These three ecologies once again bring back the importance of creating a sustainable planet, the interconnectedness between all living systems, and the need to be holistic in how issues are addressed and resolved. For many organizations, their leaders have focused on the cost savings aspects of activities in the first two domains. However, an unanticipated outcome of serving society in this manner may be their revenue growth potential and their ability to attract and retain talent.

> "John Rogers . . . [manager of the] $168 million Ariel Growth fund shuns the stocks of polluters, tobacco companies, and outfits with insufficiently diverse work forces. But unlike other 'socially responsible' portfolios, Ariel hasn't had to eat the dust of less fastidious funds. Its 36.4% gain in 1997, for example, far outdistanced the 24.4% chalked up by the Russell 2500. Though the fund lagged behind its closest peers in the early 1990s, its annualized gain of 25.9% over the past three years puts it well ahead of the relevant indexes."[24]

While environmental sustainability activities (a part of the physical ecology) are ideally pursued because of enlightened management, they are also carried out because they are interwoven with economic performance. Royal Dutch/Shell's gasoline sales plummeted by 50 percent at some German stations when Greenpeace derailed its efforts to sink Brent Spar, an abandoned offshore oil-storage buoy. As a result of this and other situations, Shell decided to publically report its environmental records and defend human rights in places where the company operates.[25]

Business ethics falls into the social ecology category. Its relationship to organizational performance has to do with the decisions that are made in relationship to those ethics on which the enterprise prides itself. Organizations can use any of a number of approaches to ethical decision making, employing a continuum anchored on one side by a system-centered approach and an agent-centered approach on the other.[26] A system-centered approach is based on the organization's taking responsibility for distinguishing between right and wrong through the establishment of enterprise-wide policies and rules, whereas the agent-centered approach relies on the individual to make the distinction and necessary decisions. Because ethical decisions are often ambiguous, difficult, and complex, both types of approaches need to be engaged by an organization. This may mean that an individual will make a decision that is truly best for the organization and society in the long run but is at odds with the organization's short-term objectives.

> "Today Hewlett-Packard operates in many different communities throughout the world. We stress to our people that each of these communities must be better for our presence. This means being sensitive to the needs and interests of the community; it means applying the highest standards of honesty and integrity to all our relationships with individuals and groups; it means enhancing and protecting the physical environment and building attractive plants and offices of which the community can be proud; it means contributing talent, energy, time, and financial support to community projects."[27]
>
> —David Packard, cofounder of Hewlett Packard and author of *The HP Way: How Bill Hewlett and I Built Our Company*

COMMONLY USED TOOLS AND METHODS

This section covers four of the tools and methods used in the Spiritual Awakening Field of Performance Practice—new social contract for employment, community building, social responsibility audits, and zero-emissions systems. Each of these topics was briefly introduced in chapter 1. Journals such as the *Journal for Quality and Participation* (from the Association for Quality and Participation), *Perspectives on Business and Global Change* (from the World Business Academy), and *Fast Company* are good sources for articles on these topics and the issues that pertain to this field of performance practice.

New Social Contract for Employment

A guaranteed lifetime job is an artifact of the past. The new rules of employment and the changing landscape of work suggest the need for a new type of employment contract. At the core of this new contract are a set of assumptions based on employees' actively managing their own careers, and organizations' valuing employees and working to make them employable in the long term. It is designed to provide clear definitions of everyone's rights, responsibilities, and relationships to each other, and a redefinition of the role of management and its commitments to people. In the ideal world, all parties are to be involved in the contract's development.

Just how new is this type of employment contract? And, how viable is it in today's organizations? Enterprises such as "Hewlett-Packard, Harley Davidson, and Johnson & Johnson [who] have long-standing policies of valuing their employees as resources" have been committed to this contract for a long time.[28] It is an integral part of their culture and how they manage their business. Fundamental to this new type of employment contract is the organization's ability to provide an environment in which people can reach their full potential and have the opportunity to obtain the training, tools, and skills they need now and in the future. Pay systems are being retooled so that lateral moves for skill enhancement are rewarded; downsizing is used as a last alternative in business downturns; and honest communication and high levels of mutual trust are promoted between the enterprise and its people. Job rotation programs are being initiated to address employees' changing life needs. These organizations are altering their human resources policies and approaches to retention in order to keep workers.

Until organizations begin to fully embrace these requirements, it will be challenging for employees to fully embrace their responsibilities within them. It will also be hard for employees to let go of the skepticism and anger resulting from downsizing initiatives and their ultimate impact on productivity. The employee piece of the equation, also covered in chapter 14, Enacting Your Career: Thriving in **CHAOS,** speaks to being responsible for one's own career and career development. This may include paying out of one's own pocket to obtain requisite knowledge and skills and creating career opportunities that do not appear obvious on first blush. It promotes being attentive to one's value in the employment marketplace and uncovering ways to increase it over time.

Community Building

> "There are few communities in which the entire population is involved in a massive interdependent and significant effort. One is Mauritius, a tiny island nation off the east coast of Africa, where the norm for the 1.3 million people who live there is to work together to take care of the children. . . . The community works to improve training for people in marketable skills, so there is no unemployment or homelessness. . . . They have 100 percent employment and 98 percent literacy, which puts them ahead of the top fifteen industrial nations. The nation includes people from five distinct cultures—people who value differences so highly that they even celebrate one another's religious holidays. They are a Third World, poor country, trying to move into the First World. But socially, they are way ahead of us. The police officers don't even carry guns. Their deeply integrated interdependence reflects their values of order, harmony, cooperation, synergy, and respect for all people, particularly children."[29]
>
> —Stephen R. Covey, cochairman of the Franklin Covey Company and author of *The Seven Habits of Highly Effective People*

Community building is not a new approach. It has been practiced in towns, cities, countries, religious institutions, and voluntary community organizations around the world for hundreds of years. What is fairly new, however, is its application to the workplace, especially in for-profit organizations.

Some of the specific tools and methods used to foster community in the workplace are not unique to this field. They include employee involvement approaches such as teamwork, which are critical to the deployment of the tools and methods in each of the five fields of performance practice. They also include the use of groupware technology to conduct work in any of the fields which, in turn, nurtures community building. In the Alignment and Integration Field, the creation of ideology (shared vision, mission, values, guiding principles) and the use of large group interventions encourage consistency in practice and decision making, a sense that one is part of a larger whole, and a feeling of commonality.

So why isn't the experience of community an everyday part of organizational life? The primary reason is that there may be an absence of the explicit desire to build community. Thus, fundamental organizational systems and practices needed to sustain it do not change, which causes any feeling of community to be fleeting.

To foster community internally requires organizations to alter a number of their basic practices including governance structures, information flow, the number and type of human resources policies, the creation and deployment of strategy, and financial controls. The move toward community also brings with it the need to make specialized tools and knowledge (such as those described in each of the preceding fields of performance practice) commonplace, and requires the ability to engage large groups of people in productive learning, work, and dialogue.[30] For community to take hold in the workplace, Carolyn Schaffer and Kristin Anundsen suggest the following prerequisites:

- organization-wide values alignment;
- a flat, employee-based organizational structure that supports teamwork and dispersed decision making authority;
- open communications between all individuals, independent of rank, including the ability for anyone to express concerns about the work of others;
- mutual support for getting work accomplished;
- respect for individual uniqueness and the integration of work and life; and
- ongoing renewal sessions to resolve issues, celebrate achievements, and dialogue about ideology (i.e., vision, mission, values, principles).[31]

Collectively, these items suggest that the culture-related elements of the first four fields of performance practice must be a part of everyday organizational life before sustained community can start to take root. They also suggest that those in leadership must be willing to open themselves and the enterprise up to profound change in organizational assumptions relative to work and the workplace.

Eric Klein and John Izzo suggest several ways to get started on what they call the "path of community"—sharing personal stories, dreams, and aspirations so people can learn about each other and their uniqueness; learning how to safely explore subjects that are off-limits; dismantling barriers between groups through job rotations and cocreating the future; and sharing information that might otherwise be kept from people to enhance their decisions and work accomplishment.[32] These activities also benefit the organization by unleashing pent-up energy that is a required fuel for the creation of organizational spirit, which ultimately can lead to increased productivity.

Gifford Pinchot, author of *Intrapreneuring: Why You Don't Have to Leave the Corporation to Become an Entrpreneur,* and *The Intelligent Organization: Engaging the Talent and Initiative of Everyone in the Workplace* (written with Elizabeth Pinchot), suggests that there are six steps for building community in the workplace. They are:

1. creating a common purpose for the organization;
2. supporting the gift economy (i.e., defining status based on giving instead of on what one has, as exemplified by the growth of one's personal avatar at Sun Microsystems);
3. establishing a shared environment experienced by all;
4. moving toward equality and away from status based on rank or wealth;
5. creating internal not-for-profit entities that serve the whole; and
6. caring for members by providing safety, security, and love.[33]

In his book, *The Living Organization: Transforming Teams into Workplace Communities,* John Nirenberg, Ph.D. outlines a series of activities for an organization to take if it is interested in initiating community in its workplace. These activities move from the establishment of a planning committee, through organizational assessment, to measurement, implementation, institutionalization, and ongoing feedback and learning. Community building in organizations is not happenstance; it requires forethought, planning, and coordinated efforts focused on creating and sustaining it for the long run.

In addition to the books already mentioned, there are literally hundreds of publications that speak to the development of religious communities, voluntary community organizations, and the communities in which we live. Organizations can benefit from exploring communities that arise around common interests, places, values, and relationships; studying the learnings of volunteer community organizers; reviewing the research regarding the effectiveness of towns and cities as communities; and hearing stories about their transformation.

> "The motorcycle company Harley-Davidson has been absolutely ingenious in creating an entire social organization around its product—from the chrome-rich hogs themselves to the symbol-ridden clothing that riders don and the weekend riding clubs that assuage the riders' weekday loneliness. In effect, Harley has taken its customer base, expanded it into a tribe, and provided the tribe the means to constantly reinforce its rituals. All those riding clubs lack is warpaint to complete the effect."[34]
>
> —Watts Wacker and Jim Taylor, with Howard Means, authors of *The 500 Year Delta: What Happens After What Comes Next*

Social Responsibility Audits

Perhaps the way that organizations approach measuring their social responsibility efforts needs to change. William McDonough, dean of the School of Architecture at the University of Virginia, and his business partner Michael Braungart, of William McDonough + Partners, suggest that organizations should start by measuring their legacy, not their activities—what they call "eco-effectiveness."[35] This shift in thinking causes organizations to ask different questions, and to entertain the possibility that their offerings might be their worst offense (such as those that cannot be recycled and do not decay for hundreds of years).

Three approaches for measuring social responsibility were covered in chapter 1—The Ethical Accounting Statement, the Sunshine Standards for Corporate Reporting to Stakeholders, and Social Accountability 8000, an international and interindustry standard focusing on workplace conditions and the promotion of fair and humane labor practices. A fourth approach, The Sustainability Portfolio, is a diagnostic tool for determining whether a company's strategy is consistent with product stewardship, pollution prevention, clean technology, and a vision for sustainability.[36]

These are just a sampling of the tools and systems available for assessing social responsibility behavior on the part of the organization. While industry, academics, and the general public are at the forefront of creating some of these types of systems, social responsibility measures need to become an integral part of the enterprise's organization-wide measurement system (covered in chapter 6).

Zero-Emissions Systems

> "Those who think that sustainability is only a matter of pollution control are missing the bigger picture. Even if all the companies in the developed world were to achieve zero emissions by the Year 2000, the Earth would still be stressed beyond what biologists refer to as carrying capacity. Increasingly, the scourges of the late twentieth century—depleted farmland, fisheries, and forests; choking urban pollution; poverty; infectious disease; and migration—are spilling over geopolitical borders. The simple fact is this: In meeting our needs, we are destroying the ability of future generations to meet theirs."[37]
>
> —Stuart L. Hart, faculty member in corporate strategy and the director of the Corporate Environmental Management Program at the University of Michigan Business School in Ann Arbor

Zero-emissions thinking is an outgrowth of a focus on sustainability of the planet. Its principles speak to elimination of all types of waste, using renewable energy sources, recycling an organization's products into future products, and using clean technology (e.g., chemicals that are not hazardous to the environment or people). Full attention is given to the impact of the organization on its local community and the surrounding physical environment.

Interface, Inc. an Atlanta-based organization that turns petrochemicals into textiles, has as its goal to become a "fully sustainable industrial enterprise" [that is]

100% environmentally benign" and has zero waste from every process.[38] It is teaching the principles of sustainability to its workforce of 7,300 employees and is using its products as the raw materials for future textiles. In one year, from 1995 to 1996, the company's sales grew from $800 million to $1 billion, while the amount of raw materials decreased almost 20 percent per dollar of sales, thus making sustainability and the prospect of zero emissions viable business propositions.

As organizations in the same industry strive to provide value to consumers, and consumers desire to attach themselves to socially responsible organizations, zero emissions may be a way for enterprises to strategically distinguish themselves from their competition. The pursuit of never-ending improvement resulting in zero emissions is a hidden opportunity.

WHO IS INVOLVED IN THE SPIRITUAL AWAKENING FIELD OF PERFORMANCE PRACTICE

Undoubtedly, the impact of the Spiritual Awakening Field of Performance Practice will be felt first at the individual level. This person-by-person groundswell of interest will eventually spread into enterprise-wide values, guiding principles, and mission and vision statements. As employment becomes more dependent on the individual and people seek meaningful work, they will pick and choose with whom they want to be associated. These choices will continue to push the need for organizational community and social accountability.

As members of an interconnected planet, each individual has a personal responsibility to serve society and to ensure that the planet is managed as a system that provides for improved life for everyone. Service to society is also covered in chapter 14, Enacting Your Career: Thriving in **CHAOS.**

SHORTCOMINGS WITH THE SPIRITUAL AWAKENING FIELD OF PERFORMANCE PRACTICE

The Spiritual Awakening Field of Performance Practice continues to address the linkage and interconnectedness shortcomings of both the Quality Assurance and the Problem Resolution Fields of Performance Practice. It does this by acknowledging the need to appreciate and understand the interrelationship between all living things. Thus, there is the possibility in this performance practice that an "either/or mindset" will give way to a "both/and mindset." Both of these issues were mentioned in the Consumer Obsession Field of Performance Practice.

Because this field is slowly emerging, with impact on organizational life just beginning to be felt, it is difficult to conjecture about its shortcomings. However, three issues come to mind. First, those who write about community spend more

Table 8.1

Your Organization and the Spiritual Awakening Field of Performance Practice

Directions: Record the activities your organization has and has not engaged in relative to the concepts, tools, and methods referenced in this field of performance practice, noting the degree of deployment of each item. Also document its future plans for deploying these concepts, tools, and methods throughout the enterprise.

Purpose: To serve society		**Desired Outcomes:** • The planet managed as a system • Improved life for everyone on the planet		
	What Your Organization Is Doing	**What Your Organization Is Not Doing**	**Degree of Deployment***	**Plans Your Organization Has for the Future**
Underlying Concepts • Spirituality • Organization as community • Social responsibility and accountability			 1 2 3 4 5 1 2 3 4 5 1 2 3 4 5	
Commonly Used Tools and Methods • New social contract for employment • Community building • Social responsibility audits • Zero-emissions systems			 1 2 3 4 5 1 2 3 4 5 1 2 3 4 5 1 2 3 4 5	

*Rating system: 1 = no systematic deployment is evident
2 = some deployment is evident with little or no results
3 = deployment is evident in several areas of the business with limited results
4 = deployment is evident in major portions of the business with measurable results
5 = full organization-wide deployment is evident with significant measurable results

Table 8.2

CHAOS and the Spiritual Awakening Field of Performance Practice

Directions: Note your thoughts on the future impact that the forces of **CHAOS** may have on each of the underlying concepts and the commonly used tools and methods in the Spiritual Awakening Field of Performance Practice.

CHAOS / **Underlying Concepts**	**Changing Definition of Work and the Workplace**	**Heightened Social Responsibility**	**Aging Baby Boomers**	**Overarching Demographic Change**	**Strategic Growth Through Technology and Innovation**
• Spirituality					
• Organization as community					
• Social responsibility and accountability					
Commonly Used Tools and Methods					
• New social contract for employment					
• Community building					
• Social responsibility audits					
• Zero-emissions systems					

time exploring its merits than its flaws. It is as important to understand the negative unintended side effects of creating community in the workplace as it is to understand its benefits to the organization and its stakeholders. Secondly, genuine initiatives to incorporate spirituality into the workplace will need to dodge those initiatives that occur because it is the latest management fad. Assessing performance results will be clouded by the difficulty in being able to distinguish between them. Finally, organizations may elect to engage in the approaches described in this chapter using motives that do not align with the purpose of this field of performance practice. This lip-service to the need to serve society at large may achieve performance results for an organization. But these results may not be of the breadth and depth that could be achieved if its values were aligned with this need. In addition, these motives may become obvious to stakeholders over time and elicit a backlash from them.

These three issues will work themselves out over time as the practices explored in this chapter are more fully embraced by organizations. And others will emerge. However, the immediate challenge of this field of performance practice is for it to gain the attention of senior management and to demonstrate its critical role in organizational performance.

Endnotes

1. Paula Gunn Allen, *The Sacred Hoop: Recovering the Feminine in American Indian Traditions* (Boston: Beacon Press, 1992), 55.
2. Rolf Jensen, “The Dream Society,” *THE FUTURIST* (May–June 1996), 9–10.
3. Chris Lee and Ron Zemke, “The Search for Spirit in the Workplace,” *TRAINING* (June 1993), 25.
4. World Business Academy, Annual Meeting and President’s Council Invitation, 1998.
5. Richard Barrett, “A Corporate Values Revolution,” *Perspectives on Business and Global Change,* Vol. 10, No. 3 (1996), 52.
6. Phil Jackson and Hugh Delehanty, *Sacred Hoops: Spiritual Lessons of a Hardwood Warrior* (New York: Hyperion, 1995), 3–5.
7. Michele Galen, “Companies Hit the Road Less Traveled,” *BusinessWeek* (June 5, 1995), 82.
8. Pamela Leigh, “The New Spirit at Work,” *Training & Development* (March 1997), 31.
9. David Dorsey, “The New Spirit of Work,” *Fast Company* (August 1998), 130.
10. Leigh, “The New Spirit at Work,” 31.
11. Lee and Zemke, “The Search for Spirit in the Workplace,” 26.
12. Jackson and Delehanty, *Sacred Hoops: Spiritual Lessons of a Hardwood Warrior,* 11–12.
13. Diana Whitney, “Spirituality as an Organizing Principle,” *World Business Academy Perspectives,* Vol. 9, No. 4 (1995), 51–62.
14. Galen, “Companies Hit the Road Less Traveled,” 82.
15. Dorsey, “The New Spirit of Work,” 126.
16. James Rhem, “Living as Learning,” *On Wisconsin* (May–June 1998), 22–26, 55–56.

17. Carolyn R. Schaffer and Kristin Anundsen, *Creating Community Anywhere: Finding Support and Connections in a Fragmented World* (New York: Tarcher/Perigee Books, 1993), 10.

18. Marshall Goldsmith, "Global Communities and Communities of Choice," in *The Community of the Future,* eds. Francis Hesselbein et al., (San Francisco: Jossey-Bass Inc., Publishers, 1998), 110–112.

19. Eric Klein and John B. Izzo, Ph.D., *Awakening Corporate Soul: Four Paths to Unleash the Power of People at Work* (Lions Bay, BC: Fairwinds Press, 1998), 108–109.

20. Timothy Egan, "The Swoon of the Swoosh," *The New York Times* (September 13, 1998).

21. *Malcolm Baldrige National Quality Award 1998 Criteria for Performance Excellence* (Gaithersburg, MD: National Institute of Standards and Technology, 1998), 6.

22. *Malcolm Baldrige National Quality Award 1998 Criteria for Performance Excellence,* 22.

23. Duane Elgin and Coleen LeDrew, "Signs of Global Consciousness Change," *Perspectives on Business and Global Change,* Vol. 12, No. 1 (1998), 50.

24. Lawrence A. Armour, "Who Says Virtue Is Its Own Reward?" *FORTUNE* (February 16, 1998), 186.

25. Janet Guyon, "Why Is the World's Most Profitable Company Turning Itself Inside Out?" *FORTUNE* (August 4, 1997), 122.

26. Daniel D. Singer and Raymond D. Smith, "Two Approaches to Corporate Ethics," *Perspectives on Business and Global Change,* Vol. 12, No. 2 (1998), 35–36.

27. David Packard, *The HP Way: How Bill Hewlett and I Built Our Company* (New York: HarperCollins Publishers, Inc., 1995), 166.

28. Barbara Ettorre, "Empty Promises," *Management Review* (July 1996), 18.

29. Stephen R. Covey, "The Ideal Community," in *The Community of the Future,* eds. Francis Hesselbein et al., (San Francisco: Jossey-Bass Inc., Publishers, 1998), 56.

30. Peter Block, "Finding Community at Work," *Journal for Quality and Participation* (September 1994), 25.

31. Schaffer and Anundsen, *Creating Community Anywhere: Finding Support and Connections in a Fragmented World,* 116–121.

32. Klein and Izzo, *Awakening Corporate Soul: Four Paths to Unleash the Power of People at Work,* 105–120.

33. Gifford Pinchot, "Building Community in the Workplace," in *The Community of the Future,* eds. Francis Hesselbein et al., (San Francisco: Jossey-Bass Inc., Publishers, 1998), 125–137.

34. Watts Wacker and Jim Taylor, with Howard Means, *The 500 Year Delta: What Happens After What Comes Next* (New York: HarperCollins Publishers, Inc., 1997), 27.

35. Anna Muoio, "This 'Green Dean' Has a Blueprint for Sustainability," *Fast Company* (June–July 1998), 70.

36. Stuart L. Hart, "Beyond Greening: Strategies for a Sustainable World," *Harvard Business Review* (January–February 1997), 74.

37. Hart, "Beyond Greening: Strategies for a Sustainable World," 67.

38. Charles Fishman, "I Want to Pioneer the Company of the Next Industrial Revolution," *Fast Company* (April–May 1998), 138–139.

Section

III

Preparing to Use The Starburst Model™

Section II explored The Starburst Model™ and the details behind each of the five fields of performance practice. This section covers three topics that enable individuals to employ the model in their organization. Chapter 9 addresses the foundational skills and knowledge that cut across all five fields of performance practice and those that are specific to each of them. Chapter 10 outlines a number of ways to go about acquiring the skills and knowledge described in chapter 9. Chapter 11 defines the leadership behaviors (represented by the acronym **COMPASS™**) that need to be enacted by anyone who has leadership responsibility for planning, implementing, and evaluating the five fields of performance practice or their individual components, which include attention to the forces impacting the workplace of the future.

CHAPTER 9

Skills and Knowledge Fundamental to The Starburst Model™

Chapters 4 through 8 introduced the concepts, tools, and methods found in the five fields of performance practice. This chapter presents the skills and knowledge requirements that cut across all five performance practice areas in addition to listing the skills and knowledge essential for proficiency in each specific field. Following the Pareto Principle, captured here are 20 percent of the requirements that cover 80 percent of the situations. Table 9.1 (see pp. 174–178) provides a summary of this information. Considerations specific to quality professionals are covered at the end of the chapter.

> "The real challenge is to keep up with the required learning."
> —Louis E. Schultz, President, Process Management International

It may not be possible for any one person to be competent in all of the topics shown in Table 9.1, since they cover a wide variety of disciplines. On the other hand, while specialization has its benefits, it may not be wise to be an expert in one of the tools or methods or performance fields to the exclusion of all others. This is especially true in environments that suddenly shift, causing the problems and challenges of the situation to be outside of the skill set and/or expertise of the individual asked to address them. Consider what happened to some of the early computer programmers who became very good at programming stand-alone mainframe computer systems. As more and more companies turned from stand-alone mainframes to networked

Inner Exploration

1. In which field of performance practice are you most comfortable working? Least comfortable working?
2. In which field(s) of performance practice do you need to become skilled?

PCs and customized software packages, many of these programmers found, after years of employment security, that they were competing harder for fewer jobs that were less and less desirable. Some did not survive the transition. The optimal approach appears to be one in which an individual is familiar with the concepts, tools, and methods found in each of the five fields (and whom to call on for assistance), while at the same time has developed proficiency in the approaches associated with two or three fields of performance practice.

IT'S ALL IN HOW YOU SAY IT

> "The most important skills are interpersonal and group dynamics—nothing is done without people. These are followed by project management, finance, and your technical competencies. If you cannot manage a project, you are outdated; if you cannot speak and justify projects in the language of finance, you are outdated; if you cannot deal with people and groups effectively, you are in the wrong business."
>
> —Tara Martin-Milius, CEO, Center for Corporate Learning

Performance improvement is grounded in verbal communication including one-on-one, small group, and large group conversation. "[Conversation] is the single greatest learning tool in [an] organization—more important than computers or sophisticated research."[1] It starts with being able to speak the language of the business—the organization and its industry. Being fluent in technical jargon, as well as company-specific language, including that of each of the functions within the enterprise, goes a long way in effectively verbalizing ideas to others. This includes tying communications directly to the organization's mission, vision, values, guiding principles, and strategic plan.

Each person has a particular communication style, as described by Neurolinguistic Programming (NLP). It encompasses a preference for taking in information, organizing it "in our heads," and communicating it to others around us. This unconscious preference is based on the routine use of the primary senses—the eyes, ears, and body. Some individuals prefer visual (e.g., gained through e-mail or memos) while others prefer auditory (e.g., gained through hallway conversation or phone calls) or kinesthetic (e.g., gained through touch or physical movement) information. The goal is to become adept at recognizing another person's style—one approach is to listen to the verbs the individual uses—and then adapting one's own communications to this style. Benefits to be realized through this type of communication congruence include increasing the amount and accuracy of information exchange, thus leading to enhanced rapport, trust, and achievement of work-related goals.[2]

> "The business-unit consultants in our organization (those who report directly to the general manager of a group) need to have business knowledge and experience;

understand real business issues; practice business process consulting skills such as improvement, innovation, and redesign—including the ability to analyze, change, measure and evaluate systems; and be able to engage in productive conversation using advocacy and inquiry skills to deal with assumptions and mental models. Finally they need to know systems thinking tools and concepts . . . [and] good project management skills."

—Barbara Lawton, Ph.D., Vice President,
Business and Quality Processes, StorageTek

There are a variety of techniques that can lead to productive conversation. Balancing advocacy (i.e., making your thinking and reasoning more visible to others) and inquiry (asking others to make their thinking process visible) helps individuals to arrive at new insights, especially when there are no answers available to the situation at hand.[3] Both of these skills assume that all of the parties are actively listening during the conversation. Some organizations are exploring the use of dialogue as a means of creating deeper understanding, developing new perceptions and models, and opening the doorway to fundamental individual and organizational transformation. This tool is described further in chapter 11. Metaphors and storytelling are invaluable approaches for capturing the hearts and imaginations of others. Their morals (i.e., the moral of the story . . .) are remembered longer than a description of facts and figures.

Inner Exploration

1. What is your expertise in Neurolinguistic Programming (NLP)?
2. What experience have you had participating in and/or facilitating dialogue sessions?
3. Where can you use storytelling at work?

LET YOUR WRITING DO THE WORK

The purpose of written materials is more than communicating ideas, thoughts, and information. It records a version of reality that influences history. The manner in which a document is written greatly influences its ability to accomplish these purposes. First and foremost are the planning elements—defining the purpose of the communication, assessing its audience, collecting and analyzing the information that needs to be disseminated, and outlining and organizing its contents. Attention then needs to be turned to deciding on the format, writing the first draft (without worry over sentence structure, grammar, and punctuation), editing it, and finalizing the communication for publication. Some of the techniques utilized in verbal communication—for example, metaphor and storytelling—can also be invaluable in written communications.

In general, the written communications generated as one progresses from Quality Assurance to Spiritual Awakening move from technical to nontechnical, from specific to general, and from matter-of-fact to paradoxical in nature. This change in focus is a factor in creating materials within a specific field of performance practice.

IT'S A MATTER OF CHANGE

> "More and more, we are entering the age of the generalist, that individual who is able to juggle many skills, whether technical or interpersonal, in order to help manifest the type of change for which organizations clamor. I believe the most frequently overlooked critical skill is the need for effective listening, which entails listening with one's ears, eyes, and heart. Yes, listening with the eyes and heart. Think about it."
>
> —Col. Liz Anderson, 302d Support Group Commander, 302d Airlift Wing, U.S. Air Force Reserve (Any views or opinions expressed are personal to the individual and do not represent the U.S. Air Force or any other D.O.D. component official views or positions.)

"Staying ahead of change means anticipating the new actions that external events will eventually require and taking them early, before others, before being forced, while there is still time to exercise choice about how and when and what—and time to influence, shape or redirect the external events themselves."[4] Change is an underlying theme in all of the fields of performance practice. It may involve introducing a new tool, deploying a new policy, approaching traditional work in a new way, or altering the organization's culture.

Given the rapid nature of change, being an agent of change is no longer a choice. In order to be effective, change agents must first know themselves—their strengths and weaknesses, biases and mental models. Personal qualities, such as courage and a willingness to take risks, are undeniable. To be proficient, there are a myriad of subjects that fall under the change agent umbrella, some of which are covered in this chapter (i.e., verbal and written communications, coaching, etc.) and chapter 11. At a minimum, there are individual, small group, large group, and organizational change theories, models, tools, approaches, and techniques. It is imperative to know how to build solid relationships, influence others and enlist them in change, handle resistance, and work the political system within the organization (e.g., building coalitions, mobilizing resources, handling opposition, and securing blessings[5]).

Inner Exploration

1. How effective are you as a change agent?
2. Where you have not been effective as a change agent, what challenges have you encountered?
3. What can you do to increase your capabilities as a change agent?

OPPOSITE SIDES OF THE SAME COIN—SYNTHESIS AND ANALYSIS

Synthesis and analysis are two different approaches to understanding the world. Synthesizing information involves taking divergent facts from a number of sources, bringing some sort of order to them, and extrapolating beyond the scope of the existing information. Analysis, on the other hand, involves taking an existing situation and understanding how it works. It involves breaking a situation down into subsituations, studying each of the components, and putting them back together again.

To compare them, a synthesis approach would take hundreds of contextual observations of human behavior (i.e., how people behave in a given context, such as cleaning house), find patterns in these observations that surface latent market wants and needs, and extrapolate from these wants and needs into new product innovation possibilities that address them. Used here are systems thinking tools and several of the 7 Management and Planning Tools, such as affinity diagrams, interrelationship diagraphs, and tree diagrams (all described in chapter 6). If analysis were used to study customer complaint data, it would determine the major types of complaints, the steps in the system that are producing the complaints, and the causes that influence these steps to produce them. Some of the basic tools of quality such as flowcharts, Pareto charts, and stratification can be used to analyze situations.

Both synthesis and analysis are appropriate in the right situations. In fact, many situations benefit from the application of both approaches, sometimes in alternating use. To understand an organization (a very complex system), synthesis might first be used to understand the interrelationship between the organization and a larger environment that includes its customers, suppliers, shareholders, the community in which it operates, and the institutions from which it draws its workforce. Then the internal workings of the organization could be analyzed to understand how the pieces affect its overall purpose. Finally, synthesis could be used again to figure out how the pieces align with each other to serve the interrelationships within the larger environment.

THE ART OF COACHING

> "We must embrace change, and those options and opportunities that we have to influence and drive changes. The most important skills we need to develop are the people-supporting skills. We must become better communicators and learn to talk about feelings and emotions."
>
> —Marie Baucom Williams, President and CEO, Tennessee Quality

All five fields of performance practice require individuals, groups, and the organization to change at some level. It is not enough to inform people of changes, teach them new skills and enhance their knowledge, and provide them with follow-up reading materials. The types of rapid changes organizations are undergoing today require a fundamental shift in assumptions and ways of thinking and behaving. This is causing individual and team coaching support to move from a luxury to a business necessity.

There are different types of coaching approaches that can be used, depending on the needs of the situation. Described here are coach as performance improvement champion, coach as mentor, coach as navigator, and coach as integrator and strategist.[6] Coach as performance improvement champion is the oldest of these approaches. Because coaching involves change, these approaches, and their requisite skills and knowledge, need to be a part of the repertoire of change agents.

Both "coach as work performance improvement champion" and "coach as mentor" involve one-on-one relationships. In the former, coaching is ongoing between a formal leader (i.e., supervisor, manager) and his or her direct reports and focuses on improving individual work performance. Mentoring, which may have a defined start and end point, typically occurs between a formal leader (coachee) and a peer, superior, or consultant (coach). Mentoring—the act of helping another learn[7]—may address personal, professional, and organizational transformation in the leader and often takes place within the context of an identified shift or change that impacts the organization, its processes, and it people. However, if system and work process structure truly influence individual behavior, neither of these approaches can assume (as many coaching approaches do today) that the individual is the problem.

> "Coaching in all of its forms is fundamentally a learning relationship. Learning relationships aren't just between individuals; they exist between teams, between functions, and between an organization and its market. Coaching may be an organization's most important tool for rapid change."
>
> —William H. Braswell, Jr., Vice President,
> Quality Resources, Premera Blue Cross

"Coach as navigator" and "coach as integrator and strategist" involve coach-to-team relationships. As a navigator, the coach is initially from outside the team (later replaced by the team leader, supervisor, or manager) and the relationship has a defined start and end point. Coach as navigator works on team improvement and/or transformation within the context of some identified shift or change in a business system that impacts the team. The coach who functions as integrator and strategist is typically from outside the team, and the organization. However responsibility can shift from someone external to the organization to someone internal who is not a part of the team. The coach as integrator and strategist focuses on organization-wide transformation, often causing the coaching relationship to be ongoing for a period of years.

Inner Exploration

1. What type of coaching approach are you most comfortable using? Least comfortable using?
2. What skills and knowledge do you need to develop as a coach? Who could coach you on them?
3. Who has mentored you in your career? What have you gained through this relationship? What makes mentoring work?

As one moves through these four approaches, the demands for underlying skills and knowledge increase and become more complex due to the growing scope of the situation. Any coach, however, needs to be grounded in the basics, drawing from a variety of disciplines. Self-knowledge comes first, followed by an ability to demonstrate appreciation for the individual—through interpersonal communications; feedback, including confronting difficult issues; diversity; and personality type and temperament. Building on these skills and knowledge is organizational behavior emphasizing large and small group theory, including group process factors; stages of team development; observation and intervention approaches; facilitation and conflict management; and meeting management. Intertwined with all of this is the need to understand how individuals and organizations learn, how to apply theory on variation to human behavior, and how to use systems theory specific to archetypes, mental models, and tools such as the ladder of inference and those used to assess "espoused" versus "theory-in-use" behaviors.

HELPING ADULTS LEARN

"It is said we learn and remember after a month

- "14 percent of what we hear
- "22 percent of what we see
- "30 percent of what we watch others do—demonstrations or modeling
- "42 percent of sensory redundancy—rituals that repeat seeing, hearing, and doing important skills or concepts
- "72 percent of movies of the mind—learning is linked to remembered or imagined life experiences of the learner
- "83 percent of performance of a life challenge activity—first-time or demanding action that applies the new meaning
- "92 percent of what we teach others."[8]

—Russell D. Robinson, Ph.D., *An Introduction to Helping Adults Learn and Change*

Learning occurs individually and collectively. But, what is learning? "Learning may be defined as the process of making a new or revised interpretation of the meaning of an experience, which guides subsequent understanding, appreciation, and action."[9] Learning can be psychomotor (new skills and behavior patterns), cognitive (new ways of thinking and knowing), and affective (new attitudes, values, and ways of feeling)[10] Learning is a prerequisite to performance improvement and change—it guides the realization that specific performance gaps need to be closed and that fundamental shifts must occur for transformation and renewal to be organizational possibilities.

Action learning "aims to enhance the capacities of people in everyday situations to investigate, understand, and, if they wish, to change those situations in an ongoing fashion with a minimum of external help."[11] Through the use of reflection, especially critical self-reflection, individuals become conscious of their own mental models—their assumptions, values, and actions—testing them and making alterations as needed. Organizations such as Motorola, Hewlett-Packard, IBM, Citibank, Ameritech, and Johnson & Johnson have used this approach as a vehicle for cultural change, as a way to develop people, and as a means of executing key business strategies. The book, *Action Learning: How the World's Top Companies are Re-Creating Their Leaders and Themselves,* by David Dotlich and James Noel, outlines how to put together programs of this type.

Action science as described by Chris Argyris and Donald Schön in numerous books and articles, distinguishes between single- and double-loop learning. Single-loop learning is "learning that changes strategies of action or assumptions underlying strategies in ways that leave the values of a theory of action unchanged, [whereas] double-loop learning [also] results in changes in the values of theory-in-use."[12] In their example of a thermostat, single-loop learning occurs when the thermostat is set to a predetermined point. Double-loop learning goes further, examining why the temperature should be set at a particular level and what causes the thermostat to work the way it does. Techniques for enhancing double-loop learning include balancing inquiry with advocacy (described earlier), the ladder of inference (a tool that can surface the meanings, assumptions, and conclusions that cause a person to move from observable data and experiences to oftentimes misguided beliefs and actions), and "left-hand column" writing (a tool to uncover the implicit assumptions governing conversations that may prevent them from being truly effective).

> "Cycles of learning, not just corrective action, are now important. Cycles of learning demand lessons learned and the opening of windows to gain information from outside of the organization. These cycles provide new challenges and opportunities for improvement, and force us to challenge assumptions."
>
> —Dr. Curt W. Reimann, Senior Scientist Emeritus,
> National Institute of Standards and Technology

Approaches based on action science appear more rigorous and predictable than those grounded in action learning, while action learning may be more flexible. To gain the best of both suggests incorporating action science tools into action learning. Even in technical skill and on-the-job training initiatives, these approaches are required to help individuals do more than rote memorization—to engage their critical thinking skills in helping the organization to continually improve and innovate into the future.

A third approach to learning involves the use of "communities of practice"—a term coined by Etienne Wenger and Jean Lave in their 1991 book, *Situated Learning,* and explored further in Wenger's latest book, *Communities of Practice: Learning, Meaning and Identity.*[13] At StorageTek, a company that develops and provides electronic data storage devices, communities of practice (CoPs) are defined as "informal gatherings of people in a similar profession that come together to share information, experiences, questions, and to help one another along the way."[14] In this organization, communities of practice have existed for software development, Service Engineering, and new product development. Communities of practice arise out of people regularly working together—sharing common experiences, a desire to learn from one another, and a mutual identity—and may be invisible because they are not found on organization charts. Conversations over cubicle walls, in the hallways, and in break areas can signal these informal exchanges.

In essence, they are self-organizing. These groups usually do not have names or a membership list, and may cross functional boundaries. They differ from cross-functional or natural teams in that they are not "chartered" or "launched"—they emerge from the work at hand and may continue beyond the end of a project. Thus, they are how the work gets done, not an end in and of themselves. Interventions, even those that are altruistic (e.g., upgrading computer technology), can be unintentionally harmful to a CoP's ability to continue its learnings.

Understanding what defines learning and the types of learning approaches just described are the first steps in helping adults and organizations truly learn and change at a systemic level. While some forms of learning are more formal, some of the most powerful types are informal and unplanned. It is important for organizations to embrace both of these contexts.

For those interested in the more formal learning situations, there are numerous books and articles on instructional design that describe the steps for developing discovery-based reflective learning approaches and the theory behind adult learning. Upon completion of formal learning situations, their effectiveness needs to be evaluated from a number of perspectives—participant reactions to the situation, whether or not the needed change has occurred, and whether or not the organization realized the expected results. Given the types of changes expected out of these efforts, participant coaching before, during, and after the learning situation needs to be woven into its design.

Inner Exploration

1. What is your level of experience with using the action learning approach?
2. How familar are you with action science techniques such as inquiry and advocacy, the ladder of inference, and "left-hand column" writing?
3. Of which communities of practices are you a member in your organization? What makes these groups effective?
4. What experience have you had with designing formal learning situations based on discovery learning?

> "Successful coaches and mentors understand the difference between training and helping others learn. Rather than trainer-driven teaching experiences, the individual learner is guided and supported though a discovery learning process that fosters true intrinsically motivated change. This means paying attention to all that one can know about the learner's experiences, their baseline skills and knowledge, their preferred learning styles, and their desire to learn. Any formal learning experience, and any on-the-job coaching, must be designed to enhance learning rather than to just teach."
>
> —Linda Ernst, President, Training Resource

MAKING TECHNOLOGY WORK FOR YOU

> "The network is the work . . . it is the superhighway for information referrals, what's new, alternative directions, changing expectations, and hearing the voice of the customer. No business can be without it."
>
> —Tara Martin-Milius, CEO, Center for Corporate Learning

Table 9.1

Skills and Knowledge Required by The Starburst Model™

Directions: Complete columns three and four after you have read through chapter 9. Complete column 5 once you have gone through chapter 10.

Skills and Knowledge	What Is Needed	Valuable Skills and Knowledge That I Possess	Skills and Knowledge That I Need or Want to Acquire	How I Will Acquire the Skills and Knowledge (Refer to chapter 10)
Skills and knowledge required in all five fields of performance practice	• Communicate verbally (speak the language of the business, Neurolinguistic Programming, inquiry and advocacy, active listening, dialogue, metaphors, and storytelling) • Communicate in writing (planning, formatting, drafting, editing, and finalizing the communications) • Act as an agent for change (individual, group, and organizational change theories and interventions) • Synthesize information and analyze situations • Coach teams and individuals (confronting difficult issues, personality type and temperament, small and large group theory, team development, facilitation skills, conflict management, meeting management, and systems archetypes) • Help adults learn (action learning, action science, ladder of inference, left-hand column writing, communities of practice, instructional design, and evaluating learning)			

	• Use appropriate technology (groupware, computer-based, and videoconferencing)			
Quality Assurance Field • Quality system • Standardization • Basic tools of quality • The 5S's	• Write technically • Conduct quality audits, quality surveys, and product/service audits • Guide others through a systematic approach to standardization • Create measurement plans • Select and use appropriate basic tools of quality • Guide others through the 5S's			
Problem Resolution Field • Process management • Constraint management tools • Advanced tools • Creativity tools	• Identify problems and opportunities for improvement • Guide others through problem solving and continual improvement methodologies • Select and use appropriate constraint management tools • Know and apply basic statistical theory • Select and use appropriate advanced tools • Select and use creativity tools			

Table 9.1—*Continued*

Skills and Knowledge	What Is Needed	Valuable Skills and Knowledge That I Possess	Skills and Knowledge That I Need or Want to Acquire	How I Will Acquire the Skills and Knowledge (Refer to chapter 10)
Alignment and Integration Field				
• Organizational architecture	• Cultivate large-scale organizational change • Help organizations develop their ideology • Know and apply principles associated with organizational strategy • Know and apply organizational design principles			
• Organizational partnerships	• Support organizational partnerships			
• Managing the organization as a system	• Develop a picture of the organization as a system • Identify and design missing subsystems • Help leaders manage the organization as a system • Design an organization-wide measurement system			
• Large group interventions	• Select and use appropriate large group interventions			

• Strategic planning • 7 Management and Planning Tools • Project management	• Select and use appropriate strategic planning models and methods • Facilitate strategic planning efforts • Select and use appropriate 7 Management and Planning Tools • Select and use appropriate project management tools • Schedule and manage projects			
Consumer Obsession Field • Innovation • Competitive intelligence • Relationship marketing • Brand management • Non-traditional market research techniques	 • Identify appropriate uses of a systematic approach to innovation • Guide others through a methodology for innovation • Conduct best-in-class benchmarking studies • Help design competitive intelligence systems • Synthesize and analyze data • Help design relationship marketing processes • Assess the value of an offering • Support brand management activities • Select appropriate non-traditional market research techniques and know when to use them			

Table 9.1—*Continued*

Skills and Knowledge	What Is Needed	Valuable Skills and Knowledge That I Possess	Skills and Knowledge That I Need or Want to Acquire	How I Will Acquire the Skills and Knowledge (Refer to chapter 10)
Spiritual Awakening Field • New social contract for employment • Community building • Social responsibility audits • Zero-emissions systems	• Help organizations and individuals transition to the new social contract • Guide community-building activities • Design and conduct social responsibility audits • Assist in the design of zero-emissions systems			

Technology can enable work in each of the five fields of performance practice to be accomplished more effectively. As an example, the organization's quality system documentation can be housed on an intranet where it can be easily maintained, controlled, and accessed by employees and customers. Certain types of training may also be delivered in this manner. Individuals can send broadcast messages seeking solutions to problem situations. As another example of technology, people in various locations around the world can participate in meetings via videoconferencing and use "groupware" to facilitate the synthesis of ideas and information. Or customers can be given the capability to access supplier internal databases, as they are at FedEx, where customers track packages on their own, freeing up FedEx's customer service reps for other work. The possibilities for using technology to accomplish activities in all five fields of performance practice are endless—limited only by one's willingness to consider the possibilities.

CONSIDERATIONS FOR QUALITY PROFESSIONALS

> "Quality professionals need to realize that quality tools and techniques are for getting the job of business done. They must understand the choices to be made and call upon the wisdom to use the right tools and know what expertise to call on."
>
> —Dr. Curt W. Reimann, Senior Scientist Emeritus,
> National Institute of Standards and Technology

The **SHIFT** identified in chapter 2—quality goes **S**ofter, quality goes into **H**iding, quality goes **I**ntegrative, quality goes **F**ar-flung, and quality goes **T**echnical—has far-reaching implications for quality professionals. Some of them are being felt today as organizations downsize or eliminate their quality departments, leaving the individuals who worked in them questioning what they could have done differently. Other than acquiring the fundamental skills and knowledge described earlier, and that specific to each field of performance practice, what is a quality professional to do?

> "The most important skills and attributes in my work are credibility with business leaders; the ability to understand and use all the quality methodologies in a 'just-in-time' way when required to address a business situation; consulting skills; and change management skills."
>
> —Garry J. Huysse, Associate Director,
> Global Quality Improvement, Procter & Gamble

Quality professionals need to acquire a greater breadth of business experience in addition to speaking the language of the business. They must be conversant in industrywide issues and dilemmas. They must know how the tools and methods they bring to the table apply to the core work of the organization. Line experience, or experience in support functions other than quality, is the entry price for the future. Having experience solely within a quality function may limit opportunities for advancement or future employment.

"The skills and abilities that are needed are business experience, especially in finance and manufacturing."

—Richard C. Buetow, Retired Senior Vice President, Motorola, Inc., and Motorola Director of Quality

Quality professionals need to find ways to be strategically linked to the key operations that define a business instead of being connected to areas that are perceived as unimportant. Ways in which to accomplish this linkage include working for a line business rather than a corporate function and inserting oneself in business planning activities. Being strategically linked gives quality professionals the opportunity to gain credibility, demonstrate the benefits of the performance practices outlined in this book, and work with senior leaders to shape the direction of the company.

"The role of the quality professional is to lead, teach, and audit. They lead the CEO and the Management Board by helping to focus and direct management on critical issues where they need tough goals. They ask the question, 'What are the issues management should put its shoulders behind?' They help the CEO and the Management Board figure out how the organization is running and how to get the organization to 'be there first.'"

—Richard C. Buetow, Retired Senior Vice President, Motorola, Inc., and Motorola Director of Quality

Quality professionals need to visibly demonstrate the multitude of ways in which they can add value to the organization. It is no longer enough to be up to date on the latest techniques and approaches. Paramount is meeting the ongoing needs of internal customers in order to enable them to better serve their constituents. Quality professionals must explore ways to provide unique contributions to key business strategies and long-standing unresolved organizational issues. Once success has been achieved, publicize their outcomes and the approach that was used to reach them.

"I think that quality professionals need to be in tune with what the organization needs and bring those tools and skills to the forefront, rather than being solely concerned about being on the leading edge."

—Nancy M. Johnson, Ph.D., Vice President, Corporate Research and Development, American Family Insurance

These issues and the **SHIFT** occurring within the practice of quality hint at the urgent requirement to broaden the role of quality professionals. Quality professionals may no longer be designated as such, have the word "quality" in their job titles, or work in quality departments. That does not mean that they will not *practice* quality. As the world of business continues to increasingly demand better business results, quality professionals must transition from qual-

SHIFT

- Quality goes [S]ofter
- Quality goes into [H]iding
- Quality goes [I]ntegrative
- Quality goes [F]ar-flung
- Quality goes [T]echnical

ity professionals to performance improvement professionals who are also quality practitioners, incorporating what they know and what they do into the broader landscape of organizational performance.

> "Today we have a tendency to look for ways to do more with less. If we believe the theory that the quality manager is trying to work him/herself out of a job by integrating quality into everyone's job, then we had better focus on finding ways to add value if we want to keep our jobs."
>
> —Jeff Israel, Principal, SatisFaction Strategies

Endnotes

1. Peter M. Senge et al., *The Fifth Discipline Fieldbook* (New York: Doubleday, 1994), 14.
2. James Eicher, *Making the Message Clear* (Scotts Valley, CA: Grinder, Delozier, & Associates, 1993), xii.
3. Senge, *The Fifth Discipline Fieldbook,* 253–257.
4. Rosabeth Moss Kanter, *The Change Masters* (New York: Simon & Schuster, 1983), 64.
5. Kanter, *The Change Masters,* 209–240.
6. Lori L. Silverman and William H. Braswell, Jr., "The Evolution of Coaching in Today's Workplace . . . What's Next?" Presentation given at the Ohlone College Business Roundtable, May 22, 1997.
7. Chip R. Bell, *Managers as Mentors* (San Francisco: Berrett-Koehler Publishers, Inc., 1996), 3.
8. Russell D. Robinson, *An Introduction to Helping Adults Learn and Change* (West Bend, WI: Omnibook Co., 1994), 62.
9. Jack Mezirow and Associates, *Fostering Critical Reflection in Adulthood: A Guide to Transformative and Emancipatory Learning* (San Francisco: Jossey-Bass Inc., Publishers, 1990), 1.
10. Robinson, *An Introduction to Helping Adults Learn and Change,* 8.
11. G. Morgan and R. Ramirez. "Action Learning: A Holographic Metaphor for Guiding Social Change," *Human Relations,* Vol. 37, No. 1 (1983), 9.
12. Chris Argyris and Donald A. Schön, *Organizational Learning II: Theory, Method, and Practice* (Reading, MA: Addison-Wesley Publishing Company, Inc., 1996), 20–21.
13. Etienne Wenger, "Practice, Learning, Meaning, Identity," in "Communities of Practice: Learning is Social. Training is Irrelevant?" David Stamps, *TRAINING* (February 1997), 38.
14. Barbara B. Lawton, "A Whole Systems Approach to Knowledge Management: A Case Study" (unpublished paper, August 1998), 8.

CHAPTER 10

How to Acquire the Skills and Knowledge

Chapter 9 outlined the skills and knowledge required for proficiency in the five fields of performance practice. This chapter focuses on ways to acquire these capabilities, as well as those needed to anticipate the forces that will continue to shape the workplace of the future. The activities described in this chapter are readily acknowledged and easy to talk about. Their challenge is in the doing—making them a part of daily habit.

PURSUE ONGOING EDUCATION

> ". . . take classes, attend meetings, and talk to people about how they accomplish their successes. Check out workshops on facilitation, negotiation, mediation, arbitration, project management, finance for the non-financial manager, conflict management, and international business etiquette. Learning is a lifelong process—what do people pay for except your skill and expertise?"
>
> —Tara Martin-Milius, CEO, Center for Corporate Learning

Formal education (acquiring principles, theory, and concepts as opposed to skill development) is no longer age-dependent or restricted to a particular stage in an individual's career. It is not unusual for adults to return to school to get degrees or certificates on a full- or part-time basis. The issue for these individuals is how to integrate the demands of school, work, and family. In response, some universities are offering innovative options to traditional degree programs. For example, Teacher's College at Columbia University (in coordination with the University of Michigan) offers an advanced program in Organizational Development & Human Resources Management. This program is offered in three, one-week segments over a period of seven months and is taught by experts from across the United States.

> "It's a leap of faith to think the next generation of managers will understand quality well enough to lead the fast-paced improvement the marketplace will demand."
> —Dr. Curt W. Reimann, Senior Scientist Emeritus,
> National Institute of Standards and Technology

Formal education is one of several avenues for learning. Semiformal continuing education, such as short courses offered by colleges, universities, professional associations, and private firms, is also beneficial, especially since it may be further abreast of changes within specific industries and disciplines.

Often, new knowledge can be discovered by taking advantage of events sponsored by the Chamber of Commerce, visiting museums and traveling exhibits, attending meetings sponsored by local chapters of professional associations (including those that you do not belong to), and attending expos that may be in town for a short period of time. When traveling, look for similar opportunities in the local newspaper. During the summer, The Aspen Institute in Colorado sponsors no-cost evening educational opportunities that are presented by world-renowned experts in particular fields of study. Consider events specific to the region that explore issues impacting area businesses and the environment.

Inner Exploration

1. What kinds of ongoing educational events do you take advantage of?
2. What ongoing education have you delayed because of other life demands? How could you pursue these desires?
3. What opportunities for further learning are available to you in your community or organization that you are not partaking in today?

The scope encompassed by the five fields of performance practice is extremely broad and is growing each day. Disciplines as diverse as engineering, finance, human resources, marketing, organizational development, organizational behavior, psychology, quality, the social sciences, statistics, strategy, and systems dynamics have contributed to the development of each of the five fields and to the forces of **CHAOS** experienced today. Who can say whether a particular subject has applicability in the workplace—they may all have a role in promoting organizational performance. Thus it behooves individuals to enhance both the breadth and the depth of their knowledge.

Join and Participate

> "I stay linked with resources at other companies through The Conference Board's U.S. Quality Council and with academics doing research in quality organizations via the National Science Foundation's Transformation to Quality Organizations Research Program and the National Academy of Science programs. Participating in voluntary assignments—such as being a judge at the Ohio Manufacturer's Association team excellence competition—also provides opportunities for networking."
> —Garry J. Huysse, Associate Director,
> Global Quality Improvement, Procter & Gamble

Joining professional, business, and community associations and organizations is an excellent way to acquire and develop skills and knowledge in the five fields of performance practice. The decision to join should be driven by your interests and avocations. There are those that relate to a specific profession or discipline. A sampling of organizations that fall into this category include the American Marketing Association, the American Productivity and Quality Center, the American Society for Quality, the American Society for Training and Development, the American Statistical Association, the Association for Quality and Participation, the Institute of Management Consultants and the National Bureau of Professional Management Consultants (both of which certify consultants), and the Organization Development Network. Consider industry-specific business organizations—where involvement would benefit both you and your organization. Another possibility is to become a member of a business association such as the American Management Association, the Strategic Leadership Forum, the World Business Academy, the World Future Society, and local groups including the Chamber of Commerce and the Rotary Club.

> "I belong to the TQM Center and The Conference Board (these are business memberships). I also recommend the American Productivity and Quality Center."
>
> —Lawrence Schein, Director,
> Total Quality Management Center,
> The Conference Board, Inc.

However, nothing beats participation. Most professional and community organizations depend on the work of volunteers (such as yourself) to survive and function. Volunteering for committee work is a way to give something back to society and to help serve the needs of the organization's members. Volunteer work is almost always rewarding and fun—and definitely instructive—offering the opportunity to meet new and wonderful people, enhance current job skills (or obtain the next one), and round out a resume.

> "I am heavily involved in our local section of ASQ as Section Chair, which includes covering the Database Chair. I also served on the Quality Forum '97 committee and worked as a proctor on certification exams. My activity in ASQ allowed me to make the contacts that eventually resulted in my last two jobs. I have also been actively involved in my local church. I was a community volunteer in the United Way Loaned Executive program and worked on its campaign. I find that volunteer work in the church and community is very rewarding personally and professionally. On a personal note I believe that we all have an obligation to give something back to our communities."
>
> —Lon L. Barrett, Auditor, Boeing,
> and 1997–98 ASQ Spokane Section Chair

Participating in community associations can enhance awareness of the issues influencing the workplace of the future and their impact on the five fields of performance practice. In addition, these groups provide another environment in which to apply the concepts, tools, and methods associated with the five fields.

Inner Exploration

1. What types of business or professional organizations are you interested in joining? How can you find out more about them?
2. What types of nonbusiness activities are you interested in volunteering for? How can you make this happen?

When it comes to joining community associations, let inner passion drive the decision. If you are interested in gardening, join the Garden Club. If you have children who play soccer, volunteer to coach. If you belong to a religious organization, volunteer to assist with their activities. If you feel strongly about poverty, volunteer to help at a free clinic or a local shelter.

"Chairing the Los Angeles County's Quality and Productivity Manager's Network was a very rewarding experience professionally. . . . Personal involvement in schools, senior citizen centers, civic organizations, and volunteer work is [also] valuable. This has to be *integrated* to your own life activities—for example, I was president of the High School Parents Association while my two kids were attending high school. . . . It helps to have a *personal connection.* Valuable experience is gained by working with cross-sections of people who may not be of the same educational, experience, or other common characteristic which you may have. This tends to make you more *flexible* and innovative in fashioning solutions."

—George J. Gliaudys, Jr., Colonel, Staff Judge Advocate,
63rd Regional Support Command, U.S. Army Reserve
(Any views or opinions expressed are personal to the individual and do not represent the U.S. Army Reserve or any other D.O.D. component official views or positions.)

READ 'TILL YOU DROP

"Publications I find valuable in continuing to develop my knowledge base are: *Industrial Engineering Solutions, Sloan Management Review, Harvard Business Review, Quality Progress, Quality Management Journal, National Productivity Review, California Management Review, Academy of Management Review,* and *Executive.* I think that *Forbes* and *FORTUNE* type magazines are good for understanding business trends."

—D. Scott Sink, Ph.D., P. E., Learning Leader, QPM, Inc.,
Past President of the World Confederation of Productivity Science and the Institute of Industrial Engineers

One way to learn more about the disciplines contributing to the five fields of performance practice is to broaden your base of reading to stay current with the trends in each of these arenas. Applicable research (i.e., theory) is in the academic journals and publications. Knowledge of research results can prevent the misapplication of the tools and methods used in the five fields and can guide appropriate practice. Additional information about these tools and methods can be found in applied journals. However, these publications are not always in agreement with research results.

"To stay in tune with quality, the following are staples: *Quality Digest* (good overview of many areas with a human factors orientation), *Quality Progress* (ASQ's view of the world), *Systems Thinker* (systems thinking newsletter), and *Leverage* (newsletter on systems thinking applications). To keep in touch with what is/will be happening: *The Economist* (great world overview from a British point of view), *THE FUTURIST* (wonderful for spotting general trends—you supply the implications), *New Scientist* (the wonderful world of science and research and controversies), and *Discovery* (summary in layman's terms of the scientific community)."

—Tara Martin-Milius, CEO, Center for Corporate Learning

Table 10.1 lists publications that the authors read. This is in addition to reviewing several nonfiction business books each month. Reading does not require imbibing every word of what is written. It may mean scanning the table of contents of a journal, tearing out articles of interest, and filing them for future reference, or browsing through a book to get a feel for the contents and shelving it by topic area. Or, it might imply going to a publication's Web site to skim through an article or publication, then downloading a particular item (as allowed by copyright law) if it appears to be useful. Amazon.com regularly pushes articles on topics of noted interest and informs users of other publications obtained by those who have purchased a particular item. Our personal business libraries, which contain over a thousand books each, function as a network, enabling ready access to information and individual author contacts to further explore a topic.

Inner Exploration

1. What publications do you currently receive? Read?
2. How can you make better use of those that you receive or read today?
3. What publications do you want to add to your reading list?
4. Who could read and report on various publications for you?

"[I read] *FORTUNE* and the *Wall Street Journal* to know how business works, *Fast Company* and *Wired* to find out what's on the edge, and *Quality Progress* from ASQ."

—Alan Backus, Quality Manager, Exide Electronics

Do not limit what is read: Elements of the five fields of performance practice can be found in fiction as well as nonfiction. Read materials specific to an industry and let hobbies and interests guide the search into other areas. Many times an idea spoken about in a nonbusiness publication can be translated into a wonderful idea applicable to any organization.

"When I read, I just page through looking for ideas, not how-to's. Because of my interest in wines and wine-making, I read wine magazines and get some great ideas from them too."

—Richard C. Buetow, Retired Senior Vice President,
Motorola, Inc., and Motorola Director of Quality

Table 10.1
Publications That the Authors Read

For general applied business information: *BusinessWeek* *Fast Company* (always on the leading edge of what's new in business) *FORTUNE* *Nation's Business* (U.S. Chamber of Commerce) *The Economist* *Your Company* (American Express Small Business)	**For applied tools and methods as well as new approaches to business management:** *Harvard Business Review* *Journal of Business Strategy* *National Productivity Review* *Sloan Management Review* *Strategy & Business* *The Systems Thinker* *TRAINING* Magazine	**Journals from professional associations:** *Across the Board* (The Conference Board) *Bulletin of Psychological Type* (Association for Psychological Type) *Journal of Psychological Type* (Association for Psychological Type) *Journal of Quality and Participation* (Association for Quality and Participation) *Management Review* (American Management Association) *OD Practitioner* (Organization Development Network) *Perspectives on Business and Global Change* (World Business Academy) *Quality Progress* (American Society for Quality) *Strategy & Leadership* (Strategic Leadership Forum) *THE FUTURIST* (World Future Society) *Training & Development* (American Society for Training & Development)
For general interest and conversation: *Condé Nast Traveler* *People* *Reader's Digest* *TV Guide* *Golf Digest* *Golf for Women* *House Beautiful* *Official Airline Guide (OAG) Magazine* various airline magazines	**For local business issues:** *Pittsburgh Prospects* (Pittsburgh, PA) *Illinois Manufacturer* *InBusiness* (Madison, WI) *Journal of Business* (Spokane, WA)	**For general news:** *USA Today* *Wall Street Journal* local papers in cities in which we work
To keep up with technology: *Inside WordPerfect* *Wired* *Journal of Quality Technology*	**For information on the field of quality:** *Quality Digest* *Quality Engineering* *Quality Management Journal* *Technometrics*	**To stay on top of current research:** *Journal of Applied Behavioral Science* *Group and Organization Management* *Human Resource Development Quarterly* *Journal of Market Research* Marketing Science Institute publications

THE POWER OF NETWORKING

> "Today we need to continually learn and change—never-ending self-improvement. There are two kinds of networking: Networking for contact development and relationship building, and networking for data-gathering and skills/opportunity assessment. Networking is a life-skill in today's world."
>
> —Jeff Israel, Principal, SatisFaction Strategies

Through networking it is possible to discover what is happening in other organizations, in a particular community, in targeted industries or markets, and in specific professions. Sometimes networking can reliably transmit information on what is happening in one's own organization! A network can be used as a part of a targeted information search, bringing to light new skills, novel approaches, and innovative ideas.

> "I network through my involvement in two groups—the Manufacturer's Alliance and Productivity Improvement Group and the Quality Council for The Conference Board."
>
> —Richard C. Buetow, Retired Senior Vice President,
> Motorola, Inc., and Motorola Director of Quality

> "Being a Tennessee Quality Award examiner for five years was a great learning experience exposing me directly with progressive companies and a great network of professionals across the state. It has taught me practical approaches first hand that are proven and renews my faith in what we are trying to achieve."
>
> —Alan Backus, Quality Manager, Exide Electronics

Everyone knows that networking is important, but not all are as good at it as they would like to be. Here are a few tips gleaned through personal networking experiences.

1. Talk to people everywhere—on the plane, at conferences, in the grocery store, at the local gym. You may be surprised by whom you might meet. The most informative additions to your network will be those who do not know any others in your network. Find out what expertise they possess and learn more about what they are doing with it.
2. Always exchange business cards with the people you meet. Cultivate these relationships by following up with a quick note or e-mail (within a week or two). Better yet, offer to send them something (an article, the name of a book, the name of a contact) and then do it. They will remember you.
3. Regularly contact the people in your network. Send them a copy of an article that applies to their work or e-mail them the title of an interesting book. Refer people who can assist each other back and forth across your network. Make a plan to join them at conferences and professional association meetings. Call them—personal voice contact is in short supply these days.

> "The Conference Board has been a very good experience for me. Whenever I have a problem, there is this whole pool of people I can draw on for ideas and advice. I just pick up the phone and call them. I always know they'll respond."
>
> —David Luther, Vice President of Finance and Administration, Green Mountain Energy Resources; Principal, Luther Quality Associates; Past President and Past Chairman, American Society for Quality

4. Be available to help with personal and professional challenges. Help people to think through a perplexing problem at work and offer to review a resume before it is sent to a potential employer.
5. Write papers and speak at conferences. If you share a similar interest or perspective with someone in your network, write a paper on the topic and submit it to a journal or newsletter for publication. Better yet, submit it as a proposal to a local group or nationwide conference. The benefits of speaking are twofold—normally conference attendance fees are waived for presenters, and there is the opportunity to capture feedback on your thoughts and ideas.
6. Keep your list of contacts current. Record information about how and where you met the individual, what you talked about, what you initially sent to the person, and how to reach the individual. Update this information on a regular basis.

Inner Exploration

1. In what sorts of networking activities are you currently engaged?
2. What networking opportunities are available to you that you are not currently taking advantage of?
3. How can you become more effective in your networking activities?

> "My network of contacts is actually very small. It is comprised of people whom I learn with. This network has grown slowly because of the level of trust and intimacy that is required to participate. (P.S. I am an introvert.)"
>
> —William H. Braswell, Jr., Vice President, Quality Resources, Premera Blue Cross

MUTUAL LEARNING

> "Mutual learning is not simply benchmarking, nor is it industrial tourism. It's openly sharing training materials, data, and anecdotes with other companies and learning to work differently, based on their experience."[1]
>
> —John Petrolini, Director of TQM Technology, Teradyne, Inc.

Mutual learning, as defined by Thomas Lee, President Emeritus of the Center for Quality of Management (CQM), "is a way to implement the collective phenomena."[2] Mutual learning occurs in groups of people that have specific reasons to come together. For example, a group of business leaders may want to study social accounting statements and their potential impact on members' businesses; two businesses may come together to address issues, such as new product development cycle time; or several businesses may desire to implement similar approaches to innovation. At CQM, senior executive groups exchange best practices through study groups and roundtables; others conduct, implement, and analyze research; teach courses; write journal articles; and direct seminars.[3] Participating in this type of mutual learning benefits all participants and their organizations. Those who supply information on a particular approach are moved to record their learning history—what was done, what was experienced, what was achieved, what was learned, and what will be done differently in the future—before sharing it with others. Recipients are able to reduce research and implementation cycle time, accelerate their own learning, enhance commitment to the approach through its use elsewhere, and avoid pitfalls experienced by others.

Another technique for creating a community of mutual learning is a Master Mind Alliance.[4] A Master Mind Alliance is a self-organizing collection of people with a common purpose. It begins with a single individual, who "carefully enrolls another on-purpose, friendly individual. The two people add other unanimously agreed-upon individuals who are willing to work in total harmony for the good of each other and for the good of the group."[5] The purpose of the group is to make a profound difference in the life of each individual, providing the person with incredible strength, power, and possibility. At every meeting, each person (1) shares something positive or good that has happened since the last meeting, (2) shares a problem or opportunity and the support that is desired, and (3) provides support to others by taking that problem or opportunity and visualizing its conclusion or realization. Groups are encouraged to meet at least once a week for 60 to 90 minutes. They typically work best with two to six members. Large groups (e.g., over 12) do not work well because of time constraints.

Inner Exploration

1. What types of mutual learning experiences are you engaged in today?
2. What mutual learning opportunities exist in your organization? What can you do to capitalize on them?
3. If you are not currently a member of a Master Mind Alliance, who is the first person you would invite to join you in this endeavor?

Both of the mutual learning techniques presented here speak to the concept of community. They believe in the power of the individuals who participate to collectively achieve more than the sum of their individual efforts. These approaches can be used to explore each of the individual components of the five fields of performance practice. Undoubtedly, mutual learning approaches will become even more important as the forces of **CHAOS** increase in intensity and speed.

CHAOS

- [C]hanging definition of work and the workplace
- [H]eightened social responsibility
- [A]ging baby boomers
- [O]verarching demographic change
- [S]trategic growth through technology and innovation

TECHNOLOGY ENABLED LEARNING

> "When specific topics interest me, or I need to know more about one, I'll use the Internet. ASQ has a Web site located at http://www.asq.org and for members at http://www.asqnet.org. I will also use a search engine such as YAHOO to locate sites with information on specific topics."
>
> —Lon L. Barrett, Auditor, Boeing
> and 1997–98 ASQ Spokane Section Chair

The possibilities of technology in learning are endless: the Internet, the intranet, e-mail, videoconferencing, and satellite downlink. Through these vehicles one can deliver or receive education (distance learning), communicate with others through chat groups, find resources and references, network to solve a problem, and engage in group decision making. Unknowingly, technology, as demonstrated through e-mail and discussion groups, may be one of the greatest enablers of learning within community—linking together people with common needs and interests all hours of the day and night.

In order to take advantage of these opportunities, keep abreast of technological developments that are taking place. In most cases, it is sufficient to read articles about technology in business publications such as *Wired,* the *Wall Street Journal,* or computer-specific publications such as *MacWorld.* Using experts within one's personal network can help to increase awareness of impending technology issues. Trade shows are another valuable source of information on technology applications. Ask others how they engage technology in their pursuit of ongoing learning: Unknown opportunities may present themselves.

Inner Exploration

1. How do you keep up with technology advancements?
2. How do you use technology to enhance your learning?

WHERE TO GO FROM HERE

Refer again to Table 9.1 in chapter 9. Note those areas where skills and knowledge need to be acquired. For these items, complete the last column on the table titled "How I Will Acquire the Skills and Knowledge."

Endnotes

1. Toby Woll, "Mutual Learning Has Corporations Sharing Good Ideas," *Boston Business Journal,* Vol. 16, No. 41 (November 22–28, 1996).
2. George Taninecz, "Mutual Learning," *IndustryWeek* (July 7, 1997), 28.
3. Taninecz, "Mutual Learning," 28.
4. Mark Victor Hansen, "The Secret of the Super Successful: Masterminding" (Newport Beach, CA: Mark Victor Hansen & Associates), 1.
5. Hansen, "The Secret of the Super Successful: Masterminding," 2.

C H A P T E R

11

COMPASSTM: Leadership Behaviors in The Starburst ModelTM

"There is a strong need to operationally define management from first line through to the executive level. The only thing so far that has operationally defined management has been the System of Profound Knowledge. There is an increasing need for us to gain a deeper understanding of this system. The real advances in management will come out of quality management. However, this hasn't started yet."

—Howard Gitlow, Ph.D., Professor of Management Science,
School of Business Administration, University of Miami

Complete the statement, "Leadership is. . . ." Should leadership be defined in terms of followership? Or in terms of attributes such as courage, vision, credibility, and inspiration? Or as an inward sense of purpose? Or because leadership implies control, might it be the wrong concept to talk about? This chapter speaks to the importance of leadership relative to the **SHIFT** outlined in chapter 2. More specifically, it defines the leadership behaviors that need to be enacted by anyone who has leadership responsibilities for planning, implementing, and evaluating the five fields of performance practice or their individual components, which include the forces impacting the workplace of the future.

SHIFT

- Quality goes [S]ofter
- Quality goes into [H]iding
- Quality goes [I]ntegrative
- Quality goes [F]ar-flung
- Quality goes [T]echnical

LEADERSHIP AND THE FIVE FIELDS OF PRACTICE

The five fields of performance practice are rooted in several assumptions about leadership. First, leadership is purposeful—the behaviors associated with any field of performance practice are undertaken to achieve the desired outcomes for that specific field. In addition, leadership behaviors are learned behaviors. People are not born with them. Finally, as organizations evolve through the five fields, it becomes more and more imperative that all individuals associated with the enterprise be able to exhibit these behaviors.

Concepts such as never-ending improvement, special and common cause variation, customer focus, employee involvement, the impact of process structure on individual behavior, and so on are fundamental to moving organizations forward through the five fields of performance practice. Their associated tools and methods have clearly benefited those organizations that have elected to use them appropriately. Therefore, effective leadership behaviors need to be grounded in these concepts. Because these concepts are based on assumptions that differ from those underlying most traditional management approaches, their use requires a shift in mindset. For example, would there be a need for many of the human resource policies that exist today if there were a healthy understanding of how the theory of variation relates to human behavior? How would current approaches to coaching need to change to reflect an understanding of the influence of process structure on human performance?

> "Quality initiatives started in manufacturing. Then we learned how to use them in nonmanufacturing areas. The last bastion is all levels of management."
>
> —Richard C. Buetow, Retired Senior Vice President, Motorola, Inc., and Motorola Director of Quality

In this chapter, leadership is defined as "the ability to cause others to follow into areas of uncertainty."[1] The behaviors that accompany this definition speak to leadership from the inside out rather than from the outside in (i.e., delegating work to people, motivating others, etc.). Leading from the inside out suggests focusing on who the person is as a leader before the individual engages in external leadership behaviors with others.

> "Leadership is an intimate expression of who we are—our being in action. Our personhood says as much about us as leaders as our acts themselves."[2]
>
> —Kevin Cashman, author of *Seven Strategies for Mastery of Leadership from the Inside Out*

LEADERSHIP AS COMPASS™

In his book, *First Things First,* Stephen Covey uses the metaphor of a compass and the phrase "true north" to describe that which gives meaning and context to where people are, where they want to go, and how they plan to get there.[3] These language symbols provide a means for people to align their lives with what is truly important. In the following sections, the acronym **COMPASS™** is used to describe the leadership behaviors that are common to all five fields of performance practice.

Connect with Change

Not to embrace change as a fundamental part of leadership is the kiss of death in business today. The challenge is to prepare for tomorrow while continuing to do business today. Organizational change and renewal are here to stay. Additionally, they are ongoing requirements for survival. No definitive end point is in sight. Consequently, finding an organization that is "finished" with community building or value creation is an impossible task. Because of the uncertainty and anxiety that change brings to the table, it is important for leaders to help the organization know itself—its values, guiding principles, and underlying philosophies. This will help it to maintain a sense of stability around which renewal can occur.

> "When the rate of change on the outside exceeds the rate of change on the inside, the end is in sight!"[4]
>
> —Jack Welch, Chairman and Chief Executive Officer, General Electric

Dick Beckhard and Rueben Harris describe a basic change formula (that they attribute to David Gleicher) that is useful when addressing individual (including personal), group, and organizational change. In order for change to take place, the following equation must hold true: $D \times V \times F > R$, where R is resistance to change.[5] Change will occur when there is sufficient dissatisfaction (D) with the current situation, a clear sense of the vision (V) for the change, and clearly articulated first steps (F) to accomplishing it. All three elements—dissatisfaction, vision, and first steps—must be in place and must be greater than the resistance that is present in order for change to occur. Kathleen Dannemiller and her colleagues suggest that frustration will result if there is a high degree of dissatisfaction but no vision or first steps. If there is dissatisfaction and first steps, but no vision for the change, people will demonstrate actions that align with "flavor-of-the-month." And wishful thinking, resulting in passivity, comes from having a vision and first steps for the change, but no sufficient dissatisfaction with the status quo.[6]

> **Inner Exploration**
>
> 1. Select a major change that is occurring in the organization. What is the dissatisfaction? The vision for the change? The first steps for accomplishing it?
> 2. Which part of the change equation, if any, needs to be strengthened for this major change?

To achieve organization-wide change, a critical mass must share a common understanding and agreement on each of these three elements described above. Additionally, it is important to establish a sense of urgency—however, not at a level that paralyzes people and prevents them from taking action. On a personal level, leaders must be clear in their own minds on the cause of their dissatisfaction, what they perceive as the vision for the change, and what are possible first steps before attempting to transform the rest of the organization. They must undergo continual personal transformation and become comfortable with spearheading ongoing renewal.

> "What are the functions of a manager? They are to plan, operate, and manage change. Enablers such as TQM, systems thinking, benchmarking, and language technology can help one plan better. It is important to create an environment for *mutual learning* to help these individuals and their organizations learn faster, benefit from hearing how other organizations have applied the enablers in their settings, and achieve organizational progress."
>
> —Thomas H. Lee, President Emeritus,
> Center for Quality of Management

Transformational change and organizational renewal are messy processes; there is no one right way to proceed. In these situations, it is frequently more effective to rapidly turn the PDCA Cycle numerous times than to spend inordinate time in the planning step. Learning through trial and error is often more effective at producing transformational change.

Open Up—Let Go

> "Whatever is flexible and flowing will tend to grow, whatever is rigid and blocked will whither and die."[7]
>
> —Lao Tzu

To "open up and let go" has two meanings—releasing control and embracing continual learning. One paradox of life is that the more we hold onto something, the more likely we are to lose it. Identifying and questioning cherished assumptions and replacing outdated mental models with new frames of reference are both required and central to critical thinking. Giving up control to others is not an easy task, especially since it is one of life's greatest stressors. Instead of trying to externally control situations, seek inherent patterns of order that exist beneath the chaos that can be seen, and search for structures and patterns of interactions that release and intensify the energies within the system.

Inner Exploration

1. What keeps you from giving up control to others? What can you do to alter your behaviors?
2. How do you react to your own failures at work? How do you react to the failures of others in the workplace?

Rather than fighting to remove complexity in human systems, find ways to learn from it. Continual learning capitalizes upon the opportunities and possibilities that exist in everyday situations. In the workplace of the future, failure is a friend, not an enemy, providing the backdrop for learning through trial and error. For leaders, risk taking is far more desirable in these situations than trying to "save face."

Manage Polarities and Meaning

To assume that all problems are in need of a solution is a problematic belief in itself. Not all problems are solvable. Polarities, often couched as "going from" something "to" something else—from individual to team, or rigid to flexible—can only be managed. They are inherently unsolvable because the two sides of the polarity are not independent of one another. Polarity management recognizes that many problems are actually dilemmas and requires the search for the best of both opposites while avoiding their limitations.[8] In his book, *Polarity Management,* Barry Johnson outlines how to recognize the difference between a problem and a dilemma and describes how to map the polarity to maximize strengths and minimize limitations. This approach helps to replace "either/or" thinking with a "both/and" mindset. Since most leadership problems are dilemmas, leaders must personally learn how to manage them rather than attempt to address them as problems.

In and of themselves, data and information have no meaning. Meaning develops only when people engage in meaningful conversation around the data and information. For meaningfulness to occur, asking good questions through the use of inquiry skills is more important than having the right answers. As organizations become communities, the necessity for dialogue and conversation increases. Dialogue differs from discussion. The purpose of dialogue is to create common meaning and new understandings by honoring development of individuals, ideas, and organizations. Dialogue stresses "listening for contribution" rather than passing judgment. It opens the door for fundamental change—within each person (through self-reflection) and the group. Thus, wisdom emerges collectively out of deeper understandings that occur during dialogue conversations. However, dialogue in and of itself is not valuable. The results of the dialogue need to be used in order for it to provide value for all involved parties.

Inner Exploration

1. What dilemmas are you personally facing?
2. What business issues are currently being defined as problems but may actually be dilemmas?

> "The task of the boss is to convene people and engage them in the everyday challenges of how to plan, organize, discipline, and ensure that the right people are on the team and doing the right job. Bosses become convenors and clarifiers, not visionaries, role models, or motivators. . . . Defining the critical questions and deciding who needs to participate in a conversation are tasks for every moment."[9]
>
> —Peter Block, author of *Stewardship: Choosing Service Over Self-Interest*

Practice Unwavering Integrity

> "The wise leader knows that the true nature of events cannot be captured in words. So why pretend? Confusing jargon is one sure sign of a leader who does not know how things happen. But what cannot be said can be demonstrated: Be

silent, be conscious. Consciousness works. It sheds light on what is happening. It clarifies conflicts and harmonizes the agitated individual or group field. The leader also knows that all existence is a single whole. Therefore, the leader is a neutral observer who takes no sides. The leader cannot be seduced by offers or threats. Money, love, or fame—whether gained or lost—do not sway the leader from center. The leader's integrity is not idealistic. It rests on a pragmatic knowledge of how things work."[10]

—John Heider, author of *The Tao of Leadership*

Integrity is doing what you believe in your heart is the right thing to do. Personal integrity ensures that demonstrated actions are consistent with stated words. Professional integrity ensures that these actions and words are consistent with the codes of ethics prevalent within an individual's profession and the organization's industry. Integrity covers ethical behavior, trust, and honesty. Trust is a two-way street—leaders must be trustworthy and they must trust in others. Integrity includes following through on commitments, promises, and obligations. When put in a compromising situation, those who act out of the value of integrity draw on their inner strength to confront it in a sincere and direct manner.

> "One of the roles of management is to 'slay the dragons.' This includes dealing with obstacles that prevent critical initiatives from moving forward."
> —Vice President, Quality, Financial Services

Many of life's situations pose "fuzzy" integrity dilemmas. The appropriate behavior or response may depend on the interpretation of, and relationship between, a variety of factors. Because of these cloudy situations, it behooves individuals, at the very least, to achieve congruence between "the way they think they are acting" and "the way they really behave"—what Chris Argyris has described as the distinction between "espoused theory" and "theory-in-use."[11] Since these inconsistencies are quite common and occur unconsciously, leaders need to request that others provide them with direct and timely feedback at the time that they happen.

Inner Exploration

1. How do you react when you receive feedback on your personal integrity?
2. What fuzzy integrity issues are confronting you?

Attend to the Whole

In order to optimize the performance of an organization, including its relationships with suppliers, distributors, and consumers, leaders need to address the "whole" rather than focus on individual parts and pieces. For many firms, the scope surrounding the "whole" has expanded greatly because of electronic commerce and the ability to conduct business in the global marketplace. Managing an organization as a whole system (also covered in chapter 6) involves making decisions and taking actions based on an understanding of "(1) the organization's strategy, (2) how external factors—market shifts, competitive actions, regulations, the economy, and raw material supply—influence organization performance, (3) how internal factors—processes, functions, systems, policies, and people—influence organization performance, and (4) how the organization is performing in terms of appropriate measures of the organization, process, and job levels."[12]

So, what does this mean from a leadership perspective? It means linking a particular issue and its resolution to the organization's overall business strategy, including its mission and vision. This includes the recognition that cause and effect in chaotic and complex systems (i.e., today's world) are often separated from one another by both time and space. When engaging in strategic planning activities, attending to the whole requires synthesis of often disparate information early in the process, rather than ignoring or discounting information that does not seem to fit. It also requires looking for patterns of interaction within the system, seeking critical and often nonlinear relationships between seemingly unrelated items.

Inner Exploration

1. What helps you attend to the whole?
2. What prevents you from attending to the whole?
3. How experienced are you in using storytelling as a communications tool?

Attending to the whole suggests a move away from a cascade (i.e., top-down) approach to training and communications in favor of bringing large numbers of people together to engage in learning and to tackle important issues via videoconferencing, teleconferencing, or in person through large group interventions. In addition, all technical training and employee development activities must be tied directly to the organization's ideology—its philosophies, values, and guiding principles. Leaders need to become personally comfortable with these approaches and be able to engage in communications via storytelling.

Serve Others

> "Through his deeds a great leader reminds people of their possibilities. His greatness rises not upon the tower of spectacular achievement but from the foundation of the ordinary. He stands not above but among those he leads, upon the same earthy foundation, and beneath him lies the solid rock. All leaders announce themselves as servants of those they lead. For some these protestations only mask their pride. The great leader recognizes his leadership is a duty no more important than any other."[13]
>
> —Stanley Herman, author of *The Tao at Work*

The concept of servant leadership (also known today as stewardship) is not a new one. Robert K. Greenleaf, former director of management research at AT&T, first wrote about it in a 1970 essay titled "The Servant as Leader." He espoused the idea that a leader exists only to serve his or her followers and that they, in turn, grant him or her their allegiance in response to his or her servant nature.

"Stewardship is the willingness to be accountable for the well-being of the larger organization by operating in service, rather than in control, of those around us. Stated simply, it is accountability without control or compliance."[14]

—Peter Block, author of *Stewardship: Choosing Service Over Self-Interest*

Servant leaders aspire to learn and are not driven by needs for power or personal wealth. The attributes that have been used to characterize a servant leader include listening as a way of seeking to understand, helping individuals articulate their own goals and realize their true potential, getting the organization to figure out its overall purpose and vision, and making oneself approachable and available. Servant leaders demonstrate a deep devotion to others, and truly love and care for the people they lead. They believe unconditionally in them as human beings and that doing what is best for others will pay off in the long run. Leaders using this approach create value by virtue of their service to others.

"In the organization of the future it will be the job of the leader to set the values of the organization."

—David Luther, Vice President of Finance and Administration, Green Mountain Energy Resource; Principal, Luther Quality Associates; Past President and Past Chairman, American Society for Quality

This approach to leadership is akin to organizations performing as communities. In order for leaders to be able to engage in servant leadership, the organization needs to alter its view of people and employment. It also must transform its financial practices, human resource roles and systems (e.g., compensation, performance review, etc.), and management practices and structures to align itself with the concept of service, rather than self-interest. The Changing Definition of Work and the Workplace section in chapter 1 provides a fuller description of the types of changes that are required for servant leadership to take hold in an organization.

Inner Exploration

1. If others were to compare you to an exemplary servant leader, what would they say about you?

Seek Self-Knowledge

"The ultimate question is, What is your vision of a good life? In doing research for my books, I ask people for their definition of the good life. Remarkably, I keep hearing the same answer . . . You can boil it down to four elements. You live in a place where you feel you belong. You're with people you love, and your relationships are working—including your relationship with yourself. You've got the right work: You're using your talents on something you believe in, in an environment that fits who you are. And you're doing it all *on purpose:* It fits into your overall philosophy."[15]

—Richard Leider, author of *Repacking Your Bags* and *The Power of Purpose*

Taking time for reflection and introspection—what a radical thought in today's hectic world! Yet, without it each person is left to continue running on the treadmill of life, going nowhere fast. If individuals are born with a reason for being and their life here on Earth is a quest to discover that purpose, then it becomes paramount that they take time for their personal journey of self discovery.

> "What will be the greatest impact on the quality field in the near future? Whatever and whoever can reawaken thoughtfulness in American executives and managers."[16]
>
> —Peter R. Scholtes, President, Scholtes Seminars & Consulting

Leaders need to uncover and continually assess their own values, skills and abilities; preferences and interests; personality temperament; and fears. Knowing this information will allow them to make themselves truly available to others and to discover their vocation—their calling in life[17]—and their purpose—their reason for being. Without this information, it would be extremely difficult for leaders to align their personal values and aspirations with those of their employing enterprise(s). It is not unusual for the life-versus-work issue to arise out of this reflection. This is one of those dilemmas that has no answers, and as such, requires both/and integrative thinking rather than a quest for balance.

Inner Exploration

1. What is your calling in life?
2. What is your reason for being?
3. What can you do to increase the time spent on personal reflection and introspection?

WHAT TO DO ABOUT *YOU*

> "If you seek to lead, invest at least 50% of your time leading yourself—your own purpose, ethics, principles, motivation, conduct. Invest at least 20% leading those with authority over you and 15% leading your peers. If you don't understand that you work for your mislabeled 'subordinates,' then you know nothing of leadership. You know only tyranny."[18]
>
> —Dee Hock, Founder and CEO Emeritus, Visa

Take a few minutes to complete Table 11.1. Reflect on your responses. What common themes exist? How close do you come to displaying the leadership behaviors necessary in today's world and the future that is upon you? What are your strengths? Where are there gaps? We all have room for growth and learning. How will you continue to enhance your leadership behaviors? For some, it may mean scheduling personal quiet time for inward reflection and exploration. Others might engage the services of a personal coach in order to gain honest feedback. Creating a mentoring relationship can also be beneficial. In any case, each person has a responsibility to take care of himself or herself before continuing to harangue about the leadership exhibited by others.

Table 11.1

Assessing Leadership Behaviors

Directions: Use your responses to the "Inner Exploration" questions in this chapter to complete this table.

Assessment / COMPASS™	What This Set of Leadership Behaviors Means to Me	Personal Examples	Areas for Personal Growth and Plan for Accomplishment	My Overall Assessment of Leadership in My Organization and What I Can Do About This
Connect with Change				
Open Up—Let Go				
Manage Polarities and Meaning				
Practice Unwavering Integrity				
Attend to the Whole				
Serve Others				
Seek Self-Knowledge				

On the organization front, you now have ideas and feedback to share with others, as you feel appropriate. You could choose to say nothing and simply demonstrate some of the new leadership behaviors in your daily work. Or you could elect to engage in one-on-one conversations about what you have read here, and include the assessments of yourself and the leadership behaviors displayed around you. Then again, you may decide to create a dialogue session with other leaders around the **COMPASS™** model.

COMPASS

- [C]onnect with change
- [O]pen up—let go
- [M]anage polarities and meaning
- [P]ractice unwavering integrity
- [A]ttend to the whole
- [S]erve others
- [S]eek self-knowledge

This book does not suggest doing nothing at all. Doing nothing at all is not an option. In order for quality initiatives (or whatever they might be called in the future) to grow and flourish, each of us needs to lead our organization forward. This is your call to action.

Endnotes

1. William Ouchi, as quoted in H. K. Brelin, "The Role of Leadership in Total Quality Improvement," *Continuous Journey* (December 1993–January 1994), 33–36.
2. Kevin Cashman, "Seven Strategies for Mastery of Leadership from the Inside Out," *Strategy & Leadership* (September–October 1997), 53.
3. Stephen R. Covey, *First Things First* (New York: Simon & Schuster, 1994), 51.
4. Jack Welch, CEO, General Electric as quoted by Edward D. Barlow, Jr., "The Art of Looking Backwards From Tomorrow," 1997 Air Force Quality and Management Innovation Symposium Presentation.
5. Richard Beckhard and Rueben Harris, *Organizational Transitions* (Reading, MA: Addison-Wesley, 1987).
6. Dannemiller Tyson Associates, Inc., *Developing Large Scale Interactive Process Competence* (Workshop manual, Atlanta, GA, October 11–13, 1995).
7. Lao Tzu, as quoted in Kevin Cashman, "Seven Strategies for Mastery of Leadership from the Inside Out," *Strategy & Leadership* (September–October 1997), 54.
8. Barry Johnson, *Polarity Management: Identifying and Managing Unsolvable Problems* (Amherst, MA: HRD Press, Inc., 1996), xii.
9. Peter Block, "The End of Leadership," *Leader to Leader* (Winter 1997), 13.
10. John Heider, *The Tao of Leadership* (Atlanta: Humanics New Age, 1985), 111.
11. Chris Argyris, *On Organizational Learning* (Cambridge, MA: Blackwell Publishers, 1992), 89–90.
12. Alan P. Brache and Geary A. Rummler, "Managing the Organization as a System," *TRAINING* (February 1997), 71.
13. Stanley M. Herman, *The Tao at Work* (San Francisco: Jossey-Bass Inc., Publishers, 1994), 67.
14. Peter Block, *Stewardship: Choosing Service Over Self-Interest* (San Francisco: Berrett-Koehler Publishers, Inc., 1993), xx.

15. Richard Leider, as quoted in Alan M. Webber, "Are You Deciding on Purpose?" *Fast Company* (February–March 1998), 116.
16. Peter R. Scholtes, President, Scholtes Seminars & Consulting, as quoted in Marion Harmon, "Quality Leaders Predict the Future," *Quality Digest* (April 1997), 28.
17. Timothy Butler as quoted in Alan M. Webber, "Is **Your** Job Calling?" *Fast Company* (February–March 1998), 110.
18. Dee Hock, as quoted in the "The Fast Company Unit of One Anniversary Handbook," *Fast Company* (February–March 1997), 98.

Section

IV

The Starburst Model™: Implications for Your Organization

The two chapters in this section discuss what organizations can do to realize the benefits of the five fields of performance practice. Chapter 12 discusses how to use The Starburst Model™ as a framework for promoting quality and creating value throughout the enterprise. Chapter 13 outlines a process for configuring a department or function to assist management in this endeavor.

C H A P T E R

12

How to Use The Starburst Model™ in Your Organization

Chapters 4 through 8 individually highlighted the five fields of performance practice that serve as the model's core—Quality Assurance, Problem Resolution, Alignment and Integration, Consumer Obsession, and Spiritual Awakening. By bringing the fields of performance practice back together again as The Starburst Model™, this chapter introduces how the model can be used in an organizational setting. At the end of the chapter there is a discussion of some of the challenges that may be faced when employing this model, or any other model of organizational performance.

USING THE STARBURST MODEL™

> "We have gleaned a lot of learning from reviewing 10 years of Baldrige applications. Today, organizations have a better understanding of process management, a better understanding of the need to develop people and to treat them as human resources, and realize that quality is defined by the customer. Where there is significant room for improvement is in strategic integration, alignment of the performance management system (tying key processes to strategy, human resource needs, and organization-wide measures), and how to select, use, and analyze company-level information."
>
> —Harry Hertz, Director, National Quality Program,
> National Institute of Standards and Technology

Today, a number of organizations are acquainted with some (if not all) of the elements presented in the first three fields of performance practice because of the

Malcolm Baldrige National Quality Award Criteria for Performance Excellence and its adaptations throughout the world, the proliferation of books on numerous organizational performance tools and approaches, and the advent of standards such as the ISO 9000 series, QS 9000, and ISO 14000. These enterprises recognize that there is an inherent relationship between the individual concepts, tools, and methods displayed in each of the five fields of performance practice and that it is *not* advantageous for an organization to implement these items in the order in which they are presented in this book, starting with the Quality Assurance Field of Performance Practice. For example, they are aware that the concepts associated with Spiritual Awakening may cause an organization to rethink some elements of its ideology that are a part of its overall architecture (Alignment and Integration). They know that implementing a full-blown process management system (Problem Resolution) can profoundly impact the effectiveness of strategic planning (Alignment and Integration). They understand that the concept of value creation (Consumer Obsession) may alter the way in which an organization designs or refines its quality system (Quality Assurance).

Because quality and value are inseparable from each other, the concept of value needs to be incorporated into those practices associated with the Quality Assurance, Problem Resolution, and Alignment and Integration Fields of Performance Practice. Organizations are encouraged to put in place the concepts and many of the performance practices associated with these three fields of performance practice before attempting to fully implement the concepts and practices associated with the Consumer Obsession and Spiritual Awakening Fields of Performance Practice. This approach will minimize the shortcomings that may be experienced when implementing each of the five fields described at the end of chapters 4 through 8.

Following are a series of steps an organization, a business unit, and/or a division can go through to apply The Starburst Model™ to its situation. These steps help to ensure that improved business performance becomes a reality. Ideally, these steps would be carried out for an entire organization, although individual groups (such as an internal consulting group or functional department) can benefit by going through them. This work can occur over a period of several weeks or months. These steps are as follows:

1. Become acquainted with the concepts, tools, and methods presented in each of the five fields of performance practice, especially those that are new to the organization and its members.
2. Complete the "Your Organization and the _____ Field of Performance Practice" worksheets found in chapters 4 through 8 (Tables 4.2, 5.2, 6.2, 7.2, and 8.1).
3. Complete the **CHAOS** and the _____ Field of Performance Practice" worksheets found in chapters 4 through 8 (Tables 4.3, 5.3, 6.3, 7.3, and 8.2).

4. Summarize the information from Steps 2 and 3 onto Table 12.1.
5. Transfer each concept, tool, and method (i.e., component) listed on Table 3.1 onto individual Post-it® Notes. For more involved tools and methods such as quality system, process management, and organizational architecture, it is advantageous to list each of their components on separate Post-it® Notes.
6. Map the relationships that exist between each concept, tool, and method (i.e., their linkages to each other) within the context of the organization's business and how it views the relationships between these components. For example, the organization may decide that "identifying work process titles" is a prerequisite to the "standardization" of these processes and a prerequisite to the creation of a "systems map." In the following steps, this map is referred to as a relationship map. See Figure 12.1 for an example of a portion of a relationship map.
7. Add to this relationship map other concepts, tools, and methods the organization has embraced over the past five to ten years that are not directly reflected in The Starburst Model™. Also add items from Table 12.1 that are not reflected on the map. Because individuals and organizations come with different frames of reference, there is no "correct" map—a map is valuable when it provides meaning to its users.
8. Designate on the relationship map in some fashion those components that the organization has introduced and attempted to institutionalize over the past ten years, including any that are under way today (it may be useful to refer back to Tables 4.2, 5.2, 6.2, 7.2, and 8.1). Put the date initiated next to each designated component.

Once these steps have been completed, interpret the relationship map. What does it suggest about

- **a.** The field of performance practice that is best understood by the organization? Least understood?
- **b.** The field of performance practice that is most thoroughly deployed throughout the organization? Least deployed?
- **c.** The gaps that exist between initiatives that have been undertaken by the organization?
- **d.** Why specific initiatives were undertaken (i.e., how they were intended to benefit the organization, its customers, its employees, and its shareholders)?
- **e.** Initiatives that may be jeopardized because their prerequisites have not yet occurred?
- **f.** Why particular concepts, tools, and methods did not take hold and become a part of day-to-day business?
- **g.** Initiatives that need to become a part of the organization's strategic plan?

Table 12.1

Your Organization and The Starburst Model™

Assessment Summary / Fields	Summary of Your Assessment (from table noted in column 1)	Summary of Future Plans in This Field (from table noted in column 1)	How the Forces of CHAOS Impact This Field for Your Organization (refer to Tables 4.3, 5.3, 6.3, 7.3, and 8.2)
Quality Assurance Field of Performance Practice (Table 4.2)			
Problem Resolution Field of Performance Practice (Table 5.2)			
Alignment and Integration Field of Performance Practice (Table 6.2)			
Consumer Obsession Field of Performance Practice (Table 7.2)			
Spiritual Awakening Field of Performance Practice (Table 8.1)			

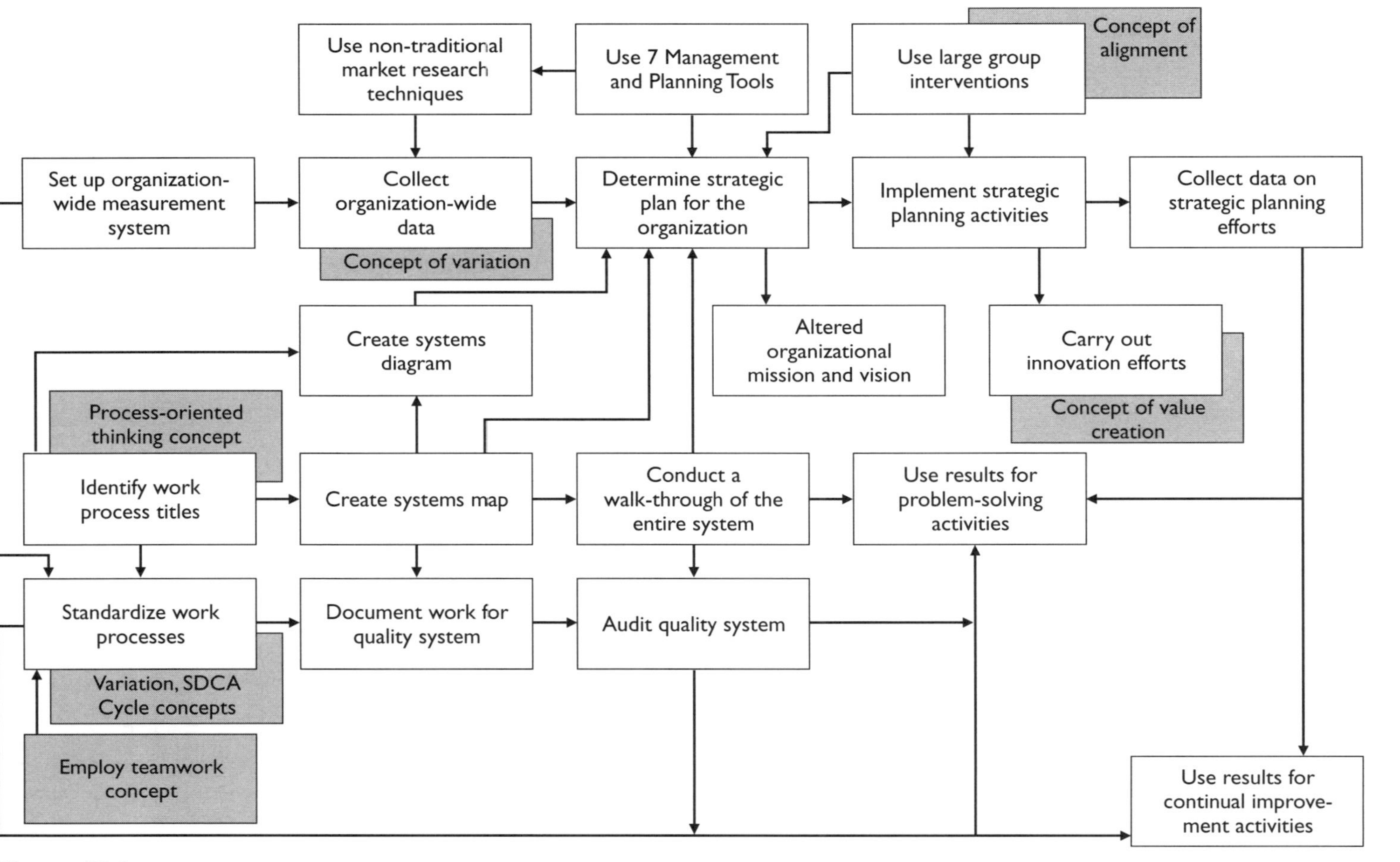

Figure 12.1
An Example of a Portion of a Relationship Map (Note: Shaded boxes denote concepts.)

h. Specific concepts, tools, and methods that are the most critical to the implementation of other components (i.e., they may be a prerequisite to several other components)?

i. The skills that people need in the organization?

j. The future role of those departments and functions whose purpose it is to assist the organization in pursuing quality and value creation for improved overall performance? (More about this topic in chapter 13.)

These questions and their responses will stimulate a variety of actions the organization needs to take to accomplish its targeted business results. Some of them may be easily fixed, some may become part of an operational plan for the coming year, others may have more strategic implications. In any case, awareness of the need to change is a move in the right direction. The vision for the change (i.e., what are things supposed to look like once implementation has occurred?) and explicit first steps for implementation need to closely follow in order for these actions to truly occur. The rest of this section provides some broad-brush recommendations, given three typical scenarios: Organizations that have engaged in very few activities that focus on the concepts, tools, and methods presented in The Starburst Model™; organizations that have used a "shotgun" approach to their implementation; and organizations that have systematically put in place many of the components described in the first three or four fields of performance practice.

> "The Starburst Model™ has helped me to change my thinking and practice. I'm working to extinguish old habits and install new ones which one day will need to be extinguished in favor of the next fundamental change. It also helped me get clear on what my group needs to do to meet business objectives in a tangible way."
>
> —William H. Braswell, Jr., Vice President,
> Quality Resources, Premera Blue Cross

"We Haven't Done a Lot Yet"

If an organization has not engaged in many activities to move the concepts, tools, and methods in the five fields of performance practice into the everyday work of all employees, it should consider implementing a serviceable quality system first (Quality Assurance Field). This quality system normally serves as the foundation for many other performance practices (and is probably noted as such on the organization's relationship map). For example, audit data can trigger problem solving activities. Having processes to ensure control of purchased services and materials begins the process of alignment, with the resulting data acting as the impetus for never-ending improvement. If a quality system is already in place, it should be evaluated to ensure that it is able to fully support activities in other fields of performance practice throughout the organization.

Simultaneous with the implementation of a quality system, the organization may want to articulate some, if not all, of the elements of organization architecture noted in the Alignment and Integration Field of Performance Practice (i.e., its assumptions, values, guiding principles, definition of quality and value, mission, and vision). This work can help to further align and integrate various aspects of the quality system so that they do not send conflicting messages to front-line leaders and employees.

If several pressing financial and consumer issues arise out of quality system data or other key indicators, the enterprise can begin to engage in pilot problem solving efforts. Recognize, however, that systemwide constraints may suboptimize or inhibit these efforts. If serious problems do not immediately surface and a serviceable quality system is in place, the organization will benefit from embracing activities in the Alignment and Integration Field while putting in place the elements of its process management system (Problem Resolution Field). In the Alignment and Integration Field, the organization can proceed with the approaches outlined in the section titled Managing the Organization as a System and walk through the remaining elements of organizational architecture. This concurrent work will ensure that the problems the organization is attempting to resolve are the "right" problems and that their solutions are aligned and integrated with the overall direction of the enterprise. It will also involve all members of the organization instead of select groups and individuals.

"We've Unknowingly Used the 'Shotgun' Approach"

Take a look at the dates associated with those concepts, tools, and methods that the organization has initiated over time. If their order of appearance does not match the linkages drawn on the map, the enterprise may have unknowingly used the shotgun approach (also known as the program-of-the-month approach) in its pursuit of performance improvement, quality, and value creation.

Using this information, ask "What groundwork is missing and preventing the full value of a particular initiative/set of initiatives (e.g., implementing self-managed teams) to be fully realized?" Groundwork includes concepts, tools, methods, and systems that appear as prerequisites on the relationship map. The organization needs to focus on these items first. Otherwise, new initiatives will not achieve expected business results, and the same issues and symptoms will continue to surface over and over again.

The organization will also want to address those concepts, tools, and methods previously introduced that have not become a part of day-to-day business. Attention to this issue will bring to the surface those components that may need to be reincorporated into future initiatives. To prevent the same situation from occurring again, the organization will want to determine what caused them not to take hold in the first place. Some of these issues are covered in the latter portion of this chapter. Once these missing components are fully deployed, the organization can continue to build on them using its relationship map.

"We've Systematically Implemented Many of the Concepts, Tools, and Methods"

Often, organizations that have systematically implemented many of the concepts, tools, and methods depicted in The Starburst Model™ have a framework that guides the implementation of current and future operational and strategic initiatives. For them, The Starburst Model™ and the relationship map are tools for critiquing this framework and making alterations to it, as needed. Thus, they function as mechanisms for continual learning.

To realize the full benefits of the concepts and practices associated with the Consumer Obsession and Spiritual Awakening Fields of Performance Practice, implement them at the same time major gaps in performance, as noted in the first three fields (Quality Assurance, Problem Resolution, and Alignment and Integration), are being eliminated or closed. This performance information should be available through the organization's quality system, its improvement initiatives, its strategic planning efforts, and other assessment/measurement systems. The reason for these gaps may be apparent in the interpretation of the organization's relationship map. There is always the possibility that gaps exists because a particular concept, tool, or method thought to be in place has not yet become habit in certain parts of the organization. Because alignment and integration needs can increase as an enterprise proceeds through the Consumer Obsession and Spiritual Awakening Fields of Performance Practice, it is imperative that the performance improvement framework used by the organization remain aligned with its long-term strategic plan.

> "During the past 10 to 20 years, the earlier indifference of American executives to practicing known-and-proven quality improvement techniques was shattered by Japanese competition in such fields as steel, ship building, automobiles, and semiconductors. In awakening, we discarded our earlier commitments to AQLs and the concept of diminishing returns and replaced these with world-class, leading-edge initiatives such as Motorola's Six Sigma policies and practices. This allowed the United States to recover part of our steel-making preeminence in specialty steels and mini-mills; almost catch up in automobile quality, surge ahead in semiconductors . . . and stay ahead in aerospace. However, the more recent industrial picture has become confused with emphasis on such competing (or counterproductive) initiatives as delayering, reengineering, agility, and numerous ISO requirements. Though the future is impossible to predict precisely, it is clear (I think) that industry, government, and academe will have to increase and expedite their quality improvement activities, even though this may be under a different banner, such as continuous improvement. The incredible changes in technology and globalization are principal drivers for such quality improvements. For properly prepared individuals and organizations, the near-term future should be very opportune—as well as very challenging!"
>
> —Thomas J. Murrin, Dean, A. J. Palumbo School of Business Administration, Duquesne University

CHALLENGES MOVING FORWARD

No matter how an organization elects to frame its initiatives, there will always be issues due to the nature of change. These challenges encompass: What to name initiatives or sets of initiatives in organizational settings; the ability to retain learning around the practices associated with the fields of performance practice; actively embracing the fundamentals in each of the five fields; and what is needed to enhance the existing concepts, tools, and methods within each performance practice.

The first hurdle speaks to the nomenclature attached to specific quality and value creation initiatives or to the umbrella statement that encompasses them. Traditional quality tools and methods are extremely beneficial and should not be carelessly abandoned. Part of a sound quality system is having an organization-wide definition of the word *quality* (and the term *value*) as a means of achieving common expectations and consistent behaviors. If the organization elects to use the phrase, "total quality management" or "continuous quality improvement," it needs to define every word in the phrase so each person (including suppliers and consumers) shares the same frame of reference. If a different umbrella "label" is used, such as "performance excellence," all of the words still need to be defined. On a personal level, when using or demonstrating the use of a quality-based approach, such as the basic tools of quality, there is no need to publicly state "this is a basic tool of quality" unless there is a purposeful reason for doing so.

The true benefits of quality management will be realized when it becomes an inseparable part of the field of management. For that reason, time needs to be spent with others exploring the relationships between quality and value creation, quality and performance improvement, and value creation and performance improvement. Fostering the integration of quality concepts, tools, and methods appropriate for the organization into its day-to-day operations will also help it to realize the benefits of the concepts, tools, and methods and achieve required objectives and targets.

> "In the future I don't see quality as a separate arena. It is one piece and function of what a business does. However, with this we will risk losing some of the gains. Ideas and approaches may be lost unless they are institutionalized in our thought process and definitions are created. We need to standardize the most basic materials and define quality as a piece of management that everyone takes on."
>
> —Barbara Lawton, Ph.D., Vice President,
> Business and Quality Processes, StorageTek

A second challenge has to do with the corporate (also referred to as "tribal") knowledge associated with quality and performance improvement methodology. For example, a number of organizations have problem solving methodologies that outline a series of steps to follow to successfully resolve an issue. However, not all organizations have documented these steps in such a manner as to (a) have them be followed by different types of learning styles (e.g., some styles require more detailed information than others); (b) have them be used by individuals with differing knowledge, skills, and abilities; (c) have them be carried out in a consistent manner throughout the organization (so that everyone is "speaking the same language"); and (d) have them be used in virtual team settings. Frequently, there is no mechanism in place to improve upon the methodology and to spread this learning quickly throughout the organization. So, what happens when the individuals who are the "experts" in this approach and its nuances leave the organization? The methodology, and the learnings associated with it, often disappear as well. Organizations need to set up and build upon systems that institutionalize learnings and recognize the knowledge losses (resulting in increased costs) brought about by turnover.

> "How do you stay the course with revolving top management? We think we've embedded quality tools and methods into everyone's daily work and then the next thing we know we lose it through turnover. When we lose senior management, the focus of attention changes; when we lose customer contact people, it causes us to start from scratch because we lose the knowledge base."
>
> —Vice President, Quality, Financial Services

> "We have also seen an increasing need for introductory material on quality. As quality departments are downsized, those left are not always fully trained in quality, thus requiring solid, basic information."
>
> —Roger Holloway, Manager, ASQ Quality Press,
> American Society for Quality

Enterprises that are actively embracing quality, performance improvement, and value creation approaches organization-wide may be unaware that they are in the minority. There appear to be more organizations not actively using the concepts, tools, and methods presented in the five fields of performance practice than those who are employing them in the day-to-day management of their enterprise. The fundamentals—the basics—cannot be ignored just because we, personally, may be familiar with them. Hence the reason the concepts associated with each field of performance practice were presented in earlier chapters of this book.

What keeps some organizations from embracing the basics? The most frequently occurring theme is whether senior leadership finds any benefit in adopting these fundamentals. Speaking the language of the business, its strategy, and its operating plans, as well as having a good grasp of the complexities of the issues faced in a particular industry and organization, are invaluable here. Role-modeling the required concepts, tools, and methods in highly visible work, and getting tangible business results, can also help an organization and its leaders to see their practical application and benefits. In order to truly actualize these approaches, they need to become an integral part of the organization's strategic plan. This requires taking a look at one's personal use of quality, performance, and value creation approaches at work.

"What is critically needed is a better integration of the business disciplines with quality techniques."

—Dr. Curt W. Reimann, Senior Scientist Emeritus,
National Institute of Standards and Technology

"In order to have effective organization-wide initiatives, you have to get them to be part of the organization's strategic plan. Quality has to start at the top in order to succeed."

—Heero Hacquebord, President,
Consulting in Continual Improvement

The final challenge acknowledges the need for continual improvement in the practices associated with each field of performance practice. Some of these required enhancements were mentioned in Chapters 4 through 8 (e.g., a need to rethink the current models of coaching and strategic planning). For this improvement to occur, some of the theory and practices in the disciplines of marketing, organizational development (also known as organizational effectiveness), and strategy must be altered. There are individuals within each of these disciplines who have written and spoken about these required changes. A few of the changes acknowledged in this book include the need to develop and use: Non-traditional market research techniques, tools and models for rapidly creating and sustaining large-scale discontinuous organizational change, tools and methods for value creation that utilize resource exchange theory, relationship marketing approaches that take into account the results of research on customer loyalty and trust, strategic planning approaches that foster follow-through and strategic innovation.

"Quality Management, in particular, and business/engineering education, in general, will move from academic to industrial universities such as Ford, Motorola, and American Express. These universities will gain accreditation and accept each others' degrees."

—Howard Gitlow, Ph.D., Professor of Management Science,
School of Business Administration, University of Miami

None of the challenges summarized here are insurmountable. In general, in the educational system, there needs to be more integration between quality, value creation, and performance improvement. At a minimum, these three subjects should be intertwined with all business disciplines. Organizationally, overcoming these challenges requires leadership that is actively involved in orchestrating what occurs, a critical mass of educated and committed individuals, an organizational desire to learn and grow, and integration of critical concepts, tools, and methods into the organization's ideology and daily business activities.

"Several years after the start of TQM approaches by individuals interested and knowledgeable in quality, a corporate Quality Department was created. The department shared and learned from other companies and initiated a corporatewide education effort focused on customer/supplier relationships and the importance of adding value in all that we did. Additionally, the company CEO participated in external quality events such as chairing National Quality Month and chairing the TQ Leadership Steering Committee. Since the start, [our] TQ effort has emphasized adding value in relationships with internal and external customers and suppliers. We have also have linked TQ principles and approaches into a restatement of the company Purpose, Values, and Principles."

—Garry J. Huysse, Associate Director,
Global Quality Improvement, Procter & Gamble

CHAPTER 13

Supporting the Organization's Performance Practices

> "There have been organizational changes within the quality area itself—primarily downsizing, and in some cases, elimination of the corporate quality office. . . . Panelists noted several ways in which the corporate quality office is changing
>
> 1. There is less involvement in day-to-day operations, including quality training.
> 2. There is much more involvement in communicating quality to external parties and in strategic planning.
> 3. The corporate office is more involved in alignment activities, including self-assessment.
> 4. The quality person needs to be well received by senior management and has to understand the direction of the company."[1]
>
> —*Quality Outlook 1996,* The Conference Board, Inc.

In the 1996 Conference Board report just cited, 80 experienced quality executives representing 74 companies in the United States, Canada, and Europe, acknowledged that the role of the corporate quality office is changing significantly. These offices are becoming more strategic in their orientation and more external in their focus. As the practice of quality **SHIFT**s, and as organizations deal with the forces of **CHAOS,** departments and functions that support performance improvement must completely rethink how to support their organizations. This activity may result in growth, downsizing, dismantling, or transformation, subsequently

SHIFT
• Quality goes [S]ofter • Quality goes into [H]iding • Quality goes [I]ntegrative • Quality goes [F]ar-flung • Quality goes [T]echnical

CHAOS

- Changing definition of work and the workplace
- Heightened social responsibility
- Aging baby boomers
- Overarching demographic change
- Strategic growth through technology and innovation

impacting the future work of its members. This chapter outlines a process for configuring an organizational unit to support or assist management in promoting quality and creating value to improve organizational performance.

DETERMINING HOW TO SUPPORT AN ORGANIZATION'S PERFORMANCE IMPROVEMENT PRACTICES

The flowchart shown in Figure 13.1 is one approach for thinking through the purpose, roles, responsibilities, relationships, structure, and work processes of a function that assists an organization with its performance improvement practices. This design process presupposes several things. It assumes that a separate function or group may not need to exist to support the organization with its performance improvement practices. Going through the first step, "develop department purpose and title," can result in no purpose statement for a group separate from other functions or departments in the organization. It also assumes that a team has been formed to go through the steps in the flowchart. Working through this process is not an individual exercise (unless you personally want to figure out your own point of view on these items). The team must be composed of those who might work within the existing function or department, and their presumed customers and suppliers (including a senior leadership representative). Finally, performing this design work is not rocket science. It does not take weeks or months to think through these steps if the team embraces the mindset of never-ending improvement. Sometimes the best learning comes from that which does not work well.

> "Quality must become integrated—it cannot be the flavor of the day. What counts is value to the customer and value to the organization. I am pleased to see the elimination of quality departments and quality councils. Quality councils have become business councils or leadership teams and are used to run the business."
>
> —Marie Baucom Williams,
> President and CEO, Tennessee Quality

It is advantageous for an organization to have gone through the steps noted in Chapter 12 before proceeding with the approach described here. The development of a relationship map and its interpretation can be used to frame the initial steps in the design process. However, this approach can be engaged without the full completion of the work outlined in chapter 12.

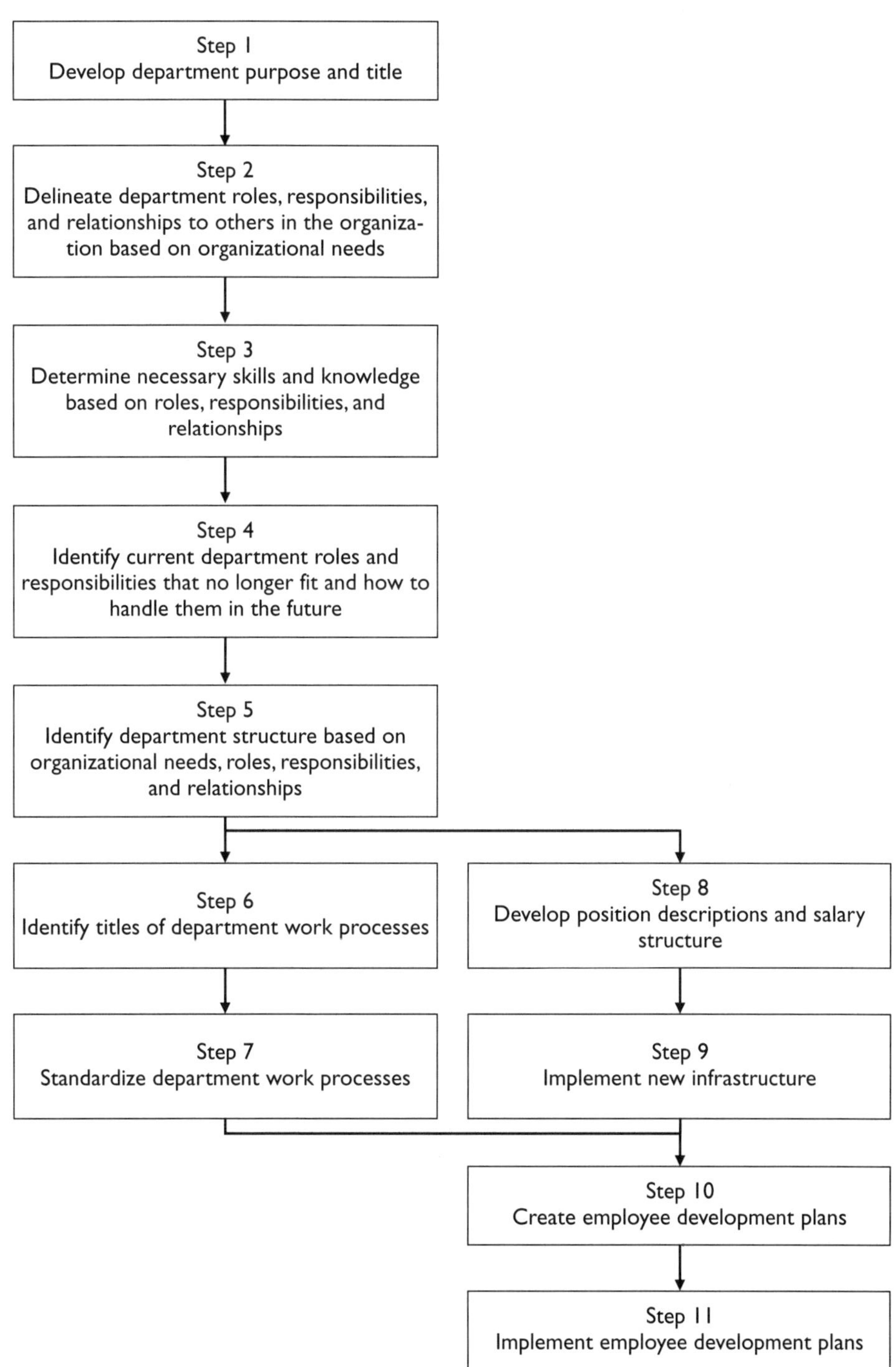

Figure 13.1
Determining How to Support an Organization's Performance Practices

Following is a description of each step in the flowchart. For the purposes of discussion, the words "department" and "function" are used interchangeably. These terms are used even though the resulting roles and responsibilities may be housed in a department or division that has primary roles other than, or in addition to, supporting performance practices that lead to improvement.

Step 1: Develop Department Purpose and Title

Before developing a purpose statement, it is important to collect and review the following types of documents: The organization's strategic and annual plans, the results of current quality/change/performance improvement efforts (including internal and external self-assessments and audits), organization-wide measurement system data, and competitive intelligence information. If a relationship map has been created, it can be used as one input to this step. These data and this information will help the team to determine whether there is a need for a distinct performance improvement function, independent of whether it is free-standing or part of another department or unit. Once the decision is made to keep, reframe, or create a separate function, the team can proceed to determine the purpose of this unit.

The purpose statement needs to answer the question, "What are we collectively paid to do and for whom?"[2] By definition, the department's purpose must be aligned with the vision and mission of the organization. In framing this purpose statement, it may be useful to consider the five fields of performance practice outlined in chapters 4 through 8.

> "In our organization, the quality department's mission is: *We provide guidance and assistance in quality, technical, informational, and process improvement for our internal customers to ensure world-class products and services that exceed customer expectations and create value.* Today, my department has no direct control of quality—no inspectors, no cops."
>
> —Alan Backus, Quality Manager, Exide Electronics

Eventually, the department purpose statement will be superseded by the collective titles of the work processes performed by the department. At this point in the process it serves as an outer boundary for ascertaining the work of the department. Once the purpose statement has been written, the team can decide on a "name" for the function.

The major challenge in this step is to define the purpose statement widely enough to allow the function to grow and thrive while not undertaking purposes that are better served by other parts of the organization. If it is discovered that the purpose statement mirrors that of another unit in the enterprise, the team will want to reassess the need for the function.

> "The mission statement for the Business and Quality Processes Department is: *to support achievement of StorageTek's goals through focused innovation and improvement around StorageTek's core business processes. We do this by accelerating the learn-*

ing and sharing of knowledge across the corporation, and actively assisting individual business units in applying this knowledge through process innovation and improvement. The business units in our organization are moving toward value creation. It is our job to enable them to do this through learning, sharing, and applying knowledge. We are also trying to build communities of practice around core learning areas (i.e., critical processes). Our focus must be on identifying the performance gaps in the business units and using the learning, sharing, and applying knowledge cycle to close the gaps. In the future we will engage in generative 'as is–to be' activities, not just problem solving."

—Barbara Lawton, Ph.D., Vice President,
Business and Quality Processes, StorageTek

Step 2: Delineate Department Roles, Responsibilities, and Relationships to Others in the Organization Based on Organizational Needs

Using the organizational documents collected in Step 1, the purpose statement for the function, and the five fields of performance practice, the team identifies the department's overall roles, and the responsibilities that fall under each of them. Part of this step includes determining the current and future needs of the organization that fall within the department's purpose statement.

"My vision for the future of my division is that there would be five roles that would fall under Corporate Research and Development. These are strategic planning, strategic research, improvement resources (which includes project management as well as facilitation of projects), innovation, and strategic information."

—Nancy M. Johnson, Ph.D., Vice President, Corporate
Research and Development, American Family Insurance

Once roles and responsibilities have been defined, it is important for the team to outline two sets of relationships. The first set is comprised of other parts of the organization that may provide related products and services. Partnering arrangements will need to be formed with these units. The second set lists the primary customers to be served by the department. Work agreements (or "contracts") will need to be collaboratively developed with these groups and/or individuals. In order to facilitate both sets of relationships, it may be helpful to have representatives from these areas become a part of the team going through this design process, if they are not already involved. The team's major challenge in this step is to not be limited by current practice and issues. This will require the team to consider the long term, be open to "out-of-the-box" thinking, and continually focus on what will provide value to consumers, employees, and shareholders.

"There are 16 individuals in our quality group. Together, we have three primary roles. The first is to collect and provide feedback each day on the voice of the customer. Part of this work includes moving beyond satisfaction to addressing customer loyalty. We have been working closely with a market research group to figure out the elements that create a loyal customer. Our second role is in integration and interdependency. We are the only group in the organization that looks across the whole system. Our third role is in knowledge management—what I call fast-cycle learning—so that people within the organization can provide high-quality service to their customers. Together these three roles allow us to add value to the organization. In order to provide value, you need to be constantly on the lookout for products that will be viewed as adding value to the organization. For example, we set up a vendor management process before the organization asked for it."

—Vice President, Quality, Financial Services

Step 3: Determine Necessary Skills and Knowledge Based on Roles, Responsibilities, and Relationships

This step focuses on the skills and knowledge required within the department to fulfill the designated roles and responsibilities, and to foster the necessary relationships. The identified skills should encompass tools, techniques, methods, approaches, and strategies. They may be technical, interpersonal, leadership, or organizational in nature. Knowledge areas include related concepts and theories. The information provided in chapter 9 is applicable in this step. As in the previous step, the challenge here is to broadly define the required skills and knowledge—and not be limited by traditional quality and/or performance improvement thinking and practices. It is quite possible that the team will need to research the required skills and knowledge through contacts with other organizations, readings, or attendance at conferences.

Step 4: Identify Current Department Roles and Responsibilities That No Longer Fit and How to Handle Them in the Future

Before beginning this step, the team needs to collect data on current roles and responsibilities if the function has been in existence prior to beginning this design process. Since position descriptions are usually not very descriptive, and may not be reflective of the work being performed today, it may be advantageous to have current staff members keep time logs for several weeks. Another good source for this information is individual calendars.

Chances are that in Step 2 the team identified a number of new roles, responsibilities, and relationships that must be undertaken by department staff. Because time is finite, one of the reasons for going through this step is to figure out where the time will come from to perform the new work. One good place to find time is to stop doing work that no longer needs to be performed. Current roles and responsibilities that do not fit with the new purpose of the department are good indicators of work that can be eliminated.

There are four ways to handle the work that needs to be eliminated. First, if the need for the role or responsibility no longer exists, the team should create a plan to phase this work out as quickly as possible. Second, if the need for the work still exists, but it is best done elsewhere, the team should develop a plan to turn over the work to the appropriate function or department as soon as possible. Third, if the need for the work still exists, but there does not seem to be a logical home for it in the organization, someone must be assigned to it for the moment. This individual is responsible for figuring out how to minimize the amount of time spent on it. At the same time, the team must delineate the steps that will be taken to find or create a place for it elsewhere in the organization. Fourth, if upon further examination, the team discovers that a particular role or responsibility is actually work that needs to be performed by the department, it may be necessary to expand the department's purpose statement.

The greatest difficulty in this step is letting go of work that personally interests department staff. Often, more importance is given to roles and responsibilities that have been carried out for a number for years. However, it cannot be forgotten that providing value to the organization's consumers is the top priority. Another issue will be the communications necessary to deploy work previously performed by department members into the hands of all employees.

Step 5: Identify Department Structure Based on Organizational Needs, Roles, Responsibilities, and Relationships

Critical to this step is the concept of "form follows function." The team needs to determine the structure of the department based on the function's primary customer relationships, and the roles and responsibilities that need to be performed to meet the needs of these constituents, both of which were identified in Step 2. Structure includes number and type of staff, the relationship between staff members, the connection between staff members and their primary customers, the amount of time required from each position, and the association between each member and the organization (i.e., employee, contractor, etc.).

Over the past ten years we have witnessed the collapsing of quality departments into human resources or strategic planning functions. In addition, some organizations have elected to expand traditional quality control/assurance functions to include areas such as organizational development, training (not necessarily specific to quality), safety, strategic planning, and industrial engineering. If the organization is serious about making the practice of quality a part of everyone's work, the structure of the department needs to reflect this philosophy. This may require attaching staff members to the core of the business rather than having them function out of a centralized area. It may also mean a leaner department.

> "Our quality directors report into the heads of the businesses. We have a small corporate quality group that has a tight relationship with all sectors and groups. We take people with business experience and bring them into the quality world. They are taught the tools of quality very quickly. It is hard to do the opposite.

These individuals are promoted into a quality role for two to three years and then are promoted out of it, typically into an operational role."

—Richard C. Buetow, Retired Senior Vice President, Motorola, Inc., and Motorola Director of Quality

Step 6: Identify Titles of Department Work Processes

Work process titles should be based on the new work of the department. One approach for determining these titles is to have the team identify all of the activities that need to be performed to fulfill the identified department roles and responsibilities, and to establish and maintain the necessary sets of relationships. If these activities are recorded on individual Post-it® Notes or index cards, they can then be categorized using affinity diagrams into work process groupings. The label for each grouping is the title of an individual work process. These titles should be recorded in verb-noun format. They eventually will replace the purpose statement articulated in Step 1. (This approach is also described in chapter 4).

Step 6 can occur simultaneously with Step 8: Develop Position Descriptions and Salary Structure.

Step 7: Standardize Department Work Processes

Standardization of work processes should occur using a systematic approach, such as that shown in chapter 4, Table 4.1. Those individuals who will be responsible for performing the work processes (rather than the team going through this design process) should be involved in standardizing them. Modifications to the recommended standardization approach may have to be made if the work process does not currently exist. This step can be time-consuming, especially for those work processes that did not exist in the past. It will be tempting to short-cut this step. However, doing so will produce less than desired results.

Step 8: Develop Position Descriptions and Salary Structure

The core items on the required position descriptions need to state the work processes served by department members; the level of responsibility and authority they hold relative to each of these work processes; and the skills, knowledge, and abilities required to perform them. They also need to include all information required by the organization's Human Resources Department. Some parts of these descriptions may not be able to be completed until work processes are defined more thoroughly in Step 7.

Ask for guidance from the organization's Human Resources Department on salary structure. You may also want to consult *Quality Progress* for the latest nationwide quality professional salary survey. Similar surveys are also conducted by other professional organizations and may be useful here, depending on the roles and responsibilities determined in Step 2 and the skills and knowledge identified in Step 3.

Step 9: Implement New Infrastructure

In Step 9, the outputs of each of the previous steps are formally implemented throughout the organization. (Note: Step 7 does not need to be completed to proceed with this step.) It is assumed at this point that the outcomes of Step 4 have already been put into motion. It is also assumed that there has been some piloting of the outputs of Steps 1, 2, 3, 5, and 7, either through discussions with others outside the team that put them together or through actual testing. The challenge associated with this step is to continue ongoing learning and to alter outputs, as appropriate.

> "We need to be on the cutting edge of the organization's problems and opportunities. Therefore, we have Business Unit Consultants who report directly to the General Manager of each group; a small pool of Business Process Consultants who the business units can draw upon; Practice Managers who convene groups of people together around critical processes (such as new product development); and several specialists with expertise in organizational learning, systems dynamics, and organizational development."
>
> —Barbara Lawton, Ph.D., Vice President,
> Business and Quality Processes, StorageTek

Step 10: Create Employee Development Plans

In order for department members to carry out the department's newly determined roles, responsibilities, and relationships, and the required skills and knowledge, they will need to assess their current knowledge, skills, and abilities against these items. Given the spirit of never-ending improvement, this assessment information is the foundation for the creation of individual development plans. These plans need to include areas for future growth and development as well as the strategies and specific time frames for their achievement.

Step 11: Implement Employee Development Plans

This step is the implementation of the development plans created in the previous step. It includes ongoing reviews, feedback, and recognition. A major issue in this step is the time required to develop new competencies.

FOOD FOR THOUGHT

Dana Gaines Robinson and James Robinson's 1995 book, *Performance Consulting: Moving Beyond Training,* spearheaded changes in the work of professional trainers and has been cited as a "must read" for all human resource development professionals. This book encourages trainers to shift their focus away from learning toward performance—what organizational members must *do* each day. Other professions, including quality, industrial and management engineering, information management, finance, organizational development, strategic planning, and marketing, are converging on the same realization from their unique perspectives. Providing value is paramount; performance management is key to its accomplishment.

There is no doubt in our minds that there will be a number of functions within an organization that will identify purposes, roles, and responsibilities related to the practice of quality, value creation, and performance management. The real question is whether they will compete with one another for internal customers, or recognize that they need to work together in a collaborative manner on behalf of the consumer. The real need is for professionals in all of these areas to become familiar with each other's theories, concepts, tools, techniques, and methods.

> "For someone involved in QI [Quality Improvement], learning about OD [Organizational Development] can add valuable process skills needed by change agents, while those involved in OD might find less 'fuzzy' QI problem solving techniques to be an effective way of initiating change. Many successful QI efforts include OD technologies to assist the change process, and there is likely to be more integration of the two fields in the future."[3]
>
> —Duke Okes, Management Consultant, APLOMET

Endnotes

1. Anna S. Powell, *Quality Outlook 1996* (New York: The Conference Board, Inc., Fall 1996), 15.
2. Maurice Hardaker and Bryan K. Ward, "How to Make a Team Work," *Harvard Business Review* (November–December 1987), 113.
3. Duke W. Okes, "Quality Improvement and Organization Development," *The Quality Management Forum* (Winter 1991).

Section

V

Your Career in Organizational Performance Improvement

The three chapters in Section V present actions that professionals who specialize in enhancing organizational performance—internal and external quality, organizational development, human resources, training, marketing, finance, engineering, and information systems professionals—can take to ensure their employability in the workplace of the future. Chapter 14 provides an approach for determining one's vocation, career, or job and the numerous steps involved in making a job and/or career change. Chapter 15 explores what it means to be an external consultant, whether to join an established firm, how to start a firm, and the daily challenges faced by those currently in this role. Chapter 16 provides the steps for creating a personal action plan.

C H A P T E R

14

Enacting Your Career: Thriving in **CHAOS**

This chapter is purposefully titled "Enacting Your Career: Thriving in **CHAOS.**" In the strategy field, the word *enact* has come to mean being actively involved in the process of "setting something into motion" or "putting something into place." In the process of enacting your career, you must take into account the forces of **CHAOS** and the **SHIFT**s taking place in the practice of quality. Doing so will prepare you to thrive in the workplace of the future.

CHAOS

- [C]hanging definition of work and the workplace
- [H]eightened social responsibility
- [A]ging baby boomers
- [O]verarching demographic change
- [S]trategic growth through technology and innovation

SHIFT

- Quality goes [S]ofter
- Quality goes into [H]iding
- Quality goes [I]ntegrative
- Quality goes [F]ar-flung
- Quality goes [T]echnical

If you are in the position of protecting your job, it is already too late. Being actively out in front of your career and working to shape its future is a much more desirable position. Protecting your job might actually be the *worst* thing for your career. Many people (including the authors) have unexpectedly lost their jobs and ended up in much better positions as a result. In fact, most of the tips offered in this chapter are things that the authors have used or learned from their friends and colleagues.

This chapter covers a variety of topics to help you enact your career. You will learn how to assess your current job and career and decide whether your current job is a good match for you. In addition, you will learn about transferring your skills and knowledge to other career choices and how to change jobs if necessary.

ASSESSING YOUR VOCATION, CAREER, AND JOB

> "There are three words that tend to be used interchangeably—and shouldn't be. They are 'vocation,' 'career,' and 'job.' Vocation is the most profound of the three, and it has to do with your calling. It's what you're doing in life that makes a difference for you, that builds meaning for you, that you can look back on in your later years and see the impact you've made on the world. . . . Career is the term you hear most often today. A career is a line of work. . . . You can have different careers at different points in your life. A job is the most specific and immediate of the three terms. It has to do with who's employing you at the moment and what your job description is for the next 6 months or so. Trying to describe what your job will be beyond 12 to 18 months from now is very dicey."[1]
>
> —Timothy Butler, Director of MBA Career Development Programs, Harvard Business School

In keeping with the definitions described here, you will approach enacting your career in a different manner than you may be used to. Instead of beginning with your vocation and deducing from that the job you want, you will begin by assessing your current job. Stephen Covey calls this putting "first things first."[2] Engage your heart and your cognitive abilities as you go through the following steps.

The first step in enacting your career is dealing with the immediate issues of your current job. Record the following information:

1. What I like about my job is . . .
2. What I do not like about my job is . . .
3. Opportunities that are available to me at work over the next few months are . . .
4. Events that could endanger my job in the next few months are . . .

Synthesize what you have written and note themes or patterns that appear. Determine how to address the issues that become apparent.

Now turn your attention to your career. The best career decisions are grounded in those areas that deeply interest you.[3] However, your deep interests may not match your skills and abilities. One tool that can help you identify your interests is the Strong Campbell Interest Inventory. A career placement office at a college or university, or a career counselor can administer this inventory for you. Record your deep interests across the top of Table 14.1. Next, brainstorm a variety of business activities—for example, tracking financial information, writing ad copy, providing patient care. Record them down the left-hand side of Table 14.1. In each cell, write down at least one possible way these two items intersect in the world of business. Once you have completed the matrix, look for patterns and synergies—the potential elements of a desirable career.

Now it is time to turn your attention to your vocation. As Timothy Butler stated earlier, your vocation is your calling. It is what brings meaning to your life.

Table 14.1
Determining Your Career Possibilities

Your Deep Interests / Business Activities						

This is your higher-order purpose statement. Two techniques that are useful in clarifying your vocation are to articulate

1. What I want people to remember me for is . . .
2. What I want written in my eulogy is . . .

Given the information presented in this book, ask yourself, "What have I learned about the role that quality plays in my job, my career, and my vocation?" Your next steps will depend on your answer to this question.

If you discover that your current job is congruent with your career and vocation assessment, continue along the path you have set out for yourself. On the other hand, you may discover that there is a mismatch between your current job and your assessments. In this case, you will have to determine what you want your next job to be. Sometimes the job you realize you want does not currently exist within the organization. You will have to either create it in your current organization or move to another one. The rest of this chapter outlines some ideas that may help you make these changes.

STAYING IN YOUR CURRENT ORGANIZATION

If you decide to stay in your organization, three different options are available to you. You can stay in your current position and enhance it, you can take on another open position, or you can create a new position in the organization for yourself.

If your career and vocational assessments are congruent with your current job, then you have no reason to change (unless, of course, the position is being eliminated from the organization or you decide you want to do something else). To prevent stagnation, find ways to enhance what you are already doing. Enhancements have to both add value to the organization and match your career and vocation. Actively seek and take on special projects. Identify unmet needs in the organization that you can fulfill, especially those that directly impact consumers.

If your career and vocational assessments are not congruent with your current job, then you need to make a decision. You may elect to stay in your current job because the time is not right to make a change. Or you can search for other positions in the organization that match your interests and needs. Now the question becomes one of where to apply the interests and the skills you enjoy using. At first glance, many of the following possibilities may not seem realistic to you. However, we suggest you take a second look.

> "I was a Quality Engineer and a Quality Manager for ten years in three different organizations before I was selected for the position I have today as a Development Consultant. My current responsibilities include coordination of education and training needs assessments, developing programs that meet these needs, conducting the classes, and monitoring and tracking performance as well as the

effectiveness of each training program. I am also expected to interact with customers and suppliers, and to interface with colleges and universities who may be able to assist us. My previous quality experiences have given me a customer-oriented view, invaluable problem solving skills (especially with regard to the interaction of variables), a healthy appreciation for attending to details (e.g., in data manipulation), and an understanding of terminology such as 'performance management,' 'associate involvement,' and 'just-in-time.'"

—Dean A. Garner, Development Consultant,
Wilson Sporting Goods

"I managed a strategic planning and quality department for about two years before I took a product manager position in the Corporate Services Division of a mid-sized commercial bank. My prior experience has given me a broad base of knowledge that I've applied to several functions of my current job. First, knowledge and understanding of process study—the ability to flowchart existing processes and then use quantifiable data methods to study and justify improvements—have been instrumental in our ability to improve client services; second, upgrading the quality and quantity of primary and secondary market research as a means of leveraging the 'voice of the customer.' I was one of the few product managers (out of eight) that could effectively evaluate and improve our products and services. Finally, knowing the power of cooperative teams, meeting management, coaching techniques, and clear delineation of roles and responsibilities have put our unit in a position to increase volumes and meet internal and external challenges. I would be remiss if I didn't say a few words about leadership. With a better understanding of effective leadership, I continue to learn and practice the skills and characteristics that help create a shared vision and develop support/committed relationships among employees."

—Randy Rossi, AVP, Business Banking Manager,
Southwest National Bank

Sometimes the search for a position in your organization that matches your desires leaves you empty-handed. In this situation, you must make the decision to leave the organization or to stay and create a new position if you believe it will add value. If you decide to stay, do not be deterred by those who tell you that it will be impossible to create a new role. Our parents taught us "Where there's a will, there's a way." Consider the following story.

"In February of 1995, I was 'volunteered' to attend a two-week seminar on decision and risk analysis (D&RA). I wasn't sure this was going to be my thing, but when I began performing the role of D&RA facilitator, it wasn't so bad. I had to facilitate meetings, gather and analyze data, and draw inferences—quality engineers know how to do that. In fact, it has been this skill that has allowed me to stay employed.

"Nearly two years ago, my company announced it would close its New England–based facilities and consolidate them with its Pittsburgh operations. Since cost reduction was the motive, there were also personnel cuts. I was not offered a position in the new organization, although for personal reasons I would not have relocated if I had been.

"My original assignment end date was June 30, 1997. At that time, because there was no demand for my usual services, I looked for other assignments. Since

I was the only active D&RA facilitator in the business unit that needed D&RA facilitation, that's what I did. In short order, my case load of D&RAs grew to consume 100% of my time. This experience not only helped me become more proficient at the task, it provided numerous opportunities for personal exposure. I became the 'go-to' guy when a D&RA was needed.

"As June approached, several of my clients initiated requests to have me extended because they saw me as adding value. A few encouraged me to submit a proposal to stay on with the company, working from an office in my home. Acting on their advice, I proposed serving as a quality engineer in support of the entire company with 50% of my time devoted to D&RA facilitation. The consequence was an extension to March 31, 1998.

"As the deadline approached, I began getting calls from a number of people within the organization—including vice presidents. They wanted me to stay, but it was too late. I had already accepted another job. I now work for a consulting company providing decision and risk analysis and quality engineering services. I like what I do, and I don't have to move."

—Nick Martino, Senior Consultant, Decision Strategies,
formerly a quality engineer at a chemicals company

What is the moral of this story? First, Nick did not refuse the new training, even though he was not sure how it related to his job or his career desires and vocational calling. His new job is rooted in what he learned during the training, the application of these skills back at work, and his prior role as quality engineer. Second, he quickly realized that many of his old skills were still relevant. Third, he practiced the new skill, even before his current job was threatened. Fourth, he was proactive in his response to the potential loss of his job. He looked for opportunities to use his skills in areas that were important to the business—perceived by his customers as adding value. Finally, he submitted an attractive proposal to the company that showed the value he was providing and presented the business case to stay. What we know from Nick is that he "really enjoys" combining a technical, statistical tool with the financial side of the business. The steps Nick followed sound pretty simple when we read his story. However, he put forth a lot of hard work and ingenuity.

Now it's your turn. If you want to stay with your current organization, discover ways you can add value and communicate this information to others. Don't hesitate to speak up. Have people who realize the value you bring to them and their consumers advocate on your behalf. Here are a few additional tips.

1. Don't take on the attitude "it's not my job." Your interests have wider applicability than you may think. Be open to accepting assignments that at first glance may appear outside your traditional role. Turn down work only if it truly does not match your interests (and you are willing to accept the consequences of this decision), or if you perceive it will not add value to the organization's consumers or those who serve them.
2. Do not wait for people to come to you. Go to others in your organization with value in hand and offer your services.

3. Perform your work in a professional manner. Never compromise quality or your personal values and principles.
4. Pay attention to how you treat others. Use people's names in conversations. Return voice, fax, and e-mail messages in a timely manner so others can move on with their work. One of the author's parents used to say "you meet the same people going up the ladder as you do going down the ladder."
5. Never stop learning. Take advantage of every reasonable opportunity: Formal education, seminars, self-study, the example of others. Become active in a community organization or professional association as a means of gaining new experiences and skills, and giving back to society.
6. Keep your resume and/or curriculum vitae up to date. Keep track of job changes, skills, personal and professional accomplishments (e.g., chair of your religious organization's entertainment committee, secretary for a professional society, Gardener of the Year Award), talks, articles, and other critical information about yourself.

"There are several key actions people can take to enhance their careers: (1) understanding the politics of the organization and how to work with that system, and figuring out how to respond to the evils of the system without destroying yourself or the system; (2) collaborating with the people who hold the power in the organization, getting buy-in and support; (3) gaining credibility in the organization by demonstrating that they are working for the good of the organization by helping others solve problems; and (4) working very hard to help others achieve the organization's objectives."

—Tim Fuller, Partner, Fuller & Propst Associates

LEAVING YOUR CURRENT ORGANIZATION

"At [my former employer], I paid for it by trying to believe that the top brass really meant that they were committed to quality when, in my heart of hearts, I knew they were not. I refused ever to give up, even when it became clear that most supervisors clearly placed personal interest above protection of loyal employees. The result was my name appearing on the short list for 'downsizing' after over 16 years of contributions, including bringing about corporate culture changes, from decisions by the seat of the pants to data-driven decisions. This culture change happened so slowly that its beneficiaries believed it was their idea. Of course, I could have done better. I could have been more patient, tactful, and polite. I could have sacrificed my principles, folded my tent, and stolen softly into the night to come back and fight again. But at every opportunity, I turned those options down, made my statement, and suffered the consequences. I must say that doing so has caused my family and me some personal turmoil, but it has always resulted in a better financial situation in the next job."

—Lynne B. Hare, Director, Applied Statistics, Nabisco, Inc.

Occasionally, when enacting your career, you may discover the need to switch organizations. Perhaps its values do not fit with yours, or perhaps you cannot meet your vocational or career needs in the current situation. You might find yourself having to decide whether you are willing to meet the demands of the organization or whether you are going to look for your next job somewhere else. Sometimes you might discover that this decision has been made for you. Whatever the chain of events that led to the need to change organizations, the result is usually the same. Find employment.

As many of us can attest to, finding a job is not easy. Often, we let the job find us, which is not usually the best-case scenario. Here are six sets of steps to help you discover meaningful employment opportunities.

Phase 1: Framing the Employment Opportunity

Respond to the following items after reflecting on them. Record your responses in writing so you can refer back to them at a later date.

- **a.** What would the ideal job look like? Describe it in detail. Refer to your responses in Table 14.1. Decide whether these possibilities can be fulfilled by an internal position anywhere or by becoming an entrepreneur (more on this topic in chapter 15). If you decide to step out for awhile and engage in other endeavors (such as going back to school or performing extended volunteer work), figure out how to support yourself during this transition time. If you decide you want an internal position, list the questions you would ask in an interview to help you determine whether a specific job meets your interests and needs.
- **b.** Determine where (i.e., in what part of the country) you want to live. Also identify where you do not want to live. There are a number of books in the career sections of libraries and bookstores that can help you to make this decision. Take into account the needs of your spouse (or significant other) and family.
- **c.** Decide how far (and how much time) you are willing to commute on a daily basis. This may impact your responses to the previous items.
- **d.** Decide whether the job you want is in the same career field, profession, and/or industry.
- **e.** Determine the kinds of opportunities you desire in your new job.
- **f.** Note the salary range and types of benefits you are looking for or are willing to accept.
- **g.** Decide how long you are willing (or able) to wait before you receive the type of employment that you are looking for.
- **h.** Prioritize your responses to the previous six items based on their level of importance. What does this information tell you about your next employment situation?

Phase 2: Getting in the Door

Many employment opportunities are usually advertised by word of mouth. Use informational interviews (i.e., meeting with individuals to learn more about what they do and the challenges they face) to ferret out potential opportunities that may not be readily apparent. When you discover an opportunity, attach a cover letter to your resume or vitae, explaining why you are the best candidate for the job. Consider the following alternatives for getting an initial interview.

a. Use a headhunter. These firms may be able to quickly get you interviews and provide you with an indication of the opportunities that are available. Be conscious of the fees that you may incur.

b. Scan the want ads (*Wall Street Journal, National Employment Weekly,* local paper, regional papers, etc.). Also look for want ads in professional journals. This search may not be very productive in terms of actually getting a job. However, it will give you information about the number and type of jobs in your profession, and sometimes an idea of the salary ranges that are being considered.

c. Use the Internet. Many professional societies, public- and private-sector organizations, recruitment firms, and newspapers now post jobs on their Web sites. Consider putting your resume in an electronic format for distribution. You may even want to create a personal Web site.

d. Work your network. Contact these individuals by phone: Something sent by mail is usually ignored. An incredible number of people obtain jobs through individuals they know—including casual acquaintances. These people may be aware of job openings before they are advertised. Ask them if you can use their names when you contact the organization.

Phase 3: Preparing for Interviews

Upon receiving an invitation to interview, there are four steps you can take to prepare yourself. By going through these steps, you will be able to speak the language of the potential employer and enhance your chances of making a good first impression. In addition, you will be able determine in advance how you can add value to the organization.

a. Research the organization and industry in which the company is located. Even if you think you already know a great deal about the organization, continue to increase your knowledge. Learn about the organization's long-term plans, its major challenges, and its key customers, suppliers, and competitors. Identify current industry issues and those that are anticipated in the future. Then, translate this information in such a way as to show how you can provide value. Use personal contacts, the Internet, and the library to enhance your knowledge. Be prepared to discuss what you have learned during the interview.

b. Prepare the questions you want to ask during the interview. Make sure your questions focus on issues pertaining to how well the job will meet your vocational and career needs. Also prepare questions that demonstrate your knowledge of the firm and its industry. Refrain from asking and responding to questions about compensation until you are offered the position and the enterprise "needs" you.

c. Rehearse answers to questions that interviewers might ask you. Work with friends or colleagues to refine your responses.

d. Prepare a portfolio of work samples to show others. Consider typing up a series of one-page success stories to leave with those who interview you. Also get testimonials of your work to distribute during your interview meetings.

Phase 4: What to Do During the Interview

Getting an interview does not ensure getting the job. How you conduct yourself before, during, and after the interview is critical to receiving an offer. It is the little things that often make the difference.

a. Dress appropriately. Even if the organization is casual, there still is an unwritten protocol about interview apparel. Do *not* wear new clothing or footwear. Road test them first.

b. Show up a few minutes early. You may be required to complete an application form prior to your scheduled meetings. Be prepared to list references—their names, addresses, and phone numbers. It is important to gain permission to use these references in advance.

c. Be confident. Use a firm handshake. Be direct and self-assured in your responses about how you can assist the organization. If you don't communicate what you can do, no one else will. Do not assume that your resume effectively communicates your accomplishments. Also mention them during the interview. Distribute your work samples and testimonials to your interviewers.

d. Ask all of the questions on your list. It helps to record the answers to them. Pay attention to nonverbal cues in the environment around you. This information will help you to determine whether this job meets your vocational and career needs.

e. Always follow up with a brief note to each individual that you interviewed with in the organization. Depending upon the person, this note may be typed or handwritten. Also take the opportunity to forward articles or information that you think will be of benefit to them.

Phase 5: Making the Decision

Taking on a new employment situation is a two-way street. A job applicant has as much a right to say "no thank you" as the potential employer. Make your decision about the employment opportunity based on your answers to the questions in Phase 1 and the data you collected in Phase 4.

Phase 6: In the Interim

"The most difficult thing for me to deal with was leaving the people that I had worked with. I had been with the previous company for almost ten years. These people felt like my family."

—Senior statistician

Time—especially waiting time for responses to resumes or interviews—can be a killer. Here are some things that you can do to make the best use of time and ease the stress that you are probably feeling about the situation.

a. If you do not get a job right away and you are not currently working, find other things to do. Use it as an opportunity to do some extra volunteer work, put in that garden you have been meaning to plant, read all those books you have been meaning to get to, and meet with friends and colleagues whom you have not spoken to in awhile.

"My job search after retiring after 22 years in the Washington Air National Guard and over 18 as a full-time civilian employee was long and difficult. It took 15 months to find a new job. I found the best way for me to cope during this time period was to get outside myself and concentrate on others. My work as a community volunteer for the United Way did several things. First and most important, it gave me a sense of purpose and a reason to get up in the morning. I was also making contacts in the business community that could (and did) add to my personal network. I was being productive and was able to regain some of my self-esteem. It also helped to fill a blank on my resume with something productive. After a couple of months, I received an offer that I accepted. All of this was because I finally decided to focus on others instead of myself. I like to think I was able to help the community at the same time."

—Lon L. Barrett, Auditor, Boeing,
and 1997–98 ASQ Spokane Section Chair

b. Rely on your friends and family for support. It can be very stressful and traumatic to be involuntarily without a job. You do not have to suffer alone. Sometimes you need someone to talk to, sometimes you need someone to scream at, sometimes you just need the proverbial "shoulder to cry on." It's okay to feel unhappy.

"Following downsizing [at my former employer], I went through . . . fear, anger, denial, and finally acceptance. It was a roller coaster of elation (at the prospect of new opportunities) and depression (at being rejected), and I doubt that I am really over it. I sought solace in my religion. Most of my family is in the ministry at some stage, and my wife and (grown) children ministered to me."

—Lynne B. Hare, Director, Applied Statistics, Nabisco, Inc.

c. Attend employment network meetings that occur in your local community. These are usually advertised in the newspaper or at grocery stores and public libraries. These meetings will give you the opportunity to exchange job hunting tips and job leads with others.

d. Take advantage of the outplacement benefits provided by the organization with whom you were previously employed. You can usually negotiate outplacement benefits if your leave-taking is due to downsizing or the business is moving out of town.

FINAL THOUGHTS

As mentioned at the beginning of this chapter, it is far better to enact your career than to wait until you no longer have control over the situation. With the changes that are occurring in the employment arena (refer to chapter 1 for a discussion of this phenomenon), it is up to us as individuals to take charge of our destiny. Every situation holds within it an opportunity. It is up to you to be able to capture it.

> "The transition from serving only external demands to meeting internal operational requirements has changed the job of the quality professional from running an independent department to a person who has become a desirable support partner to line managers (who might not be too eager to be their partners). In the past, their job was to hold to external requirements and to interpret them with fidelity. Now, they must hold to the aim of change and be creative in bringing about change without being too visible (it makes the line manager nervous)."
>
> —Paul B. Batalden, MD, Professor, Department of Pediatrics, Community, and Family Medicine, and Director, Health Care Improvement Leadership Development, Center for the Evaluative Clinical Sciences, Dartmouth Medical School; Director, Clinical Process Improvement and Leadership Development, Dartmouth-Hitchcock Medical Center; Vice President and Breech Chair, Department of Health Care Quality Improvement, Education and Research, Henry Ford Health System

Endnotes

1. Timothy Butler, as quoted in Alan M. Webber, "Is **Your** Job Calling?" *Fast Company* (February–March 1998), 110.
2. Stephen R. Covey, *The 7 Habits of Highly Effective People* (New York: Simon & Schuster Inc., 1990), 145.
3. James Waldroop, as quoted in Alan M. Webber, "Is **Your** Job Calling?" *Fast Company* (February–March 1998), 110.

C H A P T E R

15

Consulting: Becoming an External **GUIDE**

External consultants are **GUIDE**s—individuals who partner with organizations to travel through unfamiliar territory in order to reach an agreed-upon destination. As such, they offer a valuable service to those organizations that do not possess the internal resources to make the journey on their own. External consultants as **GUIDE**s need to

- [G]et a handle on the client's business,
- [U]ndertake a project only if they can add value,
- [I]ncorporate integrity into all of their interactions with others,
- [D]evelop the clients' capabilities to work on their own, and
- [E]ducate themselves continuously.

These five principles are central to our own work. Over the years, they have helped us to make tough business decisions and stay focused on clients' goals and objectives. We offer them to you as a means of summarizing what, for the authors, is at the core of consulting practice.

Being an external consultant has its own unique rewards and challenges. You will have the opportunity to enter into a wide variety of organizations to work on interesting and meaningful projects. Along the way you will meet many wonderful people who will undoubtedly stretch your thinking and increase your learning. On the other hand, weekends may turn into work days, lessening recreation and family time. Projects can disappear overnight, causing you to wonder about what went wrong.

This chapter will help you think through decisions about becoming an external consultant, whether to join an established firm, and starting up a consulting business. At the end of the chapter, you will find several types of challenges faced by those who perform this work.

DECIDING TO BECOME AN EXTERNAL CONSULTANT

"In 1994, I made a decision to leave employment as Vice President, Quality Management, in a community hospital to become an external consultant, even though I had recently been promoted. There were three main reasons that I decided to become an external consultant. (1) I received numerous calls and request for site visits from other organizations interested in what we had accomplished at the hospital in the area of performance/quality management. The thought occurred to me that these organizations might be willing to pay for this advice. (2) I knew that the health care market would get to the point where other providers (besides hospitals) would need to prove their value in the marketplace as it relates to satisfaction, outcomes, and costs. (3) I needed to broaden my experience in healthcare to include settings outside of hospitals."

—Cynthia Gentile, President, Applied Performance Strategies, Ltd.

Inner Exploration

1. Why do you want to become a consultant?
2. What unique expertise do you have?
3. Describe the nature of your desired consulting engagements.
4. Which role is most comfortable for you? Least comfortable?

The first question to address when deciding to become a consultant is "Why?" What makes you think you would be happier and more satisfied in an external capacity? Then, you must determine your area(s) of expertise and whether organizations will purchase them from you. What is unique about what you plan to offer compared to others who provide similar expertise? At the same time, consider the nature of the consulting engagement that you want to be involved in. Projects may encompass intermittent or full-time work, ranging from a day to several years in length.

Upfront, determine the consulting style that you plan to use with clients. Lippitt and Lippitt outline eight roles an external consultant (or even an internal coach) can use (see Figure 15.1).[1] These roles vary in their degree of directiveness and are not mutually exclusive. They are rather spheres of competence that may be used at any point in the consulting relationship. A good rule of thumb in systems-based consulting is to utilize the process consultation role as home base.[2] Edgar Schein defines process consultation as "a set of activities on the part of the consultant that help the client to perceive, understand, and act upon the process events that occur in the client's environment in order to improve the situation as defined by the client."[3] Depending on the needs of the situation, you may switch to an alternate role. In any case, the leaders and members of the organization, not the consultant, need to have ownership of the work that is being performed for them.

Independent of the consulting approach that you decide to use, reflect on your personal values and guiding principles and their fit with consulting. It is easy to

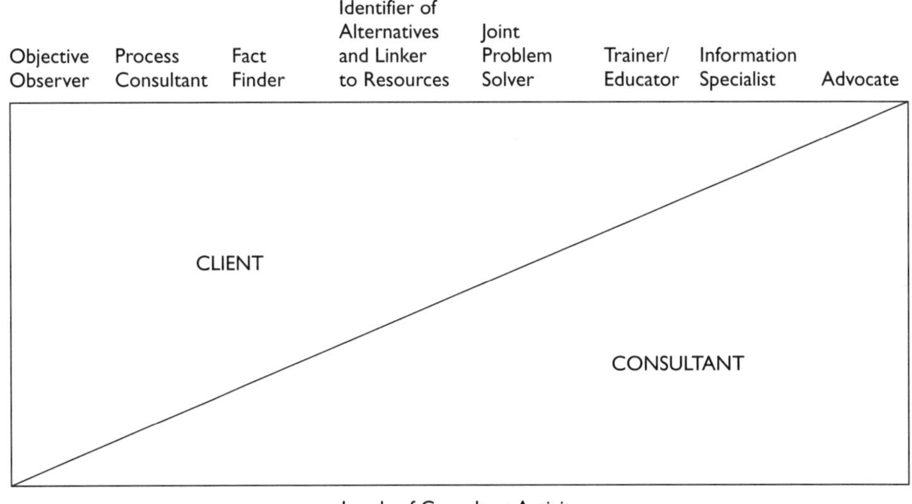

Nondirective — Directive

Raises questions for reflection	Observes problem-solving process and raises issues mirroring feedback	Gathers data and stimulates thinking	Identifies alternatives and resources for client and helps assess consequences	Offers alternatives and participates in decisions	Trains client	Regards, links, and provides policy or practice decisions	Proposes guidelines, persuades, or directs in the problem-solving process

Figure 15.1
The Consulting Continuum
Reprinted with permission from Lippitt, Gordon and Lippitt, Ronald. *The Consulting Process in Action,* second edition.

lose sight of what is important because of the overarching need to satisfy clients. Some consultants elect to be certified by organizations such as the National Bureau of Professional Management Consultants or the Institute of Management Consultants. Both organizations have a standard of conduct and a professional code of ethics. Consider interviewing external consultants who work for small, medium, and large firms. They can provide you with insights that may help you clarify your perspectives on this potential career move.

> "When I was Corporate Quality Assurance Manager at Sears, I decided early on I didn't want to retire at the mandatory retirement age. Upon studying the situation, I decided that consulting was the best option. I decided to prepare for this while I was still young. Principle #1: Do it as early as possible; don't wait until

you are 65 or 70—you may not have the energy. Then I interviewed a lot of the 'gurus.' They were still around and accessible then. Dorian Shainin said that he wanted to work for himself, not manage others. This made sense to me, so this is the model I used. When I began consulting, I started by working for someone else. This really helped me learn the business and I was in much better shape when I spun off myself."

—Robert W. Peach, Principal, Robert Peach and Associates, Inc.

DECIDING WHETHER TO JOIN AN ESTABLISHED FIRM

Once you have decided that you want to become an external consultant, there are several paths that you can take. You can (1) go into business for yourself, (2) partner with one or more individuals, (3) join a "boutique" firm (one that specializes in a particular area), (4) join a medium-size firm (i.e., one that employs between 50 to several hundred people, or (5) join a large firm where there may be thousands of consultants.

There are advantages to each of these paths. These advantages are very personal. What one person might see as essential, another person might not care about. The following remarks shed light on some of the range of benefits.

"I work in a consulting firm that employs 33 people on a full-time/part-time basis and 26 people on a contract basis. I have given a lot of thought to the benefits of working at a firm of this size and have come up with two main reasons that are important to me. First, I have control over the kind of projects I work on. I get a chance to pick projects that match my skills, abilities, and interests. As a result, I have gotten to work in some really cool places and do some really cool things. Second, I can focus on meeting the clients' needs because I am not pressured to bill all of my time to them. And, if I need to do research or collect information for a client project, I can take the necessary time to do it."

—Lynda Finn, Senior Consultant, Oriel Incorporated

"Before I worked for Cambridge I was an independent consultant for several years. Cambridge Technology Partners has 3,600 employees worldwide; Cambridge Management Consulting has 800–900. I see some big advantages to working for a firm this size. (1) Many clients still prefer to work with larger consulting firms. It is more difficult for independents to gain access to and handle the larger clients on their own. Now I have more access to large client organizations, and I am able to work on more varied projects. (2) I am able to focus on consulting work and not have to worry about the details of running a business—activities such as marketing and invoicing. (3) I have access to a pool of resources for professional growth. (4) The workload and pay is stable, without the huge swings I saw when I was on my own. (5) When I need help on client projects in terms of resources and/or knowledge, I can go wherever I want for them, even outside of Cambridge."

—Dana Ginn, Consultant, Cambridge Management Consulting

> "There are at least three major benefits to working in a large consulting firm. First, there is a large critical mass of very talented, diverse people you can harness. Even though they have diverse talents, background, and knowledge, they share a common bond and vision around the work that they do to serve clients and solve complex problems. This pool of talent creates an extremely productive and appropriate environment for ideas to flourish and be harvested. People will continue to be the number-one strategic asset in the firm. The second benefit surrounds investment capacity. The firm can afford to hire the best talent, pump significant dollars into training them, fund research and development when ideas are still embryonic, and finance technical support such as video transmissions, data exchanges, frame relay systems, and broad band networks. The third benefit has to do with the scale and magnitude of the projects that we support for our customers. The size and global nature of the enterprise makes it capable of helping other large, global organizations, especially when projects require a high degree of diverse specialized knowledge. We are able to easily reach all parts of the world."
>
> —Fernando A. Yépez, Ph.D., Arthur Andersen LLP

How do you go about deciding which path is best for you? Start with your responses to the questions in the previous section. Search out firms that meet your expectations and needs. There are books that list the characteristics of, and contact information for, medium-sized and larger firms. Call for company materials or hunt down further information on the Internet. If you discover that you want to go into business on your own or partner with someone, it may help to speak with other independent consultants, seek the services of a SCORE (Service Corps of Retired Executives) volunteer, visit a Small Business Development Center (contact the U.S. Small Business Administration), or attend short courses at a local community college on how to set up and run a business.

The rest of this chapter focuses on how to set up and run a small consulting firm. Even if you have decided to join an established organization but have never worked as a consultant, it may be useful to glance at what is presented here. It will provide you with some insights on the nature of consulting work and the issues inherent in it.

> "Life benefits of self-employment or why I work for myself rather than a boss: (1) You get to choose your customers, (2) You can be as generalized or as specialized as you like without apology, and (3) If you market yourself honestly you will not be faced with taking a job that you do not want. Customer expectations will be aligned with what you want to deliver."
>
> —A consultant in the field of statistics

STARTING A CONSULTING FIRM

> "*What is being managed is a LIFE, not a business.* Career decisions are an important part of life, but a person who is contemplating self-employment has the unique luxury of allowing his own happiness to drive all other decisions."
>
> —A consultant in the field of statistics

You will have to think through a number of items once you have made the decision to go into business on your own. These items include: Marketing your services, pricing considerations, the consulting relationship, and the image you project. The following sections briefly cover each of these topics. There are many excellent books that deal with various aspects of consulting. We recommend that you take a look at these resources; each of them offers a variety of advice and ideas.

> "Before I made the decision to go on my own, I took a class offered by the Small Business Development Center (SBDC). This helped me to formulate the key elements of a business plan. At one point I found I had to redefine the meaning of success. I've always been fully engaged in my work, but I decided financial success wasn't everything. I needed to balance my lifestyle—no more working through dinner, weekends, and holidays on a regular basis. I also had to make a decision about growth. Do I grow and hire employees, or continue as a solo act? I didn't have a formal plan, but I did have guiding principles. I felt it was important to be flexible, always look to the future, and have several options."
>
> —Jeff Israel, Principal, SatisFaction Strategies

Marketing Your Services

> "Joe Juran told me he always had the names of his next ten books. He would work on them gradually, adding chapters and ideas. As he got closer to the time to write the book, there was more substance. When he actually sat down to write the book, a lot of the work was done. I have used this model myself—not so much for books, but for papers. I tried to develop a fresh paper every six months. Speaking and writing are the foundations for effective consulting. Not only does it gain you visibility, but it deepens your understanding of the subject."
>
> —Robert W. Peach, Principal, Robert Peach and Associates, Inc.

Marketing yourself is crucial. Two of the best ways to market are to speak and to write. Both are growth opportunities, albeit painful ones for most individuals.

Speaking provides both visibility and credibility. You may want to contact your local Toastmaster's group if you need some assistance with your public speaking skills. There are a number of ways to obtain speaking engagements. These include responding to requests for proposals, contacting the local chapters of the professional associations that you belong to, and offering to speak at a meeting of the local Chamber of Commerce. The library has reference books on whom to contact at national associations for information on their conferences.

Consultants may write for conference presentation, client use, or professional publication. In addition to visibility, one of the major benefits of writing is the feedback that you will receive from others. It is usually easier to write a paper based on a talk you have already presented. It is a little more difficult to write a paper for a talk you have not given. Writing an article for a journal is more challenging. Its publication process has a much longer cycle time than writing a paper for inclusion in conference proceedings. Writing a book is the most complex and has the longest cycle time.

> "There are two abilities which are especially important in my work. One is the ability to integrate information from numerous sources (e.g., industry publications, business periodicals, marketing literature, annual reports, business plans, and internal memos and reports) quickly. Second is the ability to communicate quickly and effectively the products and services I have to offer to a prospective client. Most of my first encounters with potential clients have occurred at business meetings and conferences and lasted less than five minutes due to the nature of the function. Therefore, the window of opportunity to make a good and lasting impression is often very small. I attempt to keep both abilities up-to-date through continuous practice."
>
> —Dr. Charles Liedtke, Owner, Strategic Improvement Systems

While marketing yourself through speaking and writing are wonderful ideas, we have not yet found a small consulting firm that has claimed to get much business as the result of advertising. Most state that their best business opportunities come to them through referrals—word-of-mouth advertising.

Consider marketing your firm through your participation as a volunteer in community, civic, or professional associations. For example, if you facilitate a strategic planning session for a community group, someone in that group might become interested in what you do and contact you with a business opportunity. Another way to achieve visibility and name recognition is through a Web site. A Web site may also offer you the opportunity to distribute your writings.

We encourage external consultants to partner in some manner with institutions of higher education. There are several ways to do this. You can become an adjunct professor or lecturer in one of their programs. However, this may require up to a 16-week commitment. Or, you can teach in their executive education programs. Some of these institutions also market consultants in their local communities. Although this may involve giving up a percentage of your income in exchange for this work, there may be a benefit to having a larger institution market you under its image in the community.

> "Clients will come to you only as long as you add real value. Referrals have been my main source of business. I would advise against advertising (unless your services are really generic) because there's a big chance that the clients who will be attracted will not be an optimal match for your services; and dealing with that is a big energy drain."
>
> —A consultant in the field of statistics

To capitalize on marketing opportunities you will need several promotional pieces. You need a business card that includes your phone, fax, and voice mail numbers, and e-mail/Internet address; your mailing address, the name of your firm (more on this in the next section), and who you are. Some consultants also include the tag line for their business. Consider getting an 800/888 number for voice mail as a means of reducing costs for your clients.

You need materials such as stationary, envelopes, notepaper, Post-it® Notes, covers for training materials and papers, and mailing labels for packages that also include the information that is listed on your business card. Develop marketing materials to present yourself and your firm. At a minimum, these materials should include: Your consulting philosophy and approach, testimonials (i.e., references) from those who have benefited from your services, a list of clients who have engaged your services, the type of work your firm performs, and how your firm can (and has) provided value to its clients. You may want to develop and distribute short versions of client success stories. Don't forget that you will still need to have a resume and/or a curriculum vitae for yourself, and any other individuals who may join you in working at a client site.

> "For the first three years of our business my firm was marketed by word of mouth, speaking engagements, written information about the company, networking, and my position as an adjunct professor in the graduate program of a local university. To date, every client we have had, including my teaching appointment, resulted from a relationship. At the end of 1997, we took out a year of ad space with the local 'Business Times.' We decided to do this to enhance 'name recognition' and will be placing the ads in the health-care-focused issues. The publication is well-read by health care executives, including physicians. In addition to continuing with speaking engagements, the members of my firm are committed to publishing an article apiece in 1998. Knowing people at high levels of organizations is probably one of the most effective ways to get business. I feel that straight 'cold calling' in this field should be a last-resort effort."
>
> —Cynthia Gentile, President,
> Applied Performance Strategies, Ltd.

These marketing activities are one part of a larger strategic plan. What is unique about a strategic plan for an entrepreneurial firm is that you are the business, and as such, your personal approach to life and work are just as important as the strategies you lay out to accomplish. This plan does not need to be lengthy. It needs to clearly express the market niche that your business plans to serve and your long-term strategies, short-term goals, and specific actions to accomplish them. You will also want to add financial forecasts to this information. By putting these items on paper you will gain a sense of focus and purpose for your business and your personal life. You will be required to produce a business plan if you are planning to borrow money from a financial institution to fund your business.

Pricing Considerations

Developing an appropriate pricing strategy is a struggle for most small consulting firms. There are many ways to price your services. These include: (1) fixed time/fixed price, (2) hourly rates, (3) daily rates, (4) payment based on results achieved, and (5) percent of firm equity. Several other issues, such as billing for travel time, off-site preparation, and materials development need to be built into your pricing strategy. We encourage you to seek assistance from organizations that specialize in this area.

The Consulting Relationship

> "Whenever we go into a new organization, the focus is to do a great job for them in as short a time as possible, so they can be consultant-free and self-sustaining quickly. The work we do is always the best we can offer, with personal relationships a big part of the process. We do a free follow-up activity to make sure there are no unanswered questions or issues. This helps the organization sustain the activities and assures us that there has been systemic and sustainable change. It is also from this follow-up that we can help the organization quantify the benefits of the change—or have them tell us the impact."
>
> —Tara Martin-Milius, CEO, Center for Corporate Learning

Building a consulting relationship on mutual trust, respect, and the "policy of no surprises" is critical to success. Whether the relationship between you and the client is new or not, a contracting process should be used at the start of the consulting engagement. The contracting process needs to make explicit the expectations that you and the client organizations have for each other, the ways in which you intend to work together, and the essential elements of the consulting process. Items to be covered in the contracting process include

1. "the overall goal(s) of the initiative (including personal and political goals),
2. "the methods by which the goal(s) will be met,
3. "underlying assumptions and philosophies regarding the consulting engagement,
4. "values and guiding principles that need to be upheld by all parties,
5. "consultant and client expectations of each other (i. e., roles and responsibilities),
6. "the consulting approach required by the goal(s),
7. "issues of confidentiality,
8. "areas of apprehension and concern, and
9. "the time schedule."[4]

Although these items need to be discussed early on in the relationship between you and the client organization, revisit them on a regular basis throughout the engagement. This will ensure that issues are resolved in a timely manner and that both organizations are working together collaboratively.

After each consulting visit, we encourage you to write a trip report for the client that records your observations of what took place, concerns and issues that were surfaced, and positive actions and behaviors that occurred while you were on-site. This type of trip report can be an excellent tool for building learning into the consulting process. In addition, it is also important for you to receive feedback from your client on a regular basis. This feedback does not have to be gained in a formal manner. In fact some of the most honest feedback that you receive may be spoken in informal, relaxed situations.

"We perform monthly evaluations with clients. These are done over coffee—create an informal atmosphere and encourage clients to talk with us openly. They focus on the progress of our work together, me as a consultant, and if there was anything about our relationship that could change, what it would be. My clients always thank me and tell me that no one else does this with them."

—A service quality consultant

The Image You Project

"I have learned that relationship building is the basis for image building. I learned this after we hired a sales and marketing consultant to create an image for our business through glitzy brochures and mailings. We got less than a 1 percent return rate. For us, cold calling never worked. Today our business comes through personal contacts, referrals, or participation in conferences."

—A service quality consultant

What creates the image that your firm projects to others? We believe that there are several factors at work here. These include: The image that your company name, materials, and logo give to others; the level of success that is engendered through your client engagements; and how you and your employees/subcontractors/partners are perceived by client members in both your on- and off-site work.

In the accounting and legal professions, it is not uncommon for the name of the firm to reflect the names of its partners. For some reason, many management consulting firms follow suit. This approach is fine if "you" are the business. However, there is another path you can follow. You can elect to give your firm a name that symbolically represents its philosophies, market niche, and work focus. The following story represents the latter approach.

"Although my work and the work of my associates had been in the area of quality within a hospital setting, we wanted to avoid using that word to create our firm's image. 'Quality' in health care means different things to different people and has transitioned over the years from the policing and punitive 'quality assurance' approach to efforts to adopt the philosophies and approaches of TQM and CQI. Nevertheless, we viewed 'quality' as one piece of an overall focus on improving the 'performance' of an organization as it relates to satisfaction, outcomes, and costs. Next, we wanted our relationship with clients to be one of partnering and forming longer-term relationships while 'assisting' them with 'practical' 'strategies' or techniques for improving their organization's performance. Hence, the name 'Applied Performance Strategies.'"

—Cynthia Gentile, President, Applied Performance Strategies, Ltd.

There are several benefits to selecting a symbolic name. First, you can use this symbolism throughout your marketing materials to create brand meaning in the eyes of your consumers. Second, no one knows how large your firm is by the name you have given it. And, third, it helps organizations to self-select whether or not you can help them before meeting you. There is also one drawback. If you choose a name that has a word in it that becomes passé, you may have to alter the name of your firm.

Other image details include carefully choosing the colors you use to represent your organization; creating a "look" for your papers, training materials, and correspondence that is both professional and unique to your firm; selecting a logo that fits with the symbolic meaning of your firm's name; and selecting a tag line that is both catchy and descriptive of what you do. Pay attention to how your stationary "feels" when someone holds it and whether or not the colors that you use for your business are offensive to any culture in which you might work.

Last, but not least, pay attention at the client site to the appropriateness of your attire, how you greet people, and how prepared you are for meetings. Ensure that your materials do not have typographical errors, are free from blemishes, and are originals or first-generation copies. Off-site behaviors such as how the phone is answered and how rapidly you respond to voice, fax, and e-mail messages (the authors' rule of thumb is within 24 hours) cannot be ignored.

> "I have two mottos as the owner of a consulting firm. They are 'You never get a second chance to make a good first impression' and 'Anything worth doing is worth doing well.'"
>
> —A service quality consultant

CHALLENGES

> "The biggest challenges are (1) how to market and advertise, (2) what to do on the Web and how to do it, (3) how to match marketing and advertising of big consulting organizations when you are not big, and (4) looking fresh when there is apparently no new 'wave.'"
>
> —Heero Hacquebord, President,
> Consulting in Continual Improvement

In talking with consultants we find that the challenges they experience are threefold: There are challenges they have with their clients; there are challenges they have with regard to managing their business; and, there are challenges they have with regard to their personal needs and priorities. Client relationships can be bumpy at times. There can be confusion over the goals of the engagement, the methods used to achieve those goals, and the time line in which those goals will be achieved. There can also be personality conflicts and differing expectations about accountabilities and responsibilities. Because you are not a member or leader of the organizations to whom you are engaged, it can be frustrating to have little or no control over how things play out. Since there is often a significant amount of time between the intervention and its results, you (and the organization) may not know what impact your interventions had on the long-term performance of the organization.

> "As a consultant, I face the dilemma that I do not have any real authority over anything in the company. The real decisions are made by internal people. So I can only lead by being convincing, and this means doing solid work as well as

> communicating effectively. In every consulting relationship I have ever had, the only path to a meaningful contribution by the consultant has been through the pivotal internal person."
>
> —A consultant in the field of statistics

You will find that you need to juggle vast amounts of differing work simultaneously. In very small firms, you may have to play the roles of marketer, financier, consultant, and business leader. This leaves little time for personal learning. Because most consultants are not skilled in all of these roles, at some point it may be necessary to engage the services of others to assist in the management of the firm. If you work by yourself, you may have one additional challenge—the isolation that occurs by not having the opportunity to interface with others on a daily basis. This is when your personal network of contacts can be invaluable.

> "Working for myself has required that I wear three hats. I balance the roles of president/CEO, sales and marketing, and consultant. I must 'run the business,' 'get the business,' and 'do the consulting work.' Significant challenges faced in running the business have been in the areas of expanding the practice. The timing of adding associates and keeping the cash flow positive have been a challenge. In the area of getting the business, the significant challenge is budgeting enough time during very busy consulting times to meet with people, attend professional association meetings, send company information packets, speak at meetings, etc., to be constantly cultivating the next client relationship."
>
> —Cynthia Gentile, President,
> Applied Performance Strategies, Ltd.

> "My biggest challenges are: (1) mastering computers and technology—they allow us to do more and be competitive, but the time required to be proficient is substantial, (2) overcoming isolation and building a sense of community with clients—I overcome this by avoiding arm's-length relationships with my clients. I see a strong parallel between the situation of an external consultant and the telecommuting employee. Both require special effort to be effectively integrated within the host organization."
>
> —Jeff Israel, Principal, SatisFaction Strategies

Experiencing these challenges first-hand may cause you to rethink your decision to be on the outside of an organization. This decision often arises out of the conflicts that ensue between personal values and priorities, and the realities of the consulting world. When these conflicts arise, it is time to reevaluate the decision to be an external consultant. Thus, you may find yourself coming back full circle to where you once started—as an internal employee.

> "I made my decision to go internal six years ago. That was at the leading edge of the change for the quality professional, when many consulting organizations were beginning to downsize. Yet, that was not the key factor in my decision. Rather, I was motivated by my own need to 'settle down,' that is, not travel and to work with one organization long enough to see meaningful results. I got tired of saying

good-bye! A secondary reason for moving internal that I now recognize is that it has been a better environment for gaining management experience not typically a part of the quality professional's world. It is one thing to consult with management and another thing to do it."

—Sharon Lutz, Ph.D., Director, Integrated Analysis Team, Fairview Hospital and Healthcare Services

All of the challenges expressed here can be overcome in one way or another. Being an effective **GUIDE** requires that you address them real-time and do not let them fester. Otherwise you will experience great difficulty in partnering with organizations to travel through unfamiliar territory to reach an agreed-upon destination. With this in mind,

G et a handle on the client's business,
U ndertake a project only if you can add value,
I ncorporate integrity into all of your interactions with others,
D evelop the clients' capabilities to work on their own, and
E ducate yourself continuously.

Endnotes

1. Gordon Lippitt and Ronald Lippitt, *The Consulting Process in Action* (San Diego: University Associates, 1986), 61.
2. Lori L. Silverman, "Coaching Leaders Through a Large-Scale Change Effort" (unpublished paper, 1996), 3.
3. Edgar Schein, *Process Consultation: Its Role in Organization Development* (Reading, MA: Addison-Wesley Publishing Company, 1988), 11.
4. Silverman, "Coaching Leaders Through a Large-Scale Change Effort" (unpublished paper, 1996), 4.

CHAPTER 16

Developing a Personal Action Plan

"I believe that quality professionals must spend as much time working on themselves as they do on others. . . . I am constantly working on at least one personal development project; right now it's a 365-day, self-development program on steps to knowledge. This may be the single most important development area for quality professionals—continuing to improve their personal mastery."

—D. Scott Sink, Ph.D., P. E., Learning Leader, QPM, Inc., Past President of the World Confederation of Productivity Science and of the Institute of Industrial Engineers

CHAOS

- [C]hanging definition of work and the workplace
- [H]eightened social responsibility
- [A]ging baby boomers
- [O]verarching demographic change
- [S]trategic growth through technology and innovation

SHIFT

- Quality goes [S]ofter
- Quality goes into [H]iding
- Quality goes [I]ntegrative
- Quality goes [F]ar-flung
- Quality goes [T]echnical

Throughout this book we have pushed, teased, and challenged you with the forces affecting the workplace of the future (i.e., **CHAOS**) and the trends that have emerged in the practice of quality (i.e., **SHIFT**). We have invited you to answer questions, fill in worksheets, and evaluate your organization and yourself. In this chapter we provide you with the opportunity to compile this information and to develop a personal plan of action—one that outlines what you will do differently in your current job and career, given what you have discovered during the course of reading this book.

Find your answers to the Inner Exploration questions in chapters 9, 10,

11, and 15, and the questions woven through chapter 14. Also pull out your responses to the items requested in Tables 9.1, 11.1, and 14.1. Use this information to complete Table 16.1. If you are interested in pursuing external consulting, add these reflections to the last row of this table.

Once you have completed the table, prioritize the actions you have listed in column 2 based on their importance to you, the time required to accomplish them, and your probability of success. Do not be deterred by the time it may take to accomplish an action. If you never get started on it you will never make any progress toward achieving it. Sometimes those items that appear at first blush to have the lowest probability of success actually have the possibility of working, given today's rapidly changing environment. Communicate your plans to everyone—your family, your friends, your colleagues, your boss. Verbal commitments obligate you to accomplish them. Above all, don't lose sight of what you are ultimately striving for.

> "I began with Midwest Express almost 10 years ago as a reservations agent. Although my goals and objectives were not crystal clear, I had a strategy. Part of that strategy was to learn as much about the organization as possible. I changed course several times and in ways that may not have made sense to anyone who was unaware of this strategy. I held positions in the customer service area to gain an understanding of operations. I took a position in consumer affairs to gain a deeper appreciation for my customers' expectations, and to obtain an overall understanding of the organization and the dependencies between departments. Next, I took a position in a new department as an administrative assistant to improve my organizational and computer software skills.
>
> "I am currently a team advisor who coaches, facilitates, and trains individuals and teams from the front-line to the director level. My journey has been long, but my understanding of our system is very good. Without starting with some kind of strategy, I would have never gotten to where I am today. Ten years ago I knew my strengths, that is, training and coaching. I also knew there were areas that needed improvement and tackled them over a period of time by making many lateral moves. I always stuck to my strategy and continue today to take actions in order to, like many organizations, get to that next level. I'm currently working and going to college full-time. In the short-term it may be trying. But it is long-term success that I am shooting for. I am confident that having a strategy and sticking to my action plan will get me there."
>
> —Jill Adams-Rodeberg, Team Advisor, Midwest Express Airlines

Table 16.1

My Personal Plan of Action

	1 Key Issues for Me	2 Actions I Can Take to Address These Issues	3 Help I Need (e.g., Additional or Enhanced Skills, Support from Others in the Organization Support from My Network) to Accomplish These Actions	4 Importance to Me*	5 Time Required to Accomplish*	6 Possibility of Success*
Ch. 9: Starburst Skills and Knowledge (Table 9.1 and Inner Exploration)						
Ch. 10: Acquire Skills and Knowledge (Inner Exploration)						
Ch. 11: Assess Leadership Behaviors (Table 11.1 and Inner Exploration)						
Ch. 14: Enact Your Career (Table 14.1 and questions)						
Ch. 15: External Consulting (Inner Exploration)						

*Rating scales

Column 4: 5 high importance
3 medium importance
1 low importance

Column 5: 5 short time to accomplish
3 medium time to accomplish
1 long time to accomplish

Column 6: 5 high probability of success
3 some probability of success
1 low probability of success

Opening the Dialogue . . .

We are very interested in hearing your experiences with The Starburst Model™. Your feedback and input will help us to continue our learning and research on quality and value creation practices, and other performance improvement initiatives.

Lori Silverman and Annabeth Propst
c/o ASQ Quality Press
American Society for Quality
P.O. Box 3005
Milwaukee, WI 53201-3005
Authors' e-mail: pfprogress@aol.com; alpropst@aol.com
Author's voice mail 800.253.6398

APPENDIX A

Representative Interview Questions

Trends

1. What trends have you observed over the past 10 to 20 years in the quality field?
2. What trends do you foresee in the quality arena over the next five to ten years?

Initiatives

3. How has your organization changed since the inception of its quality initiative?
4. What long-standing issues has your quality initiative not been able to fully address?
5. What have you or your department done to move the organization and its leadership toward value creation?
6. Is the quality initiative within your organization an organization-wide or department/project-specific initiative? If the initiative is organization-wide, how do you, your department, and the organization handle the change management portion of the initiative? What specific tools and methods have you used that have been particularly useful?
7. How has your organization embedded quality concepts, tools, and methods into everyone's daily work?

The Quality Function

8. What (are) the name of the department(s) that is (are) responsible for quality in your organization? What are the overall purpose, roles, and responsibilities of the department(s) within your organization?

9. What are the overall roles and responsibilities of those who perform a quality function within your organization?
10. What projects has, or is, your "quality" department currently involved in? How does the department ensure its alignment with organizational priorities and strategic plans?

Internal Quality Professionals

11. What skills and abilities are the most important in your work? What activities do you engage in to keep these skills and abilities up to date?
12. What publications would you recommend to others to stay on the leading edge of (a) quality, and (b) what is (or will be) happening in organizations and the world at large?
13. How important is your network of contacts? How do you use your network and what benefits have you and others received from this usage?
14. What professional associations would you recommend to others to stay on the leading edge of (a) quality, and (b) what is (or will be) happening in organizations and the world at large?
15. What involvement do you have in community activities and organizations (including roles you may have at the local or national level of a professional organization)? How has this involvement benefited your work in quality and you as an individual?
16. Have you chosen to leave a job in the quality department (or a quality function within the department you were in) and move elsewhere within the same organization? A different organization? What caused you to make this move? What position did you take and why?
17. Have you ever been forced (through lay-off, downsizing, etc.) to leave an organization where you had a job in quality? What advanced warning did you receive? How did you feel about the decision? What quality initiatives did the organization continue with after your (and/or others') departure? How did you approach your job search?

External Quality Professionals

18. How did you decide to become an external consultant?
19. Does your firm have a strategic plan? If yes, how did you go about its development? How important has strategic planning been to your firm's success?
20. How did your firm create its image (image includes selecting a name, firm marketing materials, etc.)?
21. How do you market your firm?

22. How do you create long-term relationships (define long-term) with clients? How has this benefited your firm and its clients?
23. What affiliations and partnerships has your organization formed with others (i.e., individuals and/or other firms/institutions)? What caused you to form these relationships? How have these relationships benefited all parties involved in them (including the client)?
24. What significant challenges have you experienced as a consultant? How have you handled these challenges?

Bibliography

Ackerman Anderson, Linda, with Dean Anderson and Martin Marquardt. "Development, Transition or Transformation: Bringing Change Leadership Into the 21st Century." *OD Practitioner,* Vol. 28, No. 4 (1997): 5–16.

Ackoff, Russell. Keynote presentation given at the Upsizing the Organization Conference sponsored by the Indiana Quality and Productivity Improvement Council, September 1997.

Akao, Yoji, ed. *Hoshin Kanri: Policy Deployment for Successful TQM.* Cambridge, MA: Productivity Press, 1991.

Allen, Paula Gunn. *The Sacred Hoop: Recovering the Feminine in American Indian Traditions.* Boston: Beacon Press, 1992.

Altov, H. *The Art of Inventing: And Suddenly the Inventor Appeared.* Translated and adapted by Lev Shulyak, Worcester, MA: Technical Innovation Center, 1994.

Altshuller, Genrikh. *Creativity as an Exacting Science: The Theory of the Solution of Inventive Problems.* Translated by Anthony Williams. New York: Gordon and Breach, 1984.

Argyris, Chris. *Knowledge in Action: A Guide to Overcoming Barriers to Organizational Change.* San Francisco: Jossey-Bass Inc., Publishers, 1993.

Argyris, Chris, *On Organizational Learning.* Cambridge, MA: Blackwell Publishers, 1992.

Argyris, Chris, and Donald A. Schön. *Organizational Learning II: Theory, Method, and Practice.* Reading, MA: Addison-Wesley Publishing Company, Inc., 1996.

Armour, Lawrence A. "Who Says Virtue Is Its Own Reward?" *FORTUNE* (February 16, 1998): 186–187.

Aschenbach, Bernd, Hermann-Michael Hahn, and Joachim Trümper. *The Invisible Sky: Rosat and the Age of X-Ray Astronomy.* Secaucus, NJ: Copernicus Books, 1998.

Ashkenas, Ron, et al. *The Boundaryless Organization: Breaking the Chains of Organizational Structure.* San Francisco: Jossey-Bass Inc., Publishers, 1995.

ASQC Quality Cost Committee. *Principles of Quality Costs.* Milwaukee: American Society for Quality Control, 1990.

ASQC Futures Team. *Quality, the Future, and You: An ASQC Consideration of the Year 2010.* Milwaukee: American Society for Quality Control, 1996.

ASTD Models for Human Performance Improvement: Roles, Competencies, and Outputs. Alexandria, VA: ASTD, 1996.

Autry, James. *Life and Work: A Manager's Search for Meaning.* New York: Avon Books, 1995.

Bailey, Steven P., and W. H. Fellner. "Some Useful Aids for Understanding and Quantifying Process Control and Improvement Opportunities." Paper presented at the 1993 ASQC/ASA Fall Technical Conference.

Barlow, Edward D. Jr., "The Art of Looking Backwards from Tomorrow." 1997 Air Force Quality and Management Innovation Symposium Presentation, 1997.

Barner, Robert. "The New Millennium Workplace: Seven Changes That Will Challenge Management and Workers." *THE FUTURIST* (March–April 1996): 14–18.

Barrett, Richard. "A Corporate Values Revolution." *Perspectives on Business and Global Change,* Vol. 10, No. 3 (1996): 47–56.

Bassi, Lauri, George Benson, and Scott Cheney. "The Top Ten Trends." *Training & Development* (November 1996): 28–42.

Beckhard, Richard, and Rueben Harris. *Organizational Transitions.* Reading, MA: Addison-Wesley, 1987.

Beckhard, Richard, and Wendy Pritchard. *Changing the Essence: The Art of Creating and Leading Fundamental Change in Organizations.* San Francisco: Jossey-Bass Inc., Publishers 1992.

Beers, Charlotte. "Building Brands Worthy of Devotion." *Leader to Leader* (Winter 1998): 29–39.

Bell, Chip R. *Managers as Mentors.* San Francisco: Berrett-Koehler Publishers, Inc., 1996.

Berry, Leonard L. "Relationship Marketing of Services–Growing Interest, Emerging Perspective." *Journal of the Academy of Marketing Science,* Vol. 23, No. 4 (1995): 236–245.

Bersbach, Peter L., and Philip R. Wahl. "QFD on a Defense Contract," *Proceedings of the 44th Annual Quality Congress.* Milwaukee: American Society for Quality Control, (May 1990): 413–417.

Block, Peter. "The End of Leadership." *Leader to Leader* (Winter 1997):11–14.

———. "Finding Community at Work," *Journal for Quality and Participation* (September 1994): 22–25.

———. *Stewardship: Choosing Service Over Self-Interest.* San Francisco: Berrett-Koehler Publishers, Inc., 1993.

Bohl, Don L., Fred Luthans, John W. Slocum, Jr., and Richard M. Hodgetts. "Ideas That Will Shape the Future of Management Practice." *Organizational Dynamics* (Summer 1996): 7–14.

Bolman, Lee G., and Terrence E. Deal. *Leading with Soul: An Uncommon Journey of Spirit.* San Francisco: Jossey-Bass Inc., Publishers, 1995.

Bottorf, Dean L. "COQ Systems: The Right Stuff," *Quality Progress* (March 1997): 33–35.

Box, George E. P. "Some Problems of Statistics and Everyday Life." *Journal of the American Statistical Association,* Vol. 74, No. 364 (1979): 1–4.

Boyett, Joseph H., and Jimmie T. Boyett. *Beyond Workplace 2000: Essential Strategies for the New Corporation.* New York: Dutton, 1995.

Brache, Alan P., and Geary A. Rummler. "Managing the Organization as a System." *TRAINING* (February 1997): 68–74.

Brady, Teresa. "The Future Workplace and the Impact on HR Managers." *Employment Relations Today* (Winter 1995/96): 1–9.

Brassard, Michael. *The Memory Jogger Plus+.*™ Methuen, MA: GOAL/QPC, 1989.

Bridges, William. *JobShift: How to Prosper in a Workplace Without Jobs.* Reading, MA: Addison-Wesley Publishing Company, 1994.

Briskin, Allan. *The Stirring of Soul in the Workplace.* San Francisco: Jossey-Bass Inc., Publishers, 1996.

Britz, Galen, Don Emerling, Lynne Hare, Roger Hoerl, and Janice Shade. *Statistical Thinking,* a Special Publication of the Statistics Division of ASQC, (Spring 1996).

Broersma, Tom. "In Search of the Future." *Training & Development* (January 1995): 38–43.

Bronte, L., and A. Pifer. *Our Aging Society, Paradox and Promise.* New York: W. W. Norton & Company, 1986.

Brookfield, Stephan D. *Developing Critical Thinkers: Challenging Adults to Explore Alternative Ways of Thinking and Acting.* San Francisco: Jossey Bass Inc., Publishers, 1987.

Bunker, Barbara Benedict, and Billie Alban. *Large Group Interventions.* San Francisco: Jossey-Bass Inc., Publishers, 1997.

Burack, Elmer H., Marvin D. Burack, Diane M. Miller, and Kathleen Morgan. "New Paradigm Approaches in Strategic Human Resource Management." *Group and Organization Management,* Vol. 19, No. 2 (June 1994): 141–159.

Burke, W. Warner. *Organizational Development: A Process of Learning and Changing.* Reading, MA: Addison-Wesley Publishing Company, 1994.

Burley-Allen, Madelyn. *Listening: The Forgotten Skill,* 2nd ed. New York: John Wiley & Sons, Inc., 1995.

Butler, Steve. "Green Machine." *Fast Company* (June–July 1997): 114–115.

———. "What's the Core Idea? Namibia Brewers Ltd., Tsumeb, Namibia." *Fast Company* (January 1997): 114–115.

Callenbach, Ernest, et al. *EcoManagement: The Elmwood Guide to Ecological Auditing and Sustainable Business.* San Francisco: Berrett-Koehler Publishers, Inc., 1993.

Caplan, Frank. *The Quality System: A Sourcebook for Managers and Engineers.* West Chester, PA: Chilton Book Co., 1990.

Cashman, Kevin. "Seven Strategies for Mastery of Leadership from the Inside Out." *Strategy & Leadership* (September–October 1997): 53–55.

Caudron, Shari. "Wake Up to New Learning." *Training & Development* (May 1996): 30–35.

"CEO Thought Summit." *Sloan Management Review* (Spring 1995): 13–21.

Chawla, Sarita, and Jon Renesch, eds. *Learning Organizations: Developing Cultures for Tomorrow's Workplace.* Portland, OR: Productivity Press, Inc., 1995.

Chiapello, E., and M. Lebas. "The Tableau de Bord, A French Approach to Management Information." European Accounting Association (Bergen, Norway, May 2–4, 1996).

Chief Executive Quality Panel (Report 1159-96-CH). New York: The Conference Board, Inc. 1996.

Churchill, Gilbert A., Jr., and J. Paul Peter. *Marketing: Creating Value for Customers.* Burr Ridge, IL: Richard D. Irwin, Inc., 1995.

Coates, Joseph F. "Five Strategic HR Issues Of the 1990s and Beyond." *HR Horizons* (Fall 1992): 25–30.

Coates, Joseph F., John B. Mahaffie, and Andy Hines. *2025: Scenarios of U.S. and Global Society Reshaped by Science and Technology.* Greensboro, NC: Oak Hill Press, 1997.

Colvin, Geoffrey. "The Changing Art of Becoming Unbeatable." *FORTUNE* (November 24, 1997): 299–300.

"Company & Values: Welcome to the Body Shop Values Report." www.the-body-shop.com/values/valuesrep.html (1998).

Cornish, Edward. *The Cyber Future—92 Ways our Lives Will Change by the Year 2525.* Bethesda, MD: World Future Society, 1996.

———. "FUTURIST Forecasts 30 Years Later." *THE FUTURIST* (January–February 1997): 45–48.

Covey, Stephen R. *First Things First.* New York: Simon & Schuster, 1994.

———. *The 7 Habits of Highly Effective People.* New York: Simon & Schuster Inc., 1990.

Crampton, Suzanne, John Hodge, and Jitendra Mishra. "Transition–Ready or Not: The Aging of America's Work Force." *Public Personnel Management,* Vol. 25, No. 2 (Summer 1996): 243–255.

Crosby, Philip B. *Quality Is Free.* New York: New American Library, 1979.

Crouch, J. Michael. "Essential Tools for Quality Managers, Or What I Wish I Knew Before I Took This Job." *Quality Digest* (June 1997): 24–30.

Dannemiller Tyson Associates, Inc. *Developing Large Scale Interactive Process Competence.* Workshop manual, Atlanta, GA, October 11–13, 1995.

de Bono, Edward. *Serious Creativity—Using the Power of Lateral Thinking to Create New Ideas.* New York: HarperBusiness, 1992.

———. *Six Thinking Hats.* New York: Little Brown and Company, 1986.

Dent, Harry S., Jr. *The Great Boom Ahead.* New York: Hyperion, 1993.

———. *The Roaring 2000s.* New York: Simon & Schuster, 1998.

Didsbury, Howard F., Jr., ed. *FutureVision: Ideas, Insights, and Strategies.* Bethesda, MD: World Future Society, 1996.

Dobyns, Lloyd, and R. Frank. *If Japan Can, Why Can't We?* New York: NBC News, June 24, 1980.

Dorsey, David. "The New Spirit of Work." *Fast Company* (August 1998): 125–134.

Dotlich, David L., and James L. Noel. *Action Learning: How the World's Top Companies Are Re-Creating Their Leaders and Themselves.* San Francisco: Jossey-Bass Inc., Publishers, 1998.

Doyle, M. F. "Cross-Functional Implementation Teams." *Purchasing World* (February 1991): 20–21.

Dru, Jean-Marie, and Robin Lemberg. "Disrupt Your Business." *Journal of Business Strategy* (May–June 1997): 24–29.

Drucker, Peter F. "The Future that Has Already Happened." *Harvard Business Review* (September–October 1997): 20–24.

Egan, Timothy. "The Swoon of the Swoosh," *The New York Times* (September 13, 1998).

Eicher, James. *Making the Message Clear.* Scotts Valley, CA: Grinder, Delozier, & Associates, 1993.

Elgin, Duane, and Coleen LeDrew. "Signs of Global Consciousness Change." *Perspectives on Business and Global Change,* Vol. 12, No.1 (1998): 49–60.

Estes, Ralph, and Subashini Ganesan. "The Stakeholder Alliance: A New Bottom Line." *Perspectives on Business and Global Change* (December 1997): 65–76.

Ettorre, Barbara. "Empty Promises." *Management Review* (July 1996): 16–23.

———. "2020—What's the World Coming To?" *Management Review* (September 1996): 33–37.

"Everything You Ever Wanted to Know About Ben & Jerry's." www.benjerry.com/aboutbj.html (March 1998).

"The Fast Company Unit of One Anniversary Handbook." *Fast Company* (February–March 1997): 97–107.

Feitzinger, Edward, and Hau L. Lee, "Mass Customization at Hewlett-Packard: The Power of Postponement." *Harvard Business Review* (January–February 1997): 116–121.

Fishman, Charles. "I Want to Pioneer the Company of the Next Industrial Revolution," *Fast Company* (April–May 1998): 134–142.

———. "We've Seen the Future of Work and It Works, But Very Differently: How the Visionaries in Grand Rapids Are Getting Your Papers to Float, Your Desk to Travel, and Your Office to Multiply." *Fast Company* (August–September 1996): 53–62

Fournier, Susan, Susan Dobscha, and David Glen Mick. "Preventing the Premature Death of Relationship Marketing." *Harvard Business Review* (January–February 1998): 42–51.

Freedman, Daniel P. and Gerald M, Weinberg. *Handbook of Walkthroughs, Inspections, and Technical Reviews,* 3rd ed. New York: Dorset House Publishing, 1980.

Galagan, Patricia. "The Workplace in 2020: Three Scenarios." *Training & Development* (November 1996): 50–52.

Galen, Michele. "Companies Hit the Road Less Traveled," *BusinessWeek* (June 5, 1995): 82–84.

Garvin, David A. *Managing Quality: The Strategic and Competitive Edge.* New York: The Free Press, 1988.

Ghoshal, Sumantra, and Christopher A. Bartlett. *The Individualized Corporation: A Fundamentally New Approach to Management.* New York: HarperCollins, 1997.

Gilmore, James H., and B. Joseph Pine II. "The Four Faces of Mass Customization." *Harvard Business Review* (January–February 1997): 92–94.

Ginnodo, Bill. "Leading Change: A Conversation With Motorola's Bob Galvin." *Quality Digest* (November 1997): 31–34.

Gitlow, Howard S., and Process Management International, Inc. *Planning for Quality, Productivity, and Competitive Position.* Homewood, IL: Dow Jones-Irwin, 1990.

Gitlow, Howard S., and Shelly J. Gitlow. *Total Quality Management in Action.* Englewood Cliffs, NJ: PTR Prentice Hall, 1994.

Godfrey, A. Blanton. "The New CQO." *Quality Digest* (April 1997): 17.

Goldratt, Eliyahu. *Critical Chain.* Croton-on-Hudson, NY: North River Press, 1997.

———. *The Goal.* Croton-on-Hudson, NY: North River Press, 1984.

———. *It's Not Luck.* Croton-on-Hudson, NY: North River Press, 1994.

Gordon, Jack. "Work Teams: How Far Have They Come," *TRAINING* (October 1992), 59–65.

Grant, Eugene L., and Richard S. Leavenworth. *Statistical Quality Control,* 5th ed. New York: McGraw-Hill Book Company, 1980.

Greenberg, Barnett A., and Fuan Li. "Relationship Marketing: A Tactic, a Strategic Choice, or a Paradigm." *1998 AMA Winter Educators' Conference Proceedings,* Vol. 9. Chicago: American Marketing Association, 208–214.

Guaspari, John. "The Next Big Thing." *Across the Board* (March 1998): 18–25.

———. "Quality Is Not a Way of Life." *Across the Board* (November–December 1997): 43–46.

Guyon, Janet. "Why Is the World's Most Profitable Company Turning Itself Inside Out?" *FORTUNE* (August 4, 1997): 120–125.

Hackman, J. Richard. "Why Teams Don't Work." *Leader to Leader* (Winter 1998): 24–31.

Halal, William E. "The Rise of the Knowledge Entrepreneur." *THE FUTURIST* (November–December 1996): 13–16.

Hambrick, Donald C., David A. Nadler, and Michael L. Tushman. *Navigating Change: How CEOs, Top Teams, and Boards Steer Transformation.* Boston: Harvard Business School Press, 1998.

Hamel, Gary. "Strategy Innovation and the Quest for Value." *Sloan Management Review* (Winter 1998): 7–14.

Hammond, Josh, and Lew Platt. *The Stuff Americans Are Made Of.* New York: Macmillan, 1996.

Handy, Charles. *The Age of Paradox.* Boston: Harvard Business School Press, 1994.

———. *The Age of Unreason.* Boston: Harvard Business School Press, 1989.

———. *Beyond Certainty: The Changing Worlds of Organizations.* Boston: Harvard Business School Press, 1996.

———. "The Citizen Corporation." *Harvard Business Review* (September–October 1997): 26, 28.

———. *The Hungry Spirit: Beyond Capitalism: A Quest for Purpose in the Modern World.* New York, NY: Broadway Books, 1998.

Hannan, M., and J. Freeman. "The Population Ecology of Organizations." *American Journal of Sociology,* Vol. 82, No. 5 (1977): 929–940.

Hansen, Mark Victor. "The Secret of the Super Successful: Masterminding." Newport Beach, CA: Mark Victor Hansen & Associates.

Hardaker, Maurice, and Bryan K. Ward. "How to Make a Team Work." *Harvard Business Review* (November–December 1987): 112–117.

Hardie, Neil. "The Effects of Quality on Business Performance," *Quality Management Journal,* Vol. 5, No. 3 (Summer 1998), 75.

Harmon, Frederick G. *Playing for Keeps: How the World's Most Aggressive and Admired Companies Use Core Values to Manage, Energize, and Organize Their People and Promote, Advance, and Achieve Their Corporate Missions.* Somerset, NJ: John Wiley & Sons, 1996.

Harmon, Marion. "Quality Leaders Predict the Future." *Quality Digest* (April 1997): 22–28.

Hart, Stuart L. "Beyond Greening: Strategies for a Sustainable World." *Harvard Business Review* (January–February 1997): 66–76.

Hauser, John R., and Don Clausing. "The House of Quality." *Harvard Business Review,* Vol. 63, No. 3 (May–June 1988), 63–73.

Heider, John. *The Tao of Leadership.* Atlanta: Humanics New Age, 1985.

Herman, Stanley M. *The Tao at Work.* San Francisco: Jossey-Bass Inc., Publishers, 1994.

Hesselbein, Francis et al., eds. *The Community of the Future.* San Francisco: Jossey-Bass Inc., Publishers, 1998.

———. eds. *The Leader of the Future.* San Francisco: Jossey-Bass Inc., Publishers, 1996.

Hesselbein, Frances, Marshall Goldsmith, and Richard Beckhard, eds. *The Organization of the Future.* San Francisco: Jossey-Bass Inc., Publishers, 1997.

Hewson, Roger. "New Dimensions in Strategic Leadership." *Strategy & Leadership* (September–October 1997): 42–46.

Hirano, Hiroyuki. *5 Pillars of the Visual Workplace: the Sourcebook for 5S Implementation.* Portland, OR: Productivity Press, 1990.

Hofmeister, Kurt R. "QFD in the Services Environment." *The ASI Journal,* Vol. 3, No. 2 (Fall 1990): H-1–H-16.

Howard, Robert. "The CEO as Organizational Architect: An Interview with Xerox's Paul Allaire." *Harvard Business Review.* (September–October 1992): 107–121.

Hromi, John D. *The Best on Quality,* Vol. 7. Milwaukee: American Society for Quality Control, 1996.

Imparato, Nicholas, and Oren Harari. *Jumping the Curve.* San Francisco: Jossey-Bass Inc., Publishers, 1994.

Ingram, John A. *Introductory Statistics.* Menlo Park, CA: Cummings Publishing Company, 1974.

Jackson, Phil, and Hugh Delehanty. *Sacred Hoops: Spiritual Lessons of a Hardwood Warrior.* New York: Hyperion, 1995.

Jamieson, David, and Julie O'Mara. *Managing Workforce 2000: Gaining the Diversity Advantage.* San Francisco: Jossey-Bass Inc., Publishers, 1991.

Jensen, Rolf. "The Dream Society." *THE FUTURIST* (May–June 1996): 9–13.

Johnson, Barry. *Polarity Management: Identifying and Managing Unsolvable Problems.* Amherst, MA: HRD Press, Inc., 1992, 1996.

Joiner, Brian L. *Fourth Generation Management—The New Business Consciousness.* New York: McGraw-Hill, 1994.

———. "The Pros and Cons of Standardization." *Managing for Quality,* Issue 9, (Fall 1993): 3–4.

Juran, Joseph M. *A History of Managing for Quality: The Evolution, Trends, and Future Directions of Managing for Quality.* Milwaukee: American Society for Quality Control, 1995.

———. "A History of Managing for Quality, Part 1." *Quality Digest* (November 1995): 26–42.

———, ed. *Juran's Quality Control Handbook,* 4th ed. New York: McGraw-Hill, 1988.

Juran, Joseph M., and Frank M. Gryna. *Quality Planning and Analysis,* 3rd ed. New York: McGraw-Hill, 1993.

Kahaner, Larry. *Competitive Intelligence: How to Gather, Analyze, and Use Information to Move Your Business to the Top.* New York: Simon & Schuster, 1996.

Kanter, Rosabeth Moss. *The Change Masters.* New York: Simon & Schuster, 1983.

Kaplan, Robert S., and David P. Norton. *Balanced Scorecard.* Boston: Harvard Business School Press, 1996.

Katzenbach, Jon R. "Making Teams Work at the Top." *Leader to Leader* (Winter, 1998): 32–38.

Kim, Daniel H. *Systems Thinking Tools: A User's Reference Guide.* Cambridge, MA: Pegasus Communications, Inc., 1994.

Klein, Eric, and John B. Izzo, Ph.D. *Awakening Corporate Soul: Four Paths to Unleash the Power of People at Work.* Lions Bay, BC: Fairwinds Press, 1998.

Kurian, George, and Graham Molitor. *Encyclopedia of the Future, Volumes I and II.* New York: Simon & Schuster Macmillan, 1996.

Labovitz, George, Y. S. Chang, and Victor Rosansky. *Making Quality Work: A Leadership Guide for the Results-Driven Manager.* New York: HarperCollins Publishers, Inc., 1993.

Labovitz, George, and Victor Rosansky. *The Power of Alignment.* New York: John Wiley & Sons, Inc., 1997.

Larson, Elizabeth R., and Bonnie Cox. "Social Accountability 8000: Measuring Workplace Conditions Worldwide." *Quality Digest* (February 1998): 26–29.

Lawler, Edward E., et al., *Creating High Performance Organizations: Practices and Results of Employee Involvement and Total Quality Management in Fortune 1000 Companies.* San Francisco: Jossey-Bass Inc., Publishers, 1995.

———. "Organizational Capabilities: The Ultimate Competitive Advantage." Presentation given at the Strategic Leadership Forum, New York, NY, April 21, 1998.

Lawton, Barbara B. "A Whole Systems Approach to Knowledge Management: A Case Study." Unpublished paper, August 1998: 8.

Lee, Chris and Ron Zemke. "The Search for Spirit in the Workplace," *TRAINING* (June 1993): 21–28.

Leibfried, Kathleen H. J., and C. J. McNair, CMA. *Benchmarking: A Tool for Continuous Improvement.* New York: HarperCollins Publishers, Inc., 1992.

Leigh, Pamela. "The New Spirit at Work." *Training & Development* (March 1997): 31.

Lewis, James P. *Fundamentals of Project Management.* New York: American Management Association, 1995.

Lippitt, Gordon, and Ronald Lippitt. *The Consulting Process in Action.* San Diego: University Associates, 1986.

Madhavan, Ravindranath, Reshma H. Shah, and Rajiv Grover. "Motivations for and Theoretical Foundations of Relationship Marketing." *1994 AMA Winter Educators' Conference Proceedings,* Vol. 5. Chicago: American Marketing Association, 183–190.

Malcolm Baldrige National Quality Award 1998 Criteria for Performance Excellence. Gaithersburg, MD: National Institute of Standards and Technology, 1998.

Marshak, R. "Lewin Meets Confucius: A Re-View of the OD Model of Change." *Journal of Applied Behavioral Science* (December 1993): 393–415.

Matson, Eric. "Project: You." *Fast Company* (December–January 1998): 192–206.

Meyer, Christopher. "How the Right Measures Help Teams Excel." *Harvard Business Review* (May–June 1994): 95–103.

Mezirow, Jack, and Associates. *Fostering Critical Reflection in Adulthood: A Guide to Transformative and Emancipatory Learning.* San Francisco: Jossey-Bass Inc., Publishers, 1990.

Michalko, Michael. *Thinkertoys.* Berkeley, CA: Ten Speed Press, 1991.

Millett, Stephen, and William Kopp. "The Top Ten Innovative Products for 2006: Technology with a Human Touch." *THE FUTURIST* (July–August 1996): 16–19.

Mizuno, Shigeru. *Management for Quality Improvement: The Seven New QC Tools.* Cambridge, MA: Productivity Press, 1988.

Mizuno, Shigeru, and Yoji Akao, eds. *QFD: The Customer-Driven Approach to Quality Planning and Deployment.* Tokyo: Asian Productivity Organization, 1994.

Mohrman, Jr., Allan M., et al. *Large-Scale Organizational Change.* San Francisco: Jossey-Bass Inc., Publishers, 1989.

Mohrman, Susan Albers, et al. *Tomorrow's Organization: Crafting Winning Capabilities in a Dynamic World.* San Francisco: Jossey-Bass Inc. Publishers, 1998.

Møller, Kim. "Social Responsibility as a Corporate Strategy." *Perspectives on Business and Global Change,* Vol. 11, No. 1 (March 1997): 49–56.

Morgan G., and R. Ramirez. "Action Learning: A Holographic Metaphor for Guiding Social Change." *Human Relations,* Vol. 37, No. 1 (1983).

Morgan, Gareth. *Images of Organizations.* Thousand Oaks, CA: SAGE Publications, 1997.

Mowsesian, R. *Golden Goals, Rusted Realities.* Far Hills, NJ: New Horizon Press, 1986.

Muoio, Anna. "This 'Green Dean' Has a Blueprint for Sustainability." *Fast Company* (June–July 1998): 70–72.

———, ed. "Ways to Give Back." *Fast Company* (December–January 1998): 113–125.

Nadler, David A., et al. *Organizational Architecture: Designs for Changing Organizations.* San Francisco: Jossey-Bass Inc., Publishers, 1992.

Naeye, Robert. *Through the Eyes of Hubble: The Birth, Life, and Violent Death of Stars* Waukesha, WI: Kalmbach, Books, 1998.

Nathan, A. "Organization Effectiveness: Building Integrated Capabilities and Functioning for Accomplishing Desired Results." *The 1996 Annual: Volume 2, Consulting.* CA: Pfeiffer & Company (1996): 257–274.

National Institute of Standards. *Foreign/International Quality Award Descriptions.* June 22, 1998.

Nayatani, Yoshinobu, et al. *The Seven New QC Tools: Practical Applications for Managers.* Tokyo: 3A Corporation, 1984.

Naylor, Thomas H., William Willimon, and Rolf Osterberg. *The Search for Meaning in the Workplace.* Nashville: Abingdon Press, 1996.

Newstrom, John W., and Edward E. Scannell. *Games Trainers Play.* New York: McGraw Hill Book Company, 1980.

Nichols, Martha. "Does New Age Business Have a Message for Managers?" *Harvard Business Review* (March–April 1994): 52–60.

Nirenberg, John. "From Team Building to Community Building." *National Productivity Review* (Winter 1994/95): 51–62.

Nirenberg, John. Ph.D. *The Living Organization: Transforming Teams into Workplace Communities.* Burr Ridge, IL: Richard D. Irwin, 1993.

Novak, Michael. *Business as a Calling: Work and the Examined Life.* Old Tappan, NJ: The Free Press, 1996.

Ohno, Taiichi. *Toyota Production System: Beyond Large-Scale Production.* Cambridge, MA: Productivity Press, 1988.

Okes, Duke W. "Quality Improvement and Organization Development." *The Quality Management Forum* (Winter 1991).

Olesen, Douglas E. "The Top Ten Technologies for the Next Ten Years." *THE FUTURIST* (September–October 1995): 9–13.

Osada, Takashi. *The 5S's: Five Keys to a Total Quality Environment.* Tokyo: Asian Productivity Organization, 1991.

Ouchi, William. as quoted in H. K. Brelin. "The Role of Leadership in Total Quality Improvement." *Continuous Journey* (December 1993–January 1994): 33–36.

Outlook '97. Bethesda, MD: The World Future Society, 1997.

Outlook '98. Bethesda, MD: The World Future Society, 1998.

Packard, David. *The HP Way: How Bill Hewlett and I Built Our Company.* New York: HarperCollins Publishers, Inc., 1995.

Park, C. Whan, Deborah MacInnis, Steven Silverman, and Bernard Jaworski. "A Value-Based Conceptual Framework Linking the Marketing Mix and Marketplace Exchange." Unpublished working paper, January 1998.

Parker, Glenn M. *Cross-Functional Teams.* San Francisco: Jossey-Bass Inc., Publishers, 1994.

Pasmore, W. A. *Designing Effective Organizations: The Sociotechnical Systems Perspective.* New York: John Wiley & Sons, Inc., 1988.

Peters, Tom. "The Brand Called YOU™." *Fast Company* (August–September 1997): 83–94.

Pink, Daniel H. "Free Agent Nation." *Fast Company* (December–January 1998): 131–147.

———. "Metaphor Marketing." *Fast Company* (April–May, 1998): 214–229.

Pink, Daniel H., and Michael Warshaw. "Free Agent Almanac." *Fast Company* (December–January 1998): 151–160.

Plott, Curt, and John Humphrey. "Positioning Yourself for the Future: The Workplace & Learning in 2020." 1997 ASTD International Conference & Exposition Presentation.

———. "Preparing for 2020." *Training & Development* (November 1996): 46–49.

Porter, Michael. *Competitive Advantage: Creating and Sustaining Superior Performance.* New York: The Free Press, 1985.

———. *Competitive Strategy: Techniques for Analyzing Industries and Competitors.* New York: The Free Press, 1980.

Powell, Anna S. *Quality Outlook 1994.* New York: The Conference Board, Inc., Fall 1994.

———. *Quality Outlook 1996.* New York: The Conference Board, Inc., Fall 1996.

———. *Quality Outlook 1997–1998.* New York: The Conference Board, Inc., Fall 1997.

"The Price of Job Freedom." *TRAINING* (November 1997): 12.

Promise vs. Payoff: Consumer Attitudes on Quality in the Age of the Networked Society. Milwaukee: American Society for Quality Control, 1997.

Provost, Lloyd P., and Gerald J. Langley. "The Importance of Concepts in Creativity and Improvement." *Quality Progress* (March 1998): 31–38.

Pruzan, Peter. "The Ethical Accounting Statement." *World Business Academy Perspectives.* Vol. 9, No. 2 (1995): 35–45.

Pyle, Chris. "Competitive Intelligence–Get Smart!" *Fast Company* (April–May 1998): 268–279.

Quality Function Deployment—Executive Briefing. Dearborn, MI: American Supplier Institute, 1989.

Quality, the Future, and You—An ASQC Consideration of the Year 2010. Milwaukee: American Society for Quality Control, 1996.

Ray, Michael, and Alan Rinzler, eds. *The New Paradigm in Business: Emerging Strategies for Leadership and Organizational Change.* New York: G. P. Putnam's Sons, 1993.

"Report from the Futurist: John Naisbitt." *Fast Company* (December–January 1998): 44.

"Report from the Futurist: Watts Wacker." *Fast Company* (October–November, 1997): 40.

"Results of November 1997 Reader Poll." *News For a Change* (January 1998): 7.

Rhem, James. "Living as Learning." *On Wisconsin* (May–June 1998): 22–26, 55–56.

Robinson, Dana Gaines, and James C. Robinson. *Training for Impact.* San Francisco: Jossey-Bass Inc., Publishers, 1991.

Robinson, Russell D. *An Introduction to Helping Adults Learn and Change.* West Bend, WI: Omnibook Co., 1994.

Robison, Jim, and Rick Harrington. "Using Quality Costs to Drive Process Reengineering." *Quality Digest* (May 1995): 29–34.

Rucci, Anthony J., Steven P. Kirn, and Richard T. Quinn. "The Employee-Customer-Profit Chain at Sears." *Harvard Business Review* (January–February, 1998): 82–97.

Schaffer, Carolyn R., and Kristin Anundsen. *Creating Community Anywhere: Finding Support and Connections in a Fragmented World.* New York: Tarcher/Perigee Books, 1993.

Schein, Edgar H. *Organizational Culture and Leadership.* San Francisco: Jossey-Bass Inc., Publishers, 1992.

Schein, Edgar H. *Process Consultation: Its Role in Organization Development.* Reading, MA: Addison-Wesley Publishing Company, 1988.

Scholtes, Peter R. *The Leader's Handbook.* New York: McGraw-Hill, 1998.

Schonberger, Richard J. *Building a Chain of Customers.* New York: The Free Press, 1990.

"Seeking Six-Sigma Status at AlliedSignal." *Leading Voices in Quality* (Report No. 1159-96-CH). New York: The Conference Board, Inc., 1996.

Senge, Peter M., et al. *The Fifth Discipline Fieldbook.* New York: Doubleday, 1994.

Sheth, Jagdish N. "Relationship Marketing: A New School of Marketing Thought." Presentation handouts, University of Pittsburgh, April 1994.

Shewhart, Walter. *Economic Control of Quality of Manufactured Product.* New York: Van Nostrand, 1931.

———. *Statistical Method from the Viewpoint of Quality Control.* New York: Dover Publications, Inc., 1986.

Silverman, Lori L. "Coaching Leaders Through a Large-Scale Change Effort." Unpublished paper, 1995, 1996.

———. "Organizational Architecture: A Framework for Successful Transformation." Unpublished paper, May 1997.

———. *Organizational Architecture: A Framework for Successful Transformation.* Unpublished workbook, November 1994.

Silverman, Lori L., and William H. Braswell, Jr. "The Evolution of Coaching in Today's Workplace . . . What's Next?" Presentation given at the Ohlone College Business Roundtable, May 22, 1997.

Silverman, Lori L., and Dona Hotopp. "Strategic Planning: Core Elements and Enhancements." Unpublished chart, 1996, 1997.

Silverman, Lori L., and Annabeth L. Propst. "Coaching Process Improvement Teams." Paper presented at the 1991 ASQC/ASA Fall Technical Conference, October 1991.

———. *Eight Stage Approach for Developing a Current Reliable Method.* Unpublished workbook, 1995, 1997.

———. "Where Will They Fit In?" *Quality Progress* (July 1996): 33–34.

———. "Why Aren't Self-Managed Teams More Successful." Paper presented to the 1996 Spring Conference, Chicago Chapter, Association for Quality and Participation, March 13, 1996.

Silverman, Lori L., Annabeth L. Propst, and Steven N. Silverman. *Eight Stage Approach for Innovation.* Unpublished workbook, 1995.

Silverman, Steven N., and David E. Sprott. "Brands and Consumer Experience: A Multi-Method Approach for Studying Consumer-Based Brand Meaning." Unpublished working paper, October 1997.

Singer, Daniel D., and Raymond D. Smith "Two Approaches to Corporate Ethics." *Perspectives on Business and Global Change,* Vol. 12, No. 2 (1998): 33–45.

Stamps, David. "Communities of Practice: Learning is Social. Training is Irrelevant?" *TRAINING* (February, 1997): 34–42.

———. "A Conversation With Dr. Paradox." *TRAINING* (May 1997): 42–48.

Stewart, Thomas A. "Taking on the Last Bureaucracy." *FORTUNE* (January 15, 1996): 105–108.

Stratton, Brad. "More Voices Speak Out on the Future of the Quality Profession." *Quality Progress* (December 1997): 73–78.

———. "TI Has Eye on Alignment." *Quality Progress* (October 1997): 28–34.

"Surge in Global Migration." *THE FUTURIST* (January–February 1997): 40.

Taninecz, George. "Best Practices and Performances." *IndustryWeek* (December 1, 1997): 28–35, 38–43.

———. "Mutual Learning." *IndustryWeek* (July 7, 1997): 28–31.

Tomasko, Robert M. *Rethinking the Corporation: The Architecture of Change.* New York: American Management Association, 1993.

"The Tom's of Maine Story." www.toms-of-maine.com/people/tkstory.html (1995–1996).

von Oech, Roger. *A Kick in the Seat of the Pants.* New York: Harper Perennial, 1986.

———. *A Whack on the Side of the Head.* New York: Warner Books Inc., 1983.

Wacker, Watts, and Jim Taylor, with Howard Means. *The 500-Year Delta: What Happens After What Comes Next.* New York: HarperCollins Publishers, Inc., 1997.

Wadsworth, Harrison M., Kenneth S. Stephens, and A. Blanton Godfrey. *Modern Methods for Quality Control and Improvement.* New York: John Wiley & Sons, 1986.

Walmsley, Ann. "Six Sigma Enigma." *Report on Business Magazine* (October 1997).

Webber, Alan M. "Are You Deciding on Purpose?" *Fast Company* (February–March, 1998): 114–117.

———. "Is **Your** Job Calling?" *Fast Company* (February–March, 1998): 108–110.

Webster, Jr., Frederick E. *Market-Driven Management: Using the New Marketing Concept to Create a Customer-Oriented Company.* New York: John Wiley & Sons, Inc., 1994.

Webster's New World Dictionary—Third College Edition. New York: Macmillan, 1994.

Western Electric. *Statistical Quality Control Handbook.* Indianapolis: Western Electric,1956.

Wheeler, Donald. *Understanding Variation: The Key to Managing Chaos.* Knoxville, TN: SPC Press, Inc., 1993.

"When the Baby Boomers Retire." *Management Review* (June 1996): 2–4.

Whitney, Diana. "Spirituality as an Organizing Principle." *World Business Academy Perspectives,* Vol. 9, No. 4 (1995): 51–62.

Whyte, David.*The Heart Aroused: Poetry and Preservation of the Soul in Corporate America.* New York: Bantam/Doubleday, 1996.

Woll, Toby. "Mutual Learning Has Corporations Sharing Good Ideas." *Boston Business Journal,* Vol. 16, No. 41 (November 22–28, 1996).

Womack, James P., and Daniel T. Jones. *Lean Thinking: Banish Waste and Create Wealth in Your Corporation.* New York: Simon & Schuster, 1996.

———. *The Machine that Changed the World.* New York: HarperCollins Publishers, Inc., 1990.

World Business Academy, Annual Meeting and President's Council Invitation, 1998.

Wrege, Charles D., and Ronald G. Greenwood. *Frederick Taylor, The Father of Scientific Management: Myth and Reality.* Homewood, IL: Business One Irwin, 1991.

Zaltman, Gerald. "Rethinking Market Research: Putting People Back In." *Journal of Marketing Research,* Vol. XXXIV (November 1997): 424–437.

Zaltman, Gerald, and Robin A. Higie. "Seeing the Voice of the Customer: The Zaltman Metaphor Elicitation Technique." Working Paper (Report No. 93-114), Cambridge, MA: Marketing Science Institute, 1993.

Zemke, Ron. "The Call of Community." *TRAINING* (March 1996): 24–30.

Zultner, Richard E. "Software Quality Function Deployment: The First Five Years—Lessons Learned." *Proceedings of the 48th Annual Quality Congress.* Milwaukee: American Society for Quality Control, May 1994: 783–793.

Index